INTRODUCING
CULTURAL ANTHROPOLOGY

THIRD EDITION

INTRODUCING CULTURAL ANTHROPOLOGY

A CHRISTIAN PERSPECTIVE

Brian M. Howell *and* Jenell Paris

Baker Academic
a division of Baker Publishing Group
Grand Rapids, Michigan

Published by Baker Academic
a division of Baker Publishing Group
Grand Rapids, Michigan
BakerAcademic.com

Printed in the United States of America

Library of Congress Cataloging-in-Publication Data
Names: Howell, Brian M. author | Paris, Jenell Williams author
Title: Introducing cultural anthropology : a Christian perspective / Brian M. Howell and Jenell Paris.
Description: Third edition. | Grand Rapids, Michigan : Baker Academic, a division of Baker Publishing Group, [2026] | Includes bibliographical references and index.
Identifiers: LCCN 2026013587 | ISBN 9781540969798 paperback | ISBN 9781493456093 ebook | ISBN 9781493456109 pdf
Subjects: LCSH: Christianity and culture | Culture | Anthropology
Classification: LCC BR115.C8 H69 2026
LC record available at https://lccn.loc.gov/2026013587

Cover design by Paula Gibson

Baker Publishing Group publications use paper produced from sustainable forestry practices and postconsumer waste whenever possible.

26 27 28 29 30 31 32 7 6 5 4 3 2 1

CONTENTS

PREFACE TO THE THIRD EDITION

Years ago, a colleague asked me (Brian) for resources that would help her teach the concept of culture to her French class. She was teaching about modern French film and wanted students to learn how terms like "popular culture" and "subculture" were distinct from "culture." She also wanted her students to reflect on how Christians might engage film, literature, and other media in their societies.

At the time, I knew of many resources written for secular colleges, and many aimed at professional anthropologists, but I could not offer just what she needed. She was looking for a book that would explain the culture concept in academic *and* Christian terms, without assuming the reader has a professional anthropologist's training for sorting through theoretical and technical issues.

After that conversation, I envisioned authoring a short book—perhaps eighty pages—that would address the culture concept in Christian perspective. I even had a title: *Culture: A Primer for Christians*. It seemed potentially useful for Christians teaching many subjects—even modern French film.

As my sabbatical approached, I revisited this idea, but now I imagined a slightly longer book—perhaps 120 pages—that would address a cluster of key topics in addition to culture. I wanted a coauthor and was glad Jenell saw the value of the project for all the same reasons I did.

In the end, the project grew larger than our initial vision, from a modest primer to a full textbook. When we approached Baker Academic, we pointed out that there were few anthropology textbooks written by and for Christians. Those that existed were, even then, more than twenty years old. It was time for something new that would speak to contemporary audiences and incorporate current terminology, theory, and examples. We also pointed out that while anthropology has long had a strong relationship with foreign missions, it has grown in Christian higher education to support general education, cross-cultural ministry, anthropology (and sociology) majors and minors, teaching English as a second language, intercultural studies, and many other programs. There was a need for a textbook that presented anthropology as a discipline in its own right and not only as a tool to support foreign missions.

So we got to work and produced this book, which was first published in 2011. We have been gratified and grateful that it has found an audience. Many have encouraged us, giving us feedback on how they use the book with their students. Professors using the book have also passed along suggestions and critiques that we have taken into consideration. We revised the text in 2019 to produce the second edition, updating examples, changing some chapters, and refining the work.

There has been an even shorter time span between that edition and this third edition. Cultural change is accelerating in our world. What has not changed is that we strive to bring anthropology's powerful perspective and methodology to students. We have added many hands-on exercises to help students get a feel for anthropology. We have updated language and examples. We have not changed the topics of any chapters from the second edition, but large sections have been reworked. We continue to welcome feedback and are always grateful to hear from those who find this book helpful, encouraging, and strengthening for Christian faith and service.

About the Authors

Combined, we have taught Introduction to Anthropology for more than forty years. We enjoy encountering new ideas (or revising good ones) with our students and seeing students stretch their own sense of humanity, culture, and God. We see this book as an opportunity to share what we have learned and to provide resources that encourage an even stronger presence of anthropology in Christian higher education. Although we came to anthropology through different paths (described below), we have both embraced our roles as teachers and see this book as an extension of that calling.

Jenell Paris

My areas of interest include urban anthropology, race, gender, and sexuality. My path to anthropology (partly described at the beginning of chap. 1) began when I was an undergraduate at Bethel University in Minnesota. In addition to majoring in sociocultural studies, I did a month of fieldwork in Amsterdam and a semester program in Washington, DC, both of which exposed me to cultural diversity, urban life, and social science research. I also spent two summers doing urban ministry in Philadelphia with KingdomWorks (now Mission Year), which sparked interest in further studies in urban anthropology.

My dissertation research at American University was on community formation in a low-income neighborhood of Washington, DC. Since then, I have continued to research race and poverty and have expanded my interests to include conflict transformation, applied anthropology, and sex and gender.

I have invested my teaching career in Christian contexts: the American Studies Program (Washington, DC), Bethel University (St. Paul, MN), and Messiah University (Grantham, PA). This book is an outgrowth of teaching cultural anthropology in general education and major-specific settings. My hope is that it makes anthropology accessible in the wide variety of ways that Christian educational settings incorporate the discipline.

Brian M. Howell

I have worked primarily in the areas of globalization, global Christianity, short-term missions, and, to a lesser extent, race and religion in the United States. More recently, I have been interested in embodiment, gender, theater, and ritual. As I tell in my own short biography at the beginning of chapter 1, I attended Wesleyan University in Connecticut, a good liberal arts school that has long since severed ties with its Christian origins. While I received a wonderful education, there was little to help me connect my intellectual life with my faith. God provided one professor, Richard Elphick, a historian of South African Dutch missions, as a mentor. He modeled for me the life of a faithful Christian and rigorous scholar. Although God eventually drew me to anthropology rather than history, Professor Elphick showed me how important it is for Christians to connect the life of the mind with life in Christ.

After earning my master's degree at Fuller Seminary and then a PhD in anthropology from Washington University in St. Louis, I taught at Wheaton College in Illinois from 2001 until 2026. Teaching anthropology in that setting provided the same joys and challenges my colleagues faced everywhere. My students found anthropology inherently fascinating. It helped them make sense of intercultural experiences, multiculturalism, or their own background as missionary kids, ethnic and racial minorities, or simply people who questioned cultural assumptions. In the face of a discipline that emphasizes cultural and social explanations, however, those very issues sometimes raised questions about the universality of faith or the nature of God. I deeply valued the opportunity to help students connect the insights of anthropology with their faith.

Like Jenell, my publishing has been in both scholarly and popular venues. My books address global Christianity, with my primary field site in Baguio City, Philippines (hence the many Philippine examples throughout the book!), as well as short-term missions in the United States. I have enjoyed encouraging students in their own research and even published with them.

Jenell and I both see this book as an opportunity to share what we have learned in the classroom and to provide a resource that encourages the development of anthropology in Christian colleges.

Using the Third Edition

The third edition has many exciting changes. Chapter 5 (Sex, Gender, and Sexuality) is significantly revised, including more discussion of men and masculinity and updated material on diverse genders and sexualities. Chapter 6 (Economics) contains new material on neoliberalism as a cultural and economic concept, as well as a discussion of the Anthropocene. Chapter 9 (Religion and Ritual) revises our discussion of ritual theory to be more comprehensive and includes new information on witchcraft in the contemporary world. All chapters have updated examples and revisions, and some have new features on contemporary Christian anthropologists.

New "Your Turn" text boxes invite students to engage chapter themes. Instructors may adapt these activities for discussion during class, for homework, or as the basis for a writing assignment. All text boxes are revised to conclude with a brief "It's Your Turn" student engagement activity.

Instructor supports are available online through Baker Academic. All instructor supports are updated, including a test bank, chapter slide-deck presentations, and chapter outlines.

The book relies on a time-honored organizational schema. Chapters cover aspects of culture and analytical categories common to the discipline and are grouped according to what some call "cultural subcategories." The text could be taught in exactly the order in which the chapters present the material, corresponding to a standard US semester. At the same time, the chapters are structured so that they can be read or taught in any order. We anticipate professors using ethnographies, articles, and other primary sources to highlight areas of interest. With various topics, ethnographic and commercial films can be used to highlight the concepts in the text.

The book remains medium-length, keeping it affordable for students and flexible for teachers. In reaching that goal, we left some areas of cultural anthropology less developed, such as cultural aspects of aesthetics and art, environmental anthropology, and cross-cultural psychology. The material on theory and the history of the discipline could easily be twice as long. In maintaining a focus on cultural anthropology, the book's treatment of biological anthropology and archaeology is, by necessity, cursory.

Although the book is primarily geared to an undergraduate course in introductory anthropology, it also may contribute to mission courses about the history of mission, practical ministry, and ministry in both cross-cultural and domestic contexts. With devotional materials and Christian theology integrated throughout, it could serve as a helpful text for short-term mission preparation courses and cross-cultural ministry classes at local churches.

Imagining an Audience

Astute authors imagine who will read their book. This imaginary audience helps the author choose the "voice" of the book, the examples to be used, and the overall style. Every author hopes that many people will read their book, but it often helps to know the primary audience the authors have in mind. In this case, both of us tended to picture our own students: undergraduates at Christian colleges in the United States. Many of our students are European American English speakers who were born and raised in the United States, but racially and culturally diverse groups are also represented. We regularly have international students pursuing college degrees in the United States, and some are the children of missionaries or military personnel who have lived most of their lives outside the United States. Some of our students are well traveled, while others have very little firsthand experience with cultural diversity. The majority come with some, or very strong, Christian commitments and backgrounds.

Drawing on our experiences, we have worked into the text many of the questions and issues we have heard throughout the years. Some relate to Christian theology. Others are more about the cultural background many of our students bring to the table. Because both of us have done the bulk of our teaching in the United States (and we were both born and raised in the United States), the book's examples tend to draw on US cultural norms and practices. Many illustrations come from our lectures and from our students. Several ideas, ethnographic examples, and biblical explanations come from colleagues who have been kind enough to allow their words to appear here (with citation).

Many seminaries and Christian colleges around the world offer courses in anthropology, and we sincerely hope this book can be of service internationally. We hope the examples, though relative to the North American context, will be helpful for students everywhere as students and faculty adapt the book to various contexts through class discussions, lectures, films, and the like.

1

THE DISCIPLINE OF ANTHROPOLOGY

After studying this chapter, you should be able to do the following:

1. describe the four subfields of anthropology
2. describe the methods and concepts that distinguish cultural anthropology from sociology, intercultural studies, and missiology
3. explain how Christians contribute to anthropology and how anthropology contributes to Christian life and service

CHAPTER OUTLINE

Finding Cultural Anthropology

Jenell's Journey

After a summer of urban ministry in Philadelphia, I returned to my suburban Christian college in Minnesota and searched the academic catalog for classes related to race, poverty, and cities. The Department of Sociology and Anthropology offered interesting classes related to my emerging areas of passion, so I chose sociology and anthropology as a major and economics as a minor. Later, after I spent a month in an anthropology class in the Netherlands doing applied research on church planting for Youth With A Mission, I decided to become an anthropologist.

For me, anthropology has been connected with urban life and ministry. My doctoral fieldwork involved four years of life, ministry, and research in a neighborhood in the northwest quadrant of Washington, DC. I could see the US Capitol from my house, as well as the profound poverty and racial segregation that exist just blocks from that global symbol of freedom and democracy. My research question was about ghetto formation and resident activism—how urban spaces become racially homogeneous and

Jenell Paris

Jenell socializes with a key informant at a neighborhood gathering. Anthropologists participate in informal parts of everyday life as part of participant observation.

economically disadvantaged, and how residents work for neighborhood betterment. My research was motivated by my Christian faith—specifically by the question, *Who is my neighbor?* I hoped the research itself would be an act of neighborliness, telling the story of a neighborhood from residents' perspectives. Participant observation included being an involved citizen and church member while living at Esther House, a Christian residence occupied by women committed to the neighborhood. I came to see that the methodology of anthropology—living among people and listening to their stories—fit well with the Christian calling to love God and neighbor.

Brian's Journey

I got my first taste of anthropology when I was developing an undergraduate thesis project at my New England college in a program that combined government, economics, history, and social theory. I decided to do research on missions in the Philippines because that was where my United Methodist Church provided missionary support. I had not taken a single course in anthropology, but I knew I wanted to travel and spend time with people in their local contexts. With my background in social science and a lot of enthusiasm, I spent a summer doing fieldwork in a small mountain village in the northern Philippines, interviewing people and learning about the process of social change following widespread conversion to Christianity some thirty years earlier. Writing my thesis was the first time in my secular

Brian Howell

Brian and a student pose with Parno, a coconut seller in Puncak, Indonesia.

education that I really connected the social, theological, and cultural aspects of Christianity.

I wanted to continue this line of research in graduate school but did not know which discipline would work best. I considered history and political science, but neither of these seemed a good fit. At the time, I lived near Fuller Seminary in Pasadena, California, where I found anthropologists on the faculty. I realized that cultural anthropology would allow me to consider all the aspects of life I found interesting. My research was motivated by my faith as I sought to bring to the wider academic world an understanding of Christianity that is scholarly and critical but not antagonistic. During my fieldwork, I taught courses at the Philippine seminary where my family and I lived. There I came to see anthropology as a vital mode of thought for the church as well as the world.

Eventually, we met each other through the Network of Christian Anthropologists. After years of talking at conferences and even working on a colleague's book project together,[1] we became convinced that anthropology had many

1. Robert J. Priest and Alvaro L. Nieves, eds., *This Side of Heaven: Race, Ethnicity, and Christian Faith* (Oxford University Press, 2007).

important insights for Christians. Drawing from more than forty combined years of teaching Introduction to Anthropology in Christian college and seminary classrooms, and many other courses as well, we have combined our knowledge of the discipline with our understanding of the particular questions and concerns Christians often bring. In this, the third edition, we have included contemporary examples, refined our thinking in several areas, and tailored information to a new generation of students. We continue to present the discipline generally and also address distinctively Christian concerns, acknowledging points of tension and highlighting ways in which the discipline of anthropology can contribute to the church and to Christian vocations.

What Is Cultural Anthropology?

On the first day of class, we ask our students, "When you tell people you're taking a cultural anthropology class, what do they think you're studying?" Answers range widely: learning about dinosaurs, hunting down priceless artifacts on Indiana Jones–style quests, or adopting radical cultural relativism and denying ultimate truth. The first of these guesses is understandable, but wrong; the second is flattering, but not a very realistic portrayal of a different branch of anthropology; the third is an unfortunate characterization we will address in chapter 2.

Cultural anthropology is the description, interpretation, and analysis of similarities and differences in human cultures. It is a diverse discipline encompassing a wide variety of topics related to human beings. Cultural anthropologists often differentiate themselves by referring to areas of specialty such as economic anthropology, urban anthropology, or anthropology of religion, to name just a few.

As our personal stories demonstrate, anthropologists come to the discipline in a variety of ways and study an array of topics, but they share a commitment to a common perspective and method. The **anthropological perspective** refers to an approach to social research that seeks to understand culture from the point of view of the people *within* that cultural context. **Ethnographic fieldwork** is anthropology's hallmark research method, based on the anthropologist's direct experience in a culture.

What often draws Christians to the discipline is the realization that the anthropological perspective and method enable us to serve the world by better understanding it. For me (Jenell), that has included urban ministry and community development as well as helping to equip churches and Christians to engage in conflict productively over divisive issues such as human origins, sexuality, and politics. For me (Brian), anthropology shaped my ability to teach and write about global Christianity, short-term missions, and the particular dynamics of being a Christian studying Christian communities, which provides opportunities to speak to the anthropological community as a Christian while representing faith in the academy. Many Christian anthropologists study topics that have little obvious relationship to their faith, though the motivation and calling to do research and scholarship provides an opportunity for faithfully using the gifts God has given them.

Many students take only one course in anthropology, but those students with an undergraduate major in anthropology, sociology, or intercultural studies go on to serve in many different areas of society. Even a single introductory course can influence a career or open doors to options for deeper engagement. *All* Christians can benefit from understanding the methods and concepts of the discipline and connecting anthropology to service through evangelism and social action, theology and Bible study, and everyday life in a globalized world.

In this chapter, we present the four subfields of anthropology. We elaborate on the subfield of cultural anthropology, which is the focus of this text, giving an overview of its distinctive methods and concepts and distinguishing it from other disciplines. Finally, we discuss the contributions an anthropological understanding can provide Christians in our efforts to live faithful lives as members of the local and global body of Christ.

The Four Subfields of Anthropology

Simply breaking down the word "anthropology" into its parts reveals the breadth of the discipline. *Anthro* comes from the Greek *anthropos*, meaning "human," and *-ology* comes from *logos*, or "study." The term "**anthropology**" is broad because the discipline as a whole encompasses several distinct but related modes of research. Anthropology has traditionally been divided into four subfields: archaeology, linguistics, physical or biological anthropology, and cultural or social anthropology (see fig. 1.1). The four subfields each have their own method and theory, yet all share the anthropological perspective on human life and culture.

Some add a fifth branch of anthropology—**applied anthropology**—in which practitioners use anthropology in the service of particular social concerns. Others argue that applied anthropology is not a subfield because application is an integral part of each subfield and because applied anthropologists usually earn their degrees in one of the four traditional subfields. Engaged anthropology and public anthropology are additional ways of describing the application of anthropology, with different nuances regarding the purpose and the nature of application.

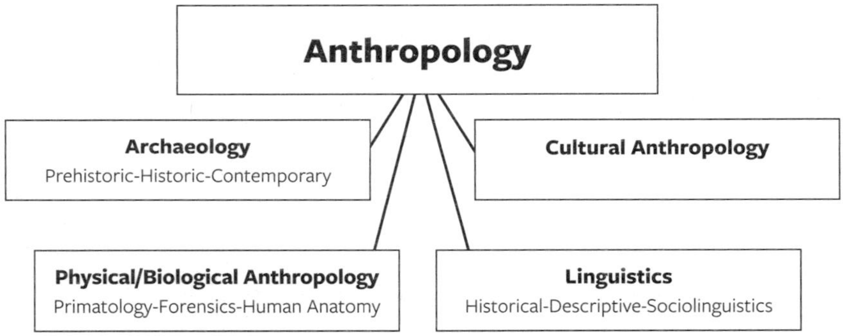

Figure 1.1. The four subfields of anthropology

Archaeology

Archaeology is the study of material artifacts to understand a people's culture or society. This could be the people of the ancient past understood through the simple stone tools or fire pits they left behind, or it could be the relatively recent past of the last century or even contemporary communities. Archaeologists have studied everything from the Underground Railroad, by which enslaved people in the Southern United States escaped to the North, to Mayan empires in Central America, to the historicity of biblical narratives, to consumption patterns of Americans based on their garbage.

The primary means of data collection for archaeologists is **excavation**, referring to methods of extracting artifacts from underground, though they may also study visible structures such as pyramids, footprints fossilized in rocks, or cave paintings. By interpreting artifacts, archaeologists are able to draw conclusions about how the people connected to those artifacts lived. For example, before Europeans arrived in what is now North America, a civilization known to us only as the "Mound Builders" constructed massive mounds in various places throughout the Great Plains and Southeastern United States.[2] Archaeologists excavating these mounds analyze bits of pottery, metal, animal bones, microscopic pollen, and the composition of the soil. They have been

2. George R. Milner, *The Moundbuilders: Ancient Peoples of Eastern North America* (Thames & Hudson, 2005); Henry Blyde Shetrone, *The Mound-Builders* (1930; repr., University of Alabama Press, 2004).

able to infer social hierarchies, trade relationships, patterns of settlement, daily diet, religious beliefs, and a great deal more. All of this comes from only the material remains; the Mound Builders left no written accounts of their lives. Various myths have circulated about the people who made these mounds, including the notion that a "lost White race" must have lived on this land long before the founding of the United States. Robert Silverberg explores how myths have grown up around archaeological remains.[3] Proper archaeological analysis can help us understand Native American prehistory and also inspire reflection on the reasons why misinformation can be so compelling.

Archaeologists may combine the analysis of material life with information taken from contemporary populations, a form of study known as **ethnoarchaeology**. Comparing the past (as seen in a material record) to the present (understood through the ethnographic methods described below) provides information about cultural change even when no written records of the past exist. Similarly, archaeologists have used artifacts to gain information about contemporary populations that is not easily accessible through ethnographic or other interactive methods.

Ned Farley teaches anthropology and archaeology at Wisconsin Lutheran College, connecting Christian faith with anthropology in the Lutheran tradition.[4] Farley has worked as part of a field crew for the Great Lakes Archaeological Research Center, where he studied the Milwaukee County Pauper Cemetery, using forensics to identify and preserve biological remains. After this, he worked with the Wichita (KS) Office of the City Archaeologist, reconstructing the history of a major transportation corridor that was slated for development. Later, he worked as a contract archaeologist on municipal projects in Connecticut. He looked at the history of early maritime communities along the northeastern American seaboard, exploring how state and federal law helps to preserve historic cultural resources. These are just a few examples of ways that an archaeologist can work in contemporary settings.

Biblical archaeology uses the methods and theories of archaeology to understand the people and cultures related to biblical texts through the

3. Robert Silverberg, *Mound Builders of Ancient America: The Archaeology of a Myth* (New York Graphic Society, 1968).

4. See Ned Farley, "Anatomical and Biochemical Evidence for *Treponema pallidum* in a 19th to Early Twentieth Century Skeletal Cadaver," *Forensic Science, Medicine and Pathology* 16, no. 3 (2020): 557–61; Ned Farley, "Environment, Diet, and Craniofacial Development: A Study of Mixed Subsistence Strategies in the Great Lakes Watershed, AD 900–1600," *International Journal of Humanities and Social Science* 5, no. 9 (2015): 29–45; Ned Farley, "Milwaukee's Early Irish and the Role of the Church in Diasporic Urban American Settlement and Assimilation, 1890–1922," *e-Keltoi* 1 (2015): 125–46.

A Cultural Perspective Brings Scripture to Life

Anthropology's subfields bring rich insight to our understanding of Scripture. Linguistic anthropologists study living languages, as well as the languages of ancient manuscripts, for Bible translation. Archaeologists discover and interpret material remains in the regions where biblical events occurred. Biblical scholars John Walton and Craig Keener, editors of the *NIV Cultural Backgrounds Study Bible*, explain that "grasping the original audience's perspective helps us understand the setting to which the inspired authors communicated their message."[a] The study helps in this Bible show images of ancient objects, buildings, and landscapes, such as a heel bone of a crucified man from the first century. Readers can picture biblical worlds rather than simply projecting their assumptions and culture into the text. The *Zondervan Handbook of Biblical Archaeology* provides a comprehensive look at artifacts, and also the processes and perspectives biblical archaeologists bring to their work.[b]

Cultural anthropologist Mary Douglas developed a general theory of religious purity and pollution, and she applied this theory to Leviticus and Numbers.[c] Douglas explains that when viewed in a cultural context, these laws express God's character, compassion, and mercy. The cultural distance is so great that the contemporary reader must work hard to interpret these texts as they were intended, resisting the impulse to avoid, reject, or misinterpret them because of the dissimilarity between their world and ours.

Christian faith can be enriched by combining a devotional reading with a studious reading. Martin Luther King Jr. (who earned a BA in sociology) encouraged Christians to cultivate a "tough mind and a tender heart," using both the rigor of critical thinking and the sincerity of an open heart to understand the gospel and to put it into practice in society.[d]

It's your turn: Which book, character, or place in the Bible do you want to know more about? How could a cultural perspective help you learn more?

a. John Walton and Craig Keener, eds., *NIV Cultural Backgrounds Study Bible* (Zondervan, 2016), x.

b. J. Randall Price and H. Wayne House, eds., *Zondervan Handbook of Biblical Archaeology: A Book by Book Guide to Archaeological Discoveries Related to the Bible* (Zondervan, 2017). See also John D. Currid, *The Case for Biblical Archaeology: Uncovering the Historical Record of God's Old Testament People* (P&R, 2020).

c. Mary Douglas, *Purity and Danger: An Analysis of Concepts of Pollution and Taboo* (Routledge, 1966); Mary Douglas, *Leviticus as Literature* (Oxford University Press, 1999).

d. Martin Luther King Jr., *Strength to Love* (Fortress, 2010), 1.

artifacts they left behind. Students of biblical archaeology develop expertise in both the science of archaeology and the study of the Bible. The Lanier Center for Archaeology at Lipscomb University is one institution that supports archaeological research in the biblical world, including the ancient Near East and the Eastern Mediterranean.[5]

Archaeology is a nonreactive measure of human behavior, meaning it does not cause subjects to change their behavior in response to the research. Thus,

5. "Lanier Center for Archaeology," Lipscomb University, accessed February 3, 2026, https://lipscomb.edu/arts-sciences/lanier-center.

archaeology is an important part of the discipline of anthropology that provides a distinctive vantage point on culture and the human experience.

Linguistics

A second subfield of anthropology, **linguistics**, involves the study of language. In some universities it remains a distinct field of study, particularly where language is studied primarily as a system of sounds and rules. Where language is studied primarily in relation to its use within larger cultural and social systems, it is known as sociolinguistics and is integrated with the study of cultural anthropology. Many Christians know of linguistics through the work of Wycliffe Bible Translators and its academic partner organization, SIL International, formerly known as the Summer Institute of Linguistics. Wycliffe and SIL International train linguists and anthropologists to translate the Bible into the thousands of languages known worldwide. Some do technical linguistic analysis, creating systems of writing and codifying the grammar of oral languages. Others engage directly with sociolinguistics, working out the metaphors, concepts, images, and poetics of the target language in order to faithfully translate Hebrew and Greek Scriptures into new linguistic contexts. SIL puts linguistics into the hands of everyday people with "A Guide for Planning the Future of Our Language," a free practical resource for local communities who want to preserve traditional languages.[6]

Today, linguistics is often considered a part of cultural anthropology, since both subfields focus on the study of meaning and culture. Linguistics, and anthropological approaches to language in general, are significant for the study of culture and society (see chap. 3).

Physical/Biological Anthropology

Physical or **biological anthropology** involves the study of human anatomy, nonhuman primates (**primatology**), and human origins. Physical anthropology illuminates how the study of physical qualities can deepen our understanding of the ways humans organize social life. Physical anthropologists often apply their expertise in medical schools, teaching courses in gross anatomy and embryology. Physical anthropologists may apply their work to health care, using comparisons of human growth patterns to understand nutrition and physical variation within a community and to otherwise aid medical practitioners in providing good care. Forensic anthropology is a

6. "A Guide for Planning the Future of Our Language," SIL, August, 2016, https://www.sil.org/guide-planning-future-our-language.

rapidly growing branch of physical anthropology in which anthropologists interpret human remains, usually for legal purposes. Forensic anthropologists work in court settings, at universities and research centers, and for human rights organizations such as the Forensic Border Coalition, where anthropologists work alongside other professionals in investigating and identifying the remains of those who die while traversing the Southern US border region.[7]

For many Christians, physical anthropology is the most controversial subfield. Because Christians, Jews, Muslims, and other religious people believe God created the world, the scientific study of human origins raises difficult issues. Some Christians hold an interpretation of Genesis that precludes the idea that humans are descended from other life-forms. Others point to Romans 5:12, where Paul writes of sin entering the world through "one man," meaning Adam must have been created separately from other animals. Even the idea of God selecting preexisting hominids to create God's image in them strikes many Christians as incompatible with scriptural accounts. At the same time, since the beginning of the church, some Christians have believed that Genesis offers theological truth, not a scientific or historical account of creation. These Christians, including ancient Christian thinkers such as Augustine as well as contemporary biblical scholars and theologians, conclude that the questions addressed by science (including evolutionary theory) are different from those answered by Genesis.[8] Today, some Christians work in areas of physical anthropology and primatology. They feel they can accept the mechanism of evolution as God's means of creating the world without compromising the authority of Scripture.

Understanding the relationship of creation to human development involves many fields of study, including theology, biblical exegesis, hermeneutics, geology, cosmology, genetics, and paleontology, as well as anthropology. For this book, with its focus on cultural anthropology, it is not necessary to settle these questions to understand how physical/biological anthropology fits within anthropology generally. Nor should questions about evolutionary theory be an insurmountable barrier for Christians to fully engage the discipline of cultural anthropology.

7. "Forensic Border Coalition," accessed February 3, 2026, https://forensicbordercoalition.org.

8. Paul Copan, Tremper Longman III, Christopher L. Reese, and Michael G. Strauss, eds., *Dictionary of Christianity and Science: The Definitive Reference for the Intersection of Christian Faith and Contemporary Science* (Zondervan, 2017); "God's Word, God's World," BioLogos, December 24, 2020, https://biologos.org/gods-word-gods-world.

Cultural Anthropology

The fourth subfield is cultural anthropology. Cultural anthropologists use the culture concept to understand human individuals and groups, especially how people shape and are shaped by dimensions of life such as family, education, religion, art, and economy. Cultural anthropology was inspired, in part, by eighteenth- and nineteenth-century reports from missionaries and colonialists about the unfamiliar people and customs they encountered in their travels. Like other contemporary social sciences, it is rooted in the Scientific Revolution, when European scientists applied newly developed scientific methods and perspectives to politics, social organization, and religion. It gained scientific rigor as standards for fieldwork, analysis, and scholarly writing developed and as university departments were founded. Still today, studying anthropology is a form of scholarly travel through which people encounter the lives of others. Anyone who enjoys reading about people around the world, or dreams of traveling to faraway places, or values engaging cultural diversity close to home has taken a step toward cultural anthropology.

Several disciplines involve detailed understandings of social organization and cultural differences, including history, geography, and sociology. Other fields of study distinctive to Christian colleges and seminaries, such as missiology, theology, and intercultural studies, connect with anthropology. One of the most distinctive features of cultural anthropology is the primary method anthropologists use in their research: ethnographic fieldwork.

Ethnography and Fieldwork

Ethnography (*ethno* = people, *graphy* = writing) refers to both the activity and the product of cultural anthropology. Cultural anthropologists engage in ethnography by studying multiple aspects of life in a particular place or among a group of people to create a picture of how those people understand and live in the world. Anthropologists write up their research in accounts called ethnographies, rich descriptions and analyses that include the anthropologists' experiences of being there. "Being there" is the ethnographic standard for legitimate anthropological knowledge.

When Elliot Liebow was preparing for fieldwork among urban Black Americans in Washington, DC, his supervisor said, "Go out there and make like an anthropologist." Anthropologists make a career of hanging out, though ethnographic training involves coursework and ethics oversight before fieldwork begins. Ethnographic research consists of living in a way that allows the anthropologist to become as integrated into daily life as possible. Even when fieldwork appears to be just "hanging out," as Liebow did for months on urban street corners, the anthropologist is always purposeful, observing and participating with care and taking notes (either on the spot or later) that will be used for analysis.[9]

The practice of long-term fieldwork emerged in the early twentieth century and reflected the belief that understanding cultural life requires observing and interacting with people as they go about their daily lives, and that this goal takes a long time to reach. Anthropologists often spend one to two years in the field, sometimes making repeated field trips over the course of their careers to correct errors, observe changes over time, and pursue new areas of interest. Unlike earlier scholars who relied on secondhand information or direct interviews with individuals outside their own social context (see chap. 2), anthropologists became committed to the notion that quality research required ethnographers to learn the languages and participate in the customs of people they wished to understand, and to spend significant time observing daily life as well as events of special social significance.

Participant observation is the primary method associated with ethnographic research. Picture a continuum with full participation at one end and detached observation at the other. Participant observation involves moving around on the continuum throughout fieldwork; it is an approach to research that combines participation and observation in various ways to optimize understanding of the culture being studied. Standing back and taking a good look around is often the way an anthropologist begins, and such detached observation yields good insight. But simultaneously and self-consciously, the anthropologist moves toward participation.

For me (Jenell), participant observation meant living, worshiping, and socializing in a low-income Black neighborhood of Washington, DC. At times I stood back and observed—for instance, at a heated meeting of community activists when I didn't yet understand the issues at hand. At other times I fully participated—having my say at community meetings, hosting community gatherings at my home, and joining a local church. Even as people came to know me as a neighbor, and sometimes as a friend, they also knew I was conducting research.

In my research on congregations in the Philippines, I (Brian) spent eighteen months participating in three congregations.[10] Having graduated from a seminary and being in a place where relatively few people were able to earn such

9. Elliot Liebow, *Tally's Corner: A Study of Negro Streetcorner Men*, 2nd ed. (Rowman & Littlefield, 2003).

10. Brian M. Howell, *Christianity in the Local Context: Southern Baptists in the Philippines* (Palgrave Macmillan, 2008).

advanced degrees, I was frequently invited to preach and lead Bible studies in congregations. Participating in this way gave me a role that people could understand more easily than "anthropologist." More importantly, sharing my faith and contributing to Christian life in these ways strengthened **rapport**, a relationship of conversational ease with individuals and groups. For all of us, good rapport allowed us to talk more honestly and intimately about our lives and perspectives on issues of culture, faith, community, and context.

For some anthropologists, participant observation may take the form of holding a job in the organization being studied, taking on an official leadership position, or even adopting a role that makes them appear to be a typical member of the community. Adopting multiple roles can be difficult since anthropologists in the United States embrace the American Anthropological Association's code of ethics, which does not allow researchers to misrepresent themselves or trick people into participating in research.[11] Yet even when anthropologists are forthcoming about their identity and research interests, it is still possible for them to become part of a community and for people to get used to the presence of an outsider. In some cases, particularly when anthropologists do not stand out in some obvious way, they can become insiders of a sort. They can occupy a place in the daily routines of life in the community they have come to study. It is through these everyday interactions that anthropologists gain insights into culture and social life.

Within the general method of participant observation, anthropologists employ a variety of techniques for obtaining information and increasing their understanding. **Ethnographic interviews** involve purposeful, documented conversation with research participants. They may be formal, including recording an interview based on a list of questions, or very informal, with questions generated on the spot and note-taking done later. Anthropologists may conduct **focus groups**, a type of interview in which small groups of people are asked to discuss a particular topic while the anthropologist takes notes. Other methods that complement participant observation include **mapping** (diagramming geographical space or human interpretation and use of space), recording a **life history** (an interview or series of interviews that document the trajectory of a single life), and conducting a **survey** (a standardized set of questions applied to numerous individuals or places).

These methods, as well as participant observation, are increasingly used in short-term research projects. Many researchers wish to glean as much benefit as possible from ethnography even when they don't have time or funding

11. "Anthropological Ethics," American Anthropological Association, accessed February 2, 2026, https://americananthro.org/about/anthropological-ethics/.

Michael Jindra

Michael Jindra (in baseball cap) discussing "death celebrations" with a group of village elders in Njindom, Cameroon.

for years in the field. **Rapid ethnographic assessment procedures** (**REAP**) involve the time-compressed use of focus groups, ethnographic interviews, mapping, and other methods within a framework of participant observation. REAP projects can occur over a period of weeks, days, or even hours. REAP researchers must always account for ways in which the short-term nature of the research limits the validity of findings, as well as ways in which ethnographic methods enhance their findings beyond what a simple questionnaire or detached observation could yield. User-experience research is a short-term, multidisciplinary approach to marketing that involves close attention to human behavior. Anthropologists contribute to this field, supporting development and implementation of products and services. The Anthropology Career Readiness Network shares resources for adapting traditional ethnographic methods to suit contemporary work and educational environments.[12]

Participant observation and its related methods highlight the extent to which cultural anthropology focuses on small-scale cases—villages, clubs, neighborhoods, congregations, families, and so on. The anthropologist draws on many aspects of life to create a holistic understanding of the situation. A **holistic understanding** assumes that all parts of human life—from birthing practices to the economy to warfare to art—are interconnected. From a very local and specific perspective, the anthropologist then discusses how the processes, features, and particularities of the case reveal something about human life more generally.

12. Anthropology Career Readiness Network, accessed February 3, 2026, https://anthrocareerready.net/.

The Anthropological Perspective

The anthropological perspective refers to the attempt by the anthropologist to explain a cultural context from the *inside*, understanding the motives, actions, and beliefs of others in their own terms. This does not mean anthropologists are trying to completely submerge themselves in the culture they are studying ("going native" is usually patronizing and unconvincing). Rather, it means they learn the context and culture to the point that they can explain how the people who reside within that culture or context understand the world and how diverse aspects of their lives come together. The methodology of long-term fieldwork is designed to allow the anthropologist to understand this complexity by spending enough time among a people not only to observe what they do but also to understand why they do it.

The culture concept (defined in detail in the next chapter) portrays all aspects of human life as interconnected, from the way people raise children to how they dress to how they classify the colors they see. Rather than isolating particular features of social life, such as political institutions or economic decision-making, anthropologists seek to understand how these interrelated aspects of life function in shaping how people live and how they make meaning of life. The anthropological perspective is broad and holistic. Margaret Mead (1901–78), an anthropologist who became a major public figure of the twentieth century, once said, "The world is my field—it's all anthropology."[13]

The anthropological perspective seeks to understand people in their own context and on their own terms. Additionally, it is in understanding people different from ourselves—the **cultural other**—that anthropologists believe we can best understand ourselves and also understand the human experience more broadly. When we realize that many things we take for granted other people construe quite differently—such as what makes a person beautiful or how many colors there are—we can more easily begin to gain insight into our own cultures. Christians, in particular, may find this helpful as we explore our own cultural assumptions that influence our reading of Scripture, relationships with fellow believers, and life and service in a globalized world.

We invite you to adopt the anthropological perspective with the "Your Turn" feature in each chapter. You can look at the world, at everyday life around you, and at your own life and context in anthropological perspective. This can even become an ethical practice when you seek to know, believe, and act with more love and wisdom. Like positive psychology, positive anthropology seeks to be hopeful (not just critical), action-oriented (not just theoretical),

13. Margaret Mead, quoted in Winthrop Sargeant, "It's All Anthropology," *New Yorker*, December 30, 1961, 31.

and available to everyone (not just to those with graduate degrees). For example, anthropologist Aaron Miller used this approach to look at college sports, recommending a "relentless positivity" in addressing problems within college sports. He encourages anthropologists to "be the change they want to see," which means doing research and discussing findings while exhibiting the very values they hope will grow as a result of their research—values such as civility, hope, reconciliation, and more.[14]

Anthropology and Related Disciplines

Because cultural anthropology draws together history, economics, politics, religion, family, and psychology to understand people's social and cultural lives, it overlaps with several disciplines, but none more than sociology. The simple answer to the question *What's the difference between sociology and anthropology?* is that, historically, sociologists have focused mainly on large-scale societies and used **quantitative research methods**—that is, hypothesis-based approaches that produce and interpret data statistically. Anthropologists more often have turned to small-scale societies outside the West and used qualitative methods to develop holistic portraits of cultural life. **Qualitative research methods** are interpretive approaches that use participant observation, interviews, document analysis, and other methods to understand the nature and meaning of social phenomena. Today, many sociologists and anthropologists use mixed-method approaches that strategically rely on both quantitative and qualitative methods to best explore a research question.

In universities and colleges, sociology and anthropology are sometimes blended in an academic department, or sociologists may teach an introductory class in cultural anthropology. Because both disciplines explore social life, cultural diversity, and group behavior, this compatibility makes good sense. Historically, the two disciplines come from some of the same philosophers and social theorists who began thinking about rapid changes in European life in the eighteenth century and the increasingly apparent differences found among people around the world (see chap. 11).

Anthropologists are more likely to study cross-culturally than sociologists. Even when studying their own culture, anthropologists compare their findings cross-culturally and employ concepts built from the ongoing comparison of

14. Aaron L. Miller, "How Can Anthropologists Be the Change They Wish to See in the World?," *Anthropology Career Readiness Network World of Work* (blog), accessed February 3, 2026, https://anthrocareerready.net/how-can-we-as-anthropologists-be-the-change-we-wish-to-see-in-the-world/.

cultural differences. Anthropologists are more committed to the use of culture as a central concept to any analysis, while sociologists are more likely to use society and institutions (see chaps. 2 and 4) as organizing ideas. Sociology proves especially useful for Christians seeking a big-picture view of religion and social life on a national or regional scale.

Anthropology is a key discipline in several interdisciplinary fields of study. Global studies relies on the theories and methods of anthropology to interpret social, political, economic, and ecological challenges and opportunities facing humanity. In Christian educational settings, intercultural studies prepares students with interpretive and communication skills for engaging across cultural difference, with anthropology as one of the foundational pillars, while missiology focuses on mission practice and theology and has long made cultural anthropology one of its core disciplines.[15] Traditional disciplines such as biblical studies and theology are enriched with integration of the methods and theories of anthropology. Andrew F. Walls, a historian of mission, writes about an "anthropology of hope" in nineteenth-century mission thinking. In theology, the word "anthropology" refers to the study of humanity in relation to God, and in social science it refers to the study of culture and humanity. Walls uses both meanings in interpreting how missionaries viewed African humanity both in social context and in relation to God.[16]

Anthropology and Missions

Effective missionaries must learn how to communicate and live effectively in the society where they serve. In addition to serving in pastoral positions, they may have medical duties, educational work, economic development projects, and more. Anthropology helps cultivate and deepen missionaries' skills in numerous ways. First, missionaries might spend time studying anthropological research on a particular group or place before they go. They not only learn about history, customs, traditions, beliefs, and values but also are able to read

15. Harvie M. Conn, *Eternal Word and Changing Worlds: Theology, Anthropology, and Mission in Trialogue* (Zondervan, 1984); Jayson Georges, *Ministering in Patronage Cultures: Biblical Models and Missional Implications* (IVP Academic, 2019); Sherwood G. Lingenfelter and Julie A. Green, *Teamwork Cross-Culturally: Christ-Centered Solutions for Leading Multinational Teams* (Baker Academic, 2022); Sherwood G. Lingenfelter and Marvin K. Mayers, *Ministering Cross-Culturally: A Model for Effective Personal Relationships* (Baker Academic, 2016); Michael Rynkiewich, *Soul, Self, and Society: A Postmodern Anthropology for Mission in a Postcolonial World* (Wipf & Stock, 2012).

16. Andrew F. Walls, "An Anthropology of Hope: Africa, Slavery, and Civilization in Nineteenth-Century Mission Thinking," *International Bulletin of Missionary Research* 39, no. 4 (2015): 225–30.

YOUR TURN

Hanging Out

You will find a "Your Turn" text box in each chapter. You may read them, do them on your own, or your professor may assign them as a course requirement.

Clifford Geertz coined the phrase "deep hanging out" to describe the ethnographic method.[a] Fieldwork is challenging and requires prolonged immersion in a different culture. It comes with all the risks and worries that may arise when initiating interactions with new people. It is rigorous—but also fun. Anthropologists often treasure the relationships and experiences they cultivate during fieldwork. Hanging out with others is how anthropologists develop the anthropological perspective.

Go hang out in a new setting, with new people—the more unfamiliar, the better. See yourself as an insider and an outsider at the same time. Participate as fully as you are able, being respectful of your setting, but also observe, and even observe yourself observing.

- What is the setting like? Take note of everything: walls, floors, furniture, and objects.
- What are people like in this setting? How do they talk, dress, sit, and move?
- What do people like and dislike? What do they describe as important or trivial?
- What allows an outsider to connect with new people? What obstacles are in the way?
- How does hanging out with new people make life better—for them and for you?

a. Clifford Geertz, "Deep Hanging Out," *New York Review of Books* 45, no. 16 (Oct. 22, 1998).

about daily life, community dynamics, and processes of change that will be critical in introducing the gospel or strengthening the church. For both long-term and short-term missions, reading ethnographies—and understanding the social and historical context of a place—is vital preparation.

Second, missionaries often study anthropological theory and method so they will be equipped to study the context personally. No matter how well researched a particular place or people may be, cultural change and local specificity make it imperative that missionaries are equipped to do their own anthropological research. Several of the largest North American seminaries have one or more anthropologists teaching in their mission education programs. Missionaries can become expert ethnographers, using participant observation, ethnographic interviews, surveys, and other research techniques to learn about another culture. They apply their research to their mission work and publish in both missiology and anthropology journals. In this way, Christian anthropologists are actively involved in helping missionaries become more effective in their calling.

Some of the earliest missionaries took anthropological research to heart in thinking about how the new converts in the places they worked could become Christians while maintaining their cultural identities. This notion, called "contextualization" or "indigenization," grew out of the interaction of anthropology and missiology as Christians throughout the world came to understand how effective communication and practice of the Christian faith rely on cultural understanding (see chap. 12).

Interactions between missionaries and anthropologists go back as far as the beginning of the discipline of anthropology. They often work together well, and sometimes missionaries provide linguistic resources and fieldwork access to new anthropologists. They sometimes collide, unfortunately, when anthropologists encounter missionaries who show insensitivity or ignorance toward cultural differences, or when missionaries see anthropologists as working for academic or career goals that do not prioritize the pressing needs of people.[17]

Despite these challenges, anthropology has made profound contributions to mission work, and many missionaries find that the tensions produce a sharpened ability to explain the Christian faith, to live peaceably with those of other faiths or no faith, and to acknowledge the failures and mistakes Christians have made. As the church expands outside European and North American contexts, the need for cross-cultural understanding on the part of Christians will only continue to grow.

Anthropology and the Christian Witness

In the first hundred years of the discipline, anthropologists and Christians not only worked well together but were often one and the same. Early anthropologists such as Maurice Leenhardt (1878–1954) conducted anthropological research in conjunction with missionary work.[18] After spending twenty-four years in New Caledonia as a Protestant missionary, Leenhardt took over as the prestigious chair of social anthropology at the École Pratique des Hautes Études, a leading French university, where he taught what he had learned during his missionary travels. Later missionary anthropologists and linguists made significant contributions to the discipline with work that flowed directly from their Christian engagement in Bible translation and evangelism, even establishing scholarly journals such as *Anthropos* and *Missiology* (formerly known as *Practical Anthropology*) with the express purpose of bringing together anthropology and missions.

17. Darrell Whiteman, *Crossing Cultures with the Gospel: Anthropological Wisdom for Effective Christian Witness* (Baker Academic, 2024). *On Knowing Humanity*, a journal that connects cultural anthropology with Christian theology, devoted an entire issue (vol. 8, no. 2 [2024]) to the theme of anthropologists and missionaries in history and dialogue.

18. James Clifford, *Person and Myth: Maurice Leenhardt in the Melanesian World* (University of California Press, 1982).

Thomas Headland

Participant observation—Agta man trying to teach Thomas Headland how to hunt with a bow and arrow; here showing the ethnographer how to lie in wait in a tree to ambush passing deer (c. 1970). No game was shot that day!

And yet, the relationship between Christianity and anthropology has not always been smooth and harmonious. Anthropologists working in various parts of the world have documented both the inadvertent and conscious cooperation of missionaries with colonial rulers, in which mission work became part of a "civilizing" and subjugating process. Christians, including Christian anthropologists, have pointed out secular assumptions often implicit in anthropological work that seem to make religious belief incompatible with anthropological research and theory. There may be some necessary strain between Christianity and anthropology, but we believe it can be a creative tension for people of either group, and even more so for individuals like us who belong to both groups. Christians are often uncomfortable with anthropology for a variety of reasons, including issues of human origins, evolution, and relativism. But at the same time, Christians have successfully integrated the study of anthropology into their colleges, universities, seminaries, and missions training programs.

In *The Slain God: Anthropologists and the Christian Faith*, historian Timothy Larsen looks at the religious lives of several major anthropologists, some of whom reject Christian faith and some of whom embrace it.[19] Edith and Victor Turner, for example, were deeply influenced by their experience of traditional

19. Timothy Larsen, *The Slain God: Anthropologists and the Christian Faith* (Oxford University Press, 2014).

African religion (Ndembu rituals in Zambia) and eventually joined the Roman Catholic Church. Edith Turner studied and interpreted the common human experience of religion, especially how religion fosters a deep sense of community and belonging (*communitas*), even as she lived a personal commitment to one religion, Christianity. The phrase "the slain God" does not mean that anthropologists kill God but rather that an anthropological perspective often prompts deep religious self-reflection (slaying what we had once believed to be God) that leads to renewed commitment. As Victor Turner described, "We are born into the faith of our fathers, we distance ourselves from it, and then, in a moment of return, we reenter it in sophisticated naivete, civilized earnestness."[20]

Christians and Basic Research in Anthropology

Christians who work in anthropology have a broad range of interests. Christian anthropologists have become world-renowned experts in areas of anthropological research that seem far from explicitly Christian concerns. Thomas Headland, an ecological anthropologist trained at the University of Hawaii and affiliated with SIL International for many years, conducted research on Agta people living in the forests of the Philippines that became central to understanding the forest ecosystem and human life for ecological anthropologists everywhere.[21] Dean Arnold, who studied at the University of Illinois and taught at Pennsylvania State University prior to teaching at Wheaton College, conducted research on potters and cultural change among Yucatec Mayan communities in Mexico. His published research became foundational for archaeologists and cultural anthropologists working with economic change and social life among Indigenous people of Latin America.[22] Patricia K. Townsend, who earned her PhD at the University of Michigan, did her doctoral research among the Saniyo-Hiyowe people in Papua New Guinea, focusing on fertility, childbirth, and child mortality. Townsend coauthored a key text in the field of medical anthropology (*Medical Anthropology in Ecological Perspective*) that has been in print for almost forty years, in addition to her more recent book *Environmental Anthropology: From Pigs to Policies*.[23]

20. Victor Turner, *Revelation and Divination in Ndembu Ritual*, quoted in Larsen, *Slain God*, 223.

21. Thomas Headland and John Early, *Population Dynamics of a Philippine Rainforest People: The Ildefonso Agta* (University of Florida Press, 1998).

22. Dean Arnold, *Ceramic Theory and Cultural Process* (Cambridge University Press, 1985).

23. Ann McElroy and Patricia K. Townsend, *Medical Anthropology in Ecological Perspective*, 6th ed. (Routledge, 2015); Patricia K. Townsend, *Environmental Anthropology: From Pigs to Policies*, 3rd ed. (Waveland Press, 2017).

Some Christian traditions prioritize service to the church or mission work, while others encourage service to the world through any profession. Throughout the history of the discipline, Christians have worked to find compatibility between faith and anthropology, and to resolve—or to engage with creatively and productively—intractable disagreements over philosophical and professional differences.

Anthropology in a Globalized World

Globalization is not simply a topic that some anthropologists study or that only globally minded Christians need to consider. Globalization is our context, a world in which local and regional systems are increasingly drawn into global systems. As local and regional systems of production and distribution are pushed and pulled toward global interconnections, people experience life with new fusions, tensions, and opportunities of the local and the global. This produces new opportunities for travel, communication, and work as well as new challenges of environmental sustainability and intensified forms of injustice, such as human trafficking.

As Christians, we are practicing a faith born in an ancient Middle Eastern context. The gospel was first preached in a language (Aramaic) we do not speak; originally recorded in yet a different language (Koine Greek); developed among a multicultural, religious minority in a now-extinct empire; passed through multiple European, African, and Asian cultures over thousands of years; and finally interpreted within the technological complexity of the twenty-first century. In other words, simply being a Christian is a cross-cultural experience.

This truth is amplified by the cultural diversity of the global church today. Christians worship in thousands of languages, use myriad instruments and musical forms, and pray in ways that can seem strange to their Christian brothers and sisters in other places. This diversity is a gift and part of God's plan for the church, but it poses challenges for being unified (see Jesus's prayer in John 17:21).

The movement of God around the world is reason for Christians everywhere to rejoice, but without the ability to relate with one another, we may become suspicious and isolated. This is true within each country or region as well, especially as migration in the era of globalization has brought people from many backgrounds close together. It is all too easy to misinterpret unfamiliar practices of other Christians and to assume they are unbiblical. Christian house blessings in the Philippines—in which the blood of a sacrificed pig is painted above the door—initially may appear to some Christians outside this context to be syncretic remnants of a pre-Christian past, while common US American Christmas traditions of giving gifts and decorating the house could seem to be pagan materialism to those unfamiliar with their meanings.[24]

Katrina Friesen

Traditional ritual ceremonies, called *kanyaw*, are seldom practiced nowadays. Due to economic and religious changes, most Ikalahan host Christian prayer services, or *gimong*, which maintain many of the elements of a *kanyaw* ritual, such as providing food for the whole community.

From such a perspective, it would be easy to think these practices will pass away as people become "mature" Christians, or even that such ceremonies reflect a lack of understanding of Christian theology. In fact, among the Ikalahan, these ceremonies are revivals of traditions that have not been practiced for decades. They reflect the desires of some younger Ikalahan, including many with theological training, to reconnect with their culture while strengthening their Christian identity. For Christians in the United States, some Christmas traditions *do* raise questions of materialism and, for some practices, concerns about non-Christian origins, but Christians also often connect gift giving among friends and relatives to God's gift of Christ to the world while viewing house decorations as making the season more meaningful.

Anthropological study strengthens perspective and research skills to help us ask insightful questions and observe more critically, as well as to think more deeply about the differences and similarities we encounter as the church continues to grow and diversify. An anthropological perspective supports an understanding of a rapidly changing world and the many ways that local and global forces come together in the human experience.

24. We use "US American" to refer to citizens of the United States, as "Americans" can properly be residents of either North or South America.

TERMS

anthropological perspective: The approach to social research that seeks to understand culture from the point of view of the people *within* that cultural context.

anthropology: The holistic study of humankind.

applied anthropology: The branch of anthropology in which practitioners use anthropology in the service of particular social concerns.

archaeology: The subfield of anthropology focused on the study of material artifacts to understand a people's culture and society, usually in the past.

cultural anthropology: The subfield of anthropology focused on the description, interpretation, and analysis of similarities and differences in human cultures.

cultural other: A term used to refer to the subjective experience of difference at the cultural level; identifying "us/me" and "them/you" through cultural symbols and markers.

ethnoarchaeology: An approach to archaeology that combines the analysis of material life with information taken from contemporary populations.

ethnographic fieldwork: Anthropology's hallmark research method, based on the anthropologist's direct experience in a culture.

ethnographic interview: Purposeful, documented conversation with research participants that may be formal or informal.

ethnography: (1) A rich description and analysis of a culture that includes the anthropologist's experience of "being there"; (2) the method of research involving firsthand fieldwork, participant observation, and other qualitative data.

excavation: A rigorous method of extracting artifacts from underground; the primary data-collection method of archaeologists.

focus groups: A type of interview in which small groups of people are asked to discuss a particular topic while the anthropologist takes notes.

globalization: The integration of economies, political systems, societies, and culture into a larger community on a global scale.

holistic understanding: The view that all parts of human life—from birthing practices to the economy to warfare to art—are interconnected.

life history: An interview or series of interviews that document the trajectory of a single life.

linguistics: The subfield of anthropology devoted to the study of language.

mapping: Diagramming geographical space or human interpretation and use of space.

participant observation: An approach to research that combines participation and observation in various ways to optimize understanding of the culture being studied.

physical (or **biological**) **anthropology:** The subfield of anthropology devoted to the study of human anatomy, nonhuman primates (primatology), and human origins.

primatology: The study of nonhuman primates.

qualitative research methods: Interpretive approaches that use participant observation, interviews, document analysis, and other methods to understand the nature and meaning of phenomena.

quantitative research methods: Measurement-based approaches that rely on mathematics, statistics, and hypotheses for producing and interpreting data.

rapid ethnographic assessment procedures (REAP): The time-compressed use of focus groups, ethnographic interviews, mapping, and other methods within a framework of participant observation.

rapport: A relationship of conversational ease with individuals and groups.

survey: A standardized set of questions applied to numerous individuals or places.

DISCUSSION QUESTIONS

1. What is it like for you to approach new places or unfamiliar people? How could anthropology support your curiosity or address your hesitations?
2. Share about a place you visited where the culture was unfamiliar. If you could revisit that place and do ethnographic fieldwork, what topics would you explore?
3. What are your impressions of how Christianity and anthropology fit together (or don't fit together)? Choose one point of tension or one point of collaboration and generate a strategy for maximizing the collaboration or for turning the tension into an asset.

ANTHROPOLOGY AND SCRIPTURE

Jesus the Participant Observer

> Jesus went through all the towns and villages, teaching in their synagogues, proclaiming the good news of the kingdom and healing every disease and sickness. When he saw the crowds, he had compassion on them, because they were harassed and helpless, like sheep without a shepherd. Then he said to his disciples, "The harvest is plentiful but the workers are few. Ask the Lord of the harvest, therefore, to send out workers into his harvest field." (Matt. 9:35–38)

The first time Matthew describes Jesus as being moved with compassion is after Jesus spent time traveling, teaching, and healing. Jesus's compassion was stirred when he *saw* the crowds. His love was not abstract or distant; Jesus lived among people, saw them, touched them, and loved them.

For Christian anthropologists, participant observation can be a spiritual practice. Anthropological research is never distant or detached. Like Jesus's ministry, anthropological research involves being close to people, speaking their language, eating their food, participating in their weddings and funerals, and caring about their concerns. In a sense, Jesus could even be described as God doing participant observation. In Jesus, God came to live among us and experience our lives as we do. Of course, just as anthropologists retain elements of their own distinctive identity, so Jesus was still Other (divine), even as he shared fully in our humanity. Although an anthropologist never "incarnates" from one context to another, like Jesus, anyone can draw closer in understanding and love through participating as fully as possible in another's world. Jesus's life and ministry provide wonderful inspiration for anthropologists doing fieldwork.

Fulfilling the Great Commission

> Then the eleven disciples went to Galilee, to the mountain where Jesus had told them to go. When they saw him, they worshiped him; but some doubted. Then Jesus came to them and said, "All authority in heaven and on earth has been given to me. Therefore go and make disciples of all nations, baptizing them in the name of the Father and of the Son and of the Holy Spirit, and teaching them to obey everything I have commanded you. And surely I am with you always, to the very end of the age." (Matt. 28:16–20)

Jesus gave his disciples the monumental task of making disciples of all nations. They took up the challenge, spending the rest of their lives spreading the gospel. Jesus's message is meant for all other believers as well, and Christians today are as challenged by the Great Commission as the eleven men who heard it spoken by Jesus.

What Jesus did not mean was to go and make some disciples *in* each country (although such a notion is not contrary to the spirit of the passage). The word translated "nations" here (*ethnos*) refers to the culture of a people—in other words, an ethnic group. Jesus calls his disciples, then and now, to help everyone understand how the gospel is meant to influence our ways of thinking, living, acting, and relating. Jesus calls his followers to make disciples of all *ethnē*. The gospel must become intimately entwined with our daily lives, not simply be an ethereal pursuit.

Sharing Jesus's message with people of all *ethnē* requires travel, language skills, and cross-cultural understanding. We must work hard to think with people in a different culture about what it would mean for them to become disciples of Jesus. Cultural anthropology helps us fulfill the Great Commission by preparing Christians to go to all *ethnē* and speak and live effectively.

2

CULTURE

After studying this chapter, you should be able to do the following:

1. understand the culture concept
2. distinguish between three types of ethnocentrism
3. evaluate common metaphors for culture
4. appreciate culture as a good part of God's creation

CHAPTER OUTLINE

Introduction

The term "culture" is often used today in words and phrases such as "multiculturalism," "cultural diversity," and "culture wars." Culture begins to seem like a real thing that simply exists. Culture is, in fact, an idea created to describe a reality that people experience: the behaviors, values, practices, technologies, and assumptions that distinguish one group from others. Culture is not simply a fixed tradition that people passively receive; it is actively made, negotiated, and contested by people. It changes in response to historical events and shifts in society's broader context. Scholars noted the similarities and differences between groups of people in different places. They saw that what seemed natural or simply human in one place was often completely unknown in another. They developed the concept of *culture*—and later, *cultures*—to explain and understand human similarities and differences.

The culture concept is both central and controversial in anthropology. It is an indispensable part of our discipline, but one that often sparks trouble. Whenever anyone—anthropologist or not—talks about culture, the question must be asked: *What exactly are we talking about?*

In this chapter, we first describe a common way of thinking about what culture is in the form of the ethnic fair model. Then we recount how anthropologists have defined culture over the course of the discipline's development. Next, we describe related concepts: cultural relativism and varieties of ethnocentrism. Finally, we conclude with a look at contemporary definitions of culture and metaphors for culture. Throughout, we see culture, and the ability to make culture, as a special part of God's good creation.

The Ethnic Fair

Imagine you are invited to participate in an ethnic fair. Your ancestors came from the Philippines, so you decide to introduce the fairgoers to Philippine culture. What do you put in your booth? You might start with the flag, hanging it prominently on the back of the booth. Then you set out a speaker playing traditional Philippine folk songs. Next, you put up a photo of a Philippine landscape, perhaps depicting something tropical or rice fields or a coastal fishing scene. Of course, you'd also want a picture of the distinctive Philippine jeepney, the common mode of transportation throughout the islands. Some lists of facts—population, the number of islands (more than seven thousand!), and a few historical notes—might appear. Finally, you'd display some food, probably *lumpia*, the fried Filipino egg roll that people everywhere find delicious.

Brian Howell

The colorful Philippine jeepney is an expression of cultural identity even though many Filipinos own their own cars, ride bicycles, or take the bus to work.

Now what if you're asked to represent the United States? No problem, just set out McDonald's hamburgers instead of *lumpia* and play country music instead of folk songs. But what about jazz? Or bluegrass? Or hip-hop? Those are all distinctively US American musical genres as well. And if you're going to show scenery, do you choose the Grand Canyon or the Appalachian Mountains? New York City or rural Iowa? Which foods, music, or landscapes really represent "US culture"?

When people reflect on their own culture, they often become aware of the differences between regions and individual experiences that make generalizations difficult. You may be a vegetarian who listens to indie British rock and have no interest in the Grand Canyon or New York City. Does that make you less of a US American? What is authentic US culture?

The same issues arise with our example earlier of Philippine culture. The millions of Philippine citizens who live in the high mountains of the north do not traditionally eat rice and fish; rather, their staple foods are sweet potato and wild deer. Many in the south are Muslims, whose style of dance and art resembles that performed in Jakarta, Indonesia, rather than Manila. Furthermore, millions of people living in the major cities are more comfortable at Starbucks than in a rice paddy behind a carabao (water buffalo). And like people all over the world, Filipinos enjoy McDonald's hamburgers (alongside the Philippine-based Jollibee's). So which is the true culture of the Philippines?

Ethnic fairs are enjoyable, and they can be educational to some extent, but this approach to culture has several problems. First, it implies that culture is primarily expressed through visible material items like food, clothing, and holiday trinkets. With an ethnic fair display, it is difficult to convey how profoundly culture shapes all parts of life, ordering our values, shaping our perceptions, and guiding our feelings. Second, it leads us to think of culture as a fixed and bounded entity, one that can be easily judged as authentic or inauthentic, and as belonging to a fairly homogeneous group of people. Moreover, it often fixes the "true" version of the culture in the past, with some traditional aspects of the society that may no longer be common among contemporary people. This tendency to see the past as more authentic than the present means that any cultural change is seen as culture *loss*, particularly for so-called traditional people. This is not to say that change is always good, or that cultures are undefinable, but the notion of culture existing as a fixed entity within specific geographic and temporal boundaries contradicts the anthropological view of culture as dynamic and fluid, with porous and fuzzy boundaries that shift over time. Third, the ethnic fair view of culture implies that each individual belongs to only one culture, when in fact many people blend elements from two, three, or more cultures into their lives in various ways.

History of the Culture Concept in Anthropology

The English word "culture" comes from the Latin *cultura*, meaning "to develop or grow." It is the root of such words as "agriculture" and "horticulture." It was present in Greek philosophy as a more abstract concept referring to the advance or growth of spirit, mind, or civilization and resurfaced among German idealist philosophers such as Georg Hegel and Johann von Herder in the eighteenth century. Despite these early roots, however, contemporary anthropological notions of **culture**, as the total way of life of a group of people, did not emerge until the nineteenth century.

Victorian-era British anthropologists began comparing reports from colonial administrators and missionaries around the world to discern patterns of behavior and belief among disparate groups (for more on these early anthropologists, see chap. 11). These first anthropologists, today often called **armchair anthropologists** for their gathering of data from travelogues and books rather than through their own direct research, were most interested in explaining why groups were so different from one another. Building on the biological theories of evolution advanced by Charles Darwin and others, these scholars assumed that all societies moved from simple to complex forms in progressive evolutionary stages. They began to develop an idea of Culture, with a capital *C*, as a capacity that all human beings possessed. These anthropologists did not talk about different *cultures*, only the *differences* in Culture. In this view, all cultural development followed a single path, or line, from simple to complex.

This view developed into the theory of **unilinear cultural evolution**, which stated that Culture, understood as all the customs, laws, behaviors, beliefs, and actions of humans, inevitably moved toward particular forms of social complexity. This "higher development" was theorized to be manifested in social and political systems such as market economies or democracy, technological innovations such as metallurgy, and complex religious beliefs in which the highest form was no religion at all, but rather a commitment to scientific atheism.[1] Not surprisingly, the Northern European scholars who developed this theory defined Northern Europeans as having progressed to possessing the most or highest Culture, while non-European people were seen as less evolved, living in a simpler, less-civilized state with less or lower Culture.

For decades, European and North American anthropologists used this idea of culture to classify societies as higher or lower on a scale of cultural development. This notion is not only repulsive to most people today but has been

1. Edward Burnett Tylor, *Primitive Culture: Researches into the Development of Mythology, Philosophy, Religion, Language, Art, and Custom*, 2 vols. (1871; repr., Dover, 2016).

thoroughly discredited by anthropologists themselves. We do retain a remnant of this view in our popular language, however. When we refer to someone as "cultured," meaning they have expensive, fancy, or rarefied tastes ("We're going to take you to the opera and get you some Culture"), we are referring to this older idea that some practices or values are "higher," and thus have more culture, than others. Some Christian traditions refer to "high church" or "low church," referring to the degree of formality and elaboration, or even to the difference between Roman Catholic and Protestant forms of worship.

Though it would ultimately lead to negative consequences for both Christians and anthropologists, many nineteenth-century Christians accepted the theory of unilinear cultural evolution. For Christians, the unilinear theory was important because it contradicted the idea of **polygenesis**, the widely held nineteenth-century belief that different groups of humans appeared or were created separately.[2] In other words, the unilinear theory fit with an understanding of all humans being a single creation of God (**monogenesis**), helping Christians argue against slavery and colonial exploitation, and for the relevance of missionary work among people who some Europeans believed were not human enough to be Christians.

Though unilinear cultural evolution supported the Christian belief that all humans originated from a single creation, it did not support the idea that all people are of equal value in God's eyes. In fact, it blended monogenesis with racism and cultural superiority. The unilinear theory questioned why some groups got "stuck" at low levels of development while others advanced. Linking with earlier theories of racial hierarchy, the unilinear theory seemed to provide scientific support to biological explanations of human difference. Put simply, many argued that some races were superior to others, leading to higher levels of Culture. For decades, anthropologists and other scientists used race theories to explore supposed biological differences between culturally distinct groups. Proponents of slavery and discrimination, advocates for eugenics, and even the Nazis used these theories to support their views. Many Christians fought vigorously against such movements, yet they often inadvertently advanced the idea that cultural differences should be ranked as

2. Historians Timothy Larsen and Daniel King tell the story of how those anthropologists arguing for monogenesis, many of whom were Christians, refuted the polygenesis argument of Victorian secularists to defend the "psychic unity of humankind" as a fundamental commitment of anthropology that persists to this day. Larsen and King, "The Dependence of Sociocultural Anthropology on Theological Anthropology," in *Theologically Engaged Anthropology*, ed. J. Derrick Lemons (Oxford University Press, 2017), 50–66. Christians would point to this as the *imago Dei*, or image of God in humanity. While many anthropologists would not link this notion to Christian theology now, it was driven by theological commitments in the early years of the discipline.

higher and lower. Thus, for some Christians, to follow Christ also meant to adopt "advanced" Culture.

While some anthropologists of these early years worked to bolster racial theories and the unilinear notion of culture, others critiqued this view. Early in the twentieth century, anthropologists moved out of their armchairs and began to promote ethnographic fieldwork as the best, if not the only, method for truly understanding different societies (see chap. 1). By immersing themselves in other cultures for long periods of time, anthropologists found that people living in supposedly simple societies actually had complex social and cultural lives. An absence of systems of elections or political office, for instance, did not mean an absence of structure, power, or authority. Supposedly racially inferior people had complex organizational systems and cultural norms that took anthropologists years to understand—hardly a strong support for notions of racial inferiority or cultural simplicity. These discoveries led anthropologists to advance the idea that differences in groups were linked not to biological predisposition but to history and environment. Differences in peoples' lives, then, were not manifestations of Culture at different stages of development but evidence of fully developed cultures shaped by and adapted to particular historical and environmental contexts.

This new theory, which would come to be called **historical particularism**, allowed anthropologists to speak of cultures in the plural (and without the capital *C*). It inspired research that looked at various cultures as complex adaptations to particular environmental and historical challenges. Within this framework, some anthropologists used materialist theories (often rooted in Marxian political economy) to explain contemporary cultures. Others focused more on psychological needs and pressures, linguistic constructs, or cognitive categories as the key to understanding how and why people in one place developed ways of thinking and living so different from people in another (for more on these theories, see chap. 11).

Today, in light of globalization, communication technologies, and urbanization, anthropologists emphasize the importance of seeing cultures as dynamic, with permeable boundaries, instead of as isolated, bounded entities. At one time, anthropologists deliberately sought out seemingly bounded societies. Several of the first well-known anthropological studies were of groups living on islands in the South Pacific; each group was literally bounded, surrounded by ocean. It seemed very clear where the limits of the culture existed. Even then, however, these boundaries were anthropological fictions, drawn according to features of language or identity the anthropologist felt were important, and studies sometimes intentionally ignored or minimized the broader political and colonial contexts that influenced life in these settings. In later years, the constructed nature of these boundaries would become even clearer as members of these remote (to us) societies traveled and communicated in the global community. The ethnic fair assumptions about cultures as neatly bounded and highly homogeneous entities simply didn't withstand scrutiny.

In addition to emphasizing the internal complexity of cultures, anthropologists now emphasize power dynamics—that is, ways in which differences in wealth and prestige (or access to wealth and prestige) shape the choices people make about their own cultures. A village in the Yucatan might seem peaceful and serene, but even there, older men might dominate younger men and women; religious specialists may use their knowledge to control nonspecialists; those with charisma might find ways to exploit others not so gifted. Today, anthropologists often employ theories of language and power to conceptualize culture as an arena where individuals and groups of individuals *within* a particular society are able to advance their own interests.

This understanding of culture—as plural, porous, and power laden—led anthropologists to reevaluate the meaning of difference across and within cultures. If there was no singular direction to "progress"—that is, if cultures were changing in response to historical events, environmental issues, and power dynamics—cultural differences must be evaluated on their own terms. In other words, cultures could only be understood relative to their own historical, ecological, and social contexts. This led to the foundational anthropological concept of cultural relativism.

Cultural Relativism

The idea of **cultural relativism** is one of the most important principles of cultural anthropology, but its meaning is contested among anthropologists and often misunderstood by others. For Christians, the word "relativism" may raise worries about secular scholars attacking Christian truth claims, or all truth claims. Understood more narrowly, however, the idea of cultural relativism poses no conflict for Christians. In fact, from a gospel perspective, a careful view of cultural relativism actually affirms Christian values. This is because cultural relativism can be understood as an empirical reality, not as a value judgment. That is, everywhere in the world people find particular and often very different ways to live in response to changing conditions. Learning to understand these differences requires a holistic understanding of cultural connection, context, and change.

The concept of cultural relativism comes from the work of historical particularists, especially Franz Boas. Arguing against the evolutionists, he held the view that various cultural practices and beliefs are best understood in relation to their own context and history. A symbol, belief, or behavior may make little sense, or even be offensive, when interpreted from an outsider's cultural perspective. Boas showed that when viewed holistically—in its own economic, historical, political, and religious contexts—what at first seemed nonsensical will appear sensible. The "relativism" in cultural relativism means that culture is relative to context.[3]

Although some of Boas's students extended his views, in this first articulation, cultural relativism did not imply that any particular belief is morally correct or beyond judgment, nor that a specific action is good simply because it is part of a culture. For example, I (Brian) recall a class in graduate school in which my professor showed slides of the Kofyar, a people who raise grains in the high plateau of Nigeria. A slide portrayed a man working alone, obviously struggling to lift large sheaves of millet[4] into a high rack used for drying. The professor remarked, "Oh yeah, this guy has to work alone. He's a Protestant." I was curious about the connection between working alone and being a Protestant. I learned that these particular Protestants were part of a church that believed drinking alcohol was taboo for Christians. The problem for these Kofyar Christians was that this belief made it difficult to mobilize help for the simultaneous labor demands of storing the millet (e.g., tossing the bundled millet to someone standing on the tall rack to catch it). Most Kofyar farmers enlisted help by having a "beer work party." Women would prepare large vats of millet beer to share with neighbors and relatives who would come to help with the harvest. This was more efficient than hiring help, as neighbors would help at a beer work party knowing they could later invite those same workers to their own beer work party.[5] Millet beer provided energy to work all day and also boosted the festive atmosphere enjoyed by the community during the days of hard labor. Beer symbolized hospitality and community; men drank from a common vessel, and women worked together to prepare the beer. By rejecting beer, the Protestants distanced themselves from the community. This made it difficult for them to gather others to do the labor necessary to harvest and store their crops efficiently.[6]

3. For a discussion of Boas's views and the ways in which his students extended his views into moral and epistemological relativism, see Henry H. Bagish, "Confessions of a Former Cultural Relativist," in *Annual Editions: Anthropology*, ed. Elvio Angeloni (Dushkin, 1983), 22–29.

4. Millet is a grain grown throughout the world. Millet must be stored and dried rapidly to prevent rain from ruining the harvested crop.

5. Robert McC. Netting, *Smallholders, Householders: Farm Families and the Ecology of Intensive, Sustainable Agriculture* (Stanford University Press, 1993), 72–75.

6. Glenn Davis Stone, *Settlement Ecology: The Social and Spatial Organization of Kofyar Agriculture* (University of Arizona Press, 1996), 112–13.

Group labor projects among the Kofyar have declined where Protestant restrictions against serving beer prevent them from offering it as an incentive to their neighbors.

Understanding the relationship between beer and work does not imply that drinking beer is a good thing or a bad thing. In many communities, alcohol consumption causes social problems. Domestic abuse, alcoholism, and traffic fatalities are linked to alcohol consumption. In some places, beer is a symbol of domineering masculinity rather than an incentive to cooperate. For these reasons (and others), some Christians teach that drinking is prohibited. What was missing in the Kofyar case, however, was an understanding of how beer tied into their economic and social life. Because Christian missionaries lacked understanding of what beer meant to these people in economic and social terms, they failed to appreciate the consequences of encouraging people to give up beer.

Cultural relativism is a helpful idea when understood straightforwardly: Aspects of culture develop relative to other aspects of that same culture. Cultural relativism is clearly distinct from moral relativism or epistemological relativism. **Moral relativism** is the idea that something is only right or wrong according to context-specific criteria. This notion is incompatible with Christian faith and ethics, and it is also incompatible with anthropology. It is also virtually impossible to put into practice. Anthropologists make moral judgments about other cultures when they see human rights violations such as genocide or torture. Even without a religious tradition or historic ethical code, anthropologists can rely on humanistic values—that is, principles common to most humans—or the ethical guidance of the American Anthropological Association to evaluate right or wrong in cross-cultural contexts.

Epistemological relativism is the belief that the validity of knowledge itself is limited to the context in which it was produced. This is the idea that some things are "true for you, but not true for me," or even "real for you, but not real for me." The epistemological relativist would argue that truth in the world of the Kofyar is different from truth among suburban US Americans. Though the Kofyar and US Americans may experience the world quite differently, the Christian doctrines of creation—that God created all humans, that we live in the world of God's creation and revelation, and that God has revealed knowledge to everyone and communicates truth consistently—counter the argument that truth itself changes with the cultural context. While it may seem kind to bow out of difficult conversations by agreeing to disagree, this isn't kind when serious matters are at stake. It's possible to take risks in conversation about different moral and ethical views, trusting that rigorous conversation can lead to the determination of truth.

Cultural relativism, understood as a truth about the nature of culture and cultural understanding, does not demand the acceptance of either moral or epistemological relativism. We can hold to Christian values and morality while acknowledging that cultures can only be understood accurately in relation to themselves. When cultural relativism is not practiced, people use the standards of their own culture to understand others, which invariably leads to misunderstanding rooted in ethnocentrism. The view that "wins the day" will often be the view of the person from a more powerful culture or the person who has more power in a given situation.

Varieties of Ethnocentrism

Ethnocentrism puts one's own culture (*ethno*) at the center (*centrism*) of interpretation, typically devaluing and invariably mischaracterizing other cultures. Ethnocentrism is inevitable because humans are socialized to see their way of life as normal, natural, and often superior. Every person needs a culture and social group at their center to guide their language, relationships, and way of life. Just imagine a person with no cultural grounding—without family and socialization, a human could never develop in the ways God designed. There is no way to rid the world of ethnocentrism, but we can understand its effects on us and thereby account for them. When we grow in cultural self-awareness, we can recognize how our own culture shapes our interpretations and interactions with others. To understand how ethnocentrism manifests in contemporary life, we can classify it in three types: xenophobia, cultural superiority, and tacit ethnocentrism.

Xenophobia

Xenophobia is an intense, irrational antipathy for people from other countries or cultures. Xenophobia is sometimes expressed in anti-immigrant views, cultural isolationism, or even discrimination or violence. The most pervasive expression of xenophobia in the world today is blatant racism. **Racism** is the belief that humans are organized into genetically valid race groupings that are different from one another in intelligence and worth. Racism asserts the superiority of some people over others, a view expressed by such US groups as the Ku Klux Klan or the neo-Nazis. Despite efforts against it, xenophobia continues to motivate massive harm around the world in ways ranging from genocide to political oppression to hate crimes to verbal cruelty.

Cultural Superiority

The second type of ethnocentrism, **cultural superiority**, is the belief that one culture is more enlightened, advanced, or civilized than another. It is often expressed with patronizing comments such as, "Those people just don't know any better," or "If we can teach these people how we live, they can be as advanced as we are." Cultural superiority can be found all over the world; no one society has a monopoly on cultural arrogance. Cultural superiority has devastating effects when a group of people has sufficient power and privilege to impose their ethnocentrism on other groups. For example, European colonial governments in North America, Africa, Asia, Australia, and elsewhere imposed their European educational systems and languages on Indigenous people and suppressed many of their important cultural, social, and economic practices. At times this was motivated by xenophobia and at other times by paternalistic cultural superiority, but either way the result has been the devastation of Indigenous cultures worldwide.

Today, many Christians reject these ethnocentric attitudes because they are so clearly in opposition to the gospel. Indeed, in the book of Acts, Paul opposed his own people's (Jews') ethnocentrism toward non-Jewish converts (see Gal. 2:1–5; also Col. 2:8–23). Across time, God has empowered brave Christians who risked their lives to lead movements against racism and xenophobia in societies around the world.

Can a Culture Be Christian?

It is true that by some criteria—efficiency or entrepreneurial incentive—some cultures have features that promote particular activities, while other cultures inhibit them. In German or US American cultures, for example, where people are taught to value punctuality and innovation, capitalism works pretty well. We can make a lot of money. Yet if we also value community cohesion, marital stability, and sexual modesty, these same cultures do not look so good.

Okay, you might reply, so perhaps cultures have strengths and weaknesses in terms of economic systems or social cohesion, but aren't some cultures more Christian than others? Isn't it true that the United States is a more Christian culture than, say, communist China?

We would argue that the question itself represents a mistaken use of the culture concept. A culture cannot be Christian because to be a Christian is to follow Christ. A culture cannot choose to give its life to Christ; people choose Christ. Certainly, a place where many people have lived as Christians for a long time has more Christian language, biblically derived concepts, and symbolism than a place that doesn't; this has led some anthropologists who study Christianity to speak of "Christian culture."[a] The problem with this idea is that it implies that there is one Christian culture, rather than a wide range of ways that people in different cultures have faithfully responded to the gospel. It also suggests that a culture deeply influenced by Christian ideas is more moral or reflects Christian behavior better than cultures where Christianity is a minority religion. For example, while more non-Christians in the United States might be informed about Christian doctrines or symbols than non-Christians in China, it is not true that US culture is more moral or faithful than other cultures. Indeed, it seems fair to say that culture in the United States values sexual freedom, individual autonomy, and materialism. Mainstream culture in China clearly values social connectedness, family loyalty, and spirituality. So is China more Christian? Of course not, but it's equally mistaken to say the United States is a more Christian culture.

The individual autonomy prized in the United States does resonate with the biblical call for individuals to follow Christ even when it means turning away from family. Those of us raised in the United States may find it easier to turn from the beliefs of a non-Christian family or non-Christian friends for the sake of Christ. The family loyalty of China may make it harder for some to leave the religion of their families, but it may also make it easier for Christians there to understand and practice the biblical metaphor of the church as family. Christians in *every* culture find themselves at odds with some things in their background, while other aspects of the same culture help them to more faithfully live in ways that honor the teachings of Christ.

a. See, for example, Joel Robbins, *Becoming Sinners: Christianity and Moral Torment in a Papua New Guinea Society* (University of California Press, 2004).

Tacit Ethnocentrism

Tacit ethnocentrism is the assumption that one's own way of life is normal and typical rather than a product of one's culture. In one sense, tacit ethnocentrism is the outcome of successful enculturation; a person has a deep sense of belonging in a group, such that the group's beliefs, values, and behaviors seem like just ordinary life. Even those opposed to xenophobia and cultural superiority may harbor tacit ethnocentrism when they assume that their view of what's normal is true for everyone, or that those who don't share their sense of normal are odd.

Tacit ethnocentrism is present, for example, when people do not see anything particularly cultural about liking ice in a glass of water, or finding a mountain lake beautiful, or wanting a soft bed off the floor. They might understand that many people from India *don't* put ice in their water but assume it must be because they are poor and do not have ice makers or have simply never experienced how wonderful cold water is. They may not hold a preference for no ice against another group, but the ones who *don't* want ice are "different," interesting perhaps, maybe a little weird. In a perspective shaped by tacit ethnocentrism, the most important question is why they do not like ice, instead of asking why we *do*. One's own culture (*ethnos*) takes center stage (*centrism*), and the other culture is understood in terms of how it is like or unlike one's own.

To take what is, for many US Americans, a more deeply held cultural ideal, consider camping. Many people in the United States find camping or other encounters with nature to be profound spiritual experiences. Christians often find that nature stirs our souls to ponder our smallness in the face of God's grandeur. We interpret these feelings as natural and human, as the testimony of creation pointing to the Creator (Job 12:7–11).

James Marohn

Such scenes may not produce these feelings at all, however, for people who actually live close to nature. They may know the lake intimately—understanding how to read wind patterns or water currents, when and where fish congregate, the most likely spots for turtles' nests—and may respect and cherish this resource, but without a soulful, spiritual response. They may also see the world as pointing to God as Creator, but in terms of how nature provides for human life rather than in sublime feelings of awe.

Similarly, people from urban subcultures in the United States often express frustration that some (usually from the dominant ethnic/racial group) insist that *everyone* should love camping: "Everyone can naturally see God better in the woods; you just have to try." One urban Black American student at a Christian college expressed it this way: "You know, in my neighborhood, people do not go camping. They say, 'I have a house. Why would I want to stay in a little tent in the woods and have bugs crawling on me?' But my [White] friends here say there's something wrong with me; that I just don't get it. I'm tired of people telling me that they're right and I'm wrong just because I don't see things their way."

This student did try camping and learned to enjoy it. His frustration came from the fact that many of his friends did not see the differences as cultural but as a flaw in him. They seemed to believe that *everyone* should love to hike into the woods, sleep in a tent, and enjoy the beauty of nature, because surely that is just natural—a God-given response to creation. Actually, a spiritual experience in nature is a culturally conditioned response. It is surely connected to something beyond culture—God and creation—but it is not the only, the best, or the natural response.

In addition to blinding us to the relevance of culture in our own lives, tacit ethnocentrism can take the form of someone saying, "I have no culture. I'm boring. I'm just a normal, average person." This might seem like a compliment to those deemed to *have* a culture, but those who call themselves cultureless tacitly suggest that the ways they feel—their judgments, their tastes, their reactions to the world—are just normal, human ones. "Others are different; I'm just normal. Others are ethnic; I'm just me."

Trying to imagine human beings without culture does not lead to a picture of a "pure" human. Our ability to interact with the world through culture is the very thing that *makes* us human. The image of human beings in the garden of Eden before the fall is of beings with language, living in a world filled with cultural meaning and social interaction. After creating Adam, God said, "It is not good for the man to be alone" (Gen. 2:18), and then God created the first cultural interaction by bringing Eve and Adam together. Adam was not supposed to be "just Adam" but Adam as created by and in communion with God, in relationship with Eve, and as part of a wider creation over which humans were to have responsibility.

God gave humans the capacity for language, relationship, and self-awareness, which we are to use to interact with the earth and shape communities; this is what theologians call the cultural mandate, part of God's good creation. The cultures we create, then, are not barriers to understanding God; they are the means through which God becomes known to us. Problems arise when one cultural expression (all of which are tainted by the fall) is seen as normal, natural, and human, and anything different is seen as substandard or sinful. Combating ethnocentrism is the place where anthropology and Christian values come together the most. Recognizing how tacit ethnocentrism plays into our assumptions should humble us into acknowledging the strengths and weaknesses of our vantage point on God's truth.

The Culture Concept Today

Culture is the total way of life of a group of people that is learned, dynamic, shared, power laden, and integrated. Each of these five characteristics reflects important elements of the culture context.

Learned

People learn culture from other people by being raised in a culture or by extended exposure to a new culture later in life. Affirming the learned aspect of culture allows anthropologists to focus on such things as the socialization of children, the organization of knowledge in a society, and how and why cultures change (or do not change) over generations. In contrast with racial or biological notions of human behavior, anthropologists agree that ethnographic data provide no support for the notion of a biological basis for cultural expressions. Neurological research suggests that our brains take shape, to some degree, in response to our social and physical environment, but at birth every brain is ready to learn any culture. Stereotypes such as "Japanese people are quiet" or "people in the United States smile a lot" may reflect some widespread cultural norm, but there is no demonstrable link between specific cultural forms and the biology of the people who practice those forms.

Dynamic

People are constantly adapting to their environments and shifting interests. Language, values, and behaviors may be understood as related to their economic, political, geographical, and historical contexts, aspects of which are always changing. Sometimes journalistic reports of societies in the rain forests of the Amazon or nomadic people of sub-Saharan Africa will describe them as "living unchanged since the beginning of time." This is flat wrong. All cultures have changed and continue to change. Some of these changes are dramatic and rapid. Some are imposed by outsiders. But even those people living relatively remote and independent lives experience cultural change in response to changes in the natural environment, social or technological innovations, or the work of charismatic leaders.

Shared

In anthropological perspective, there is no such thing as individual culture. There is individual variation, but culture can never be private. You may wake up one morning and decide to throw off the oppressive structure of English, bursting out of your room declaring, "Amtanzafna! Moockano v Stinana!" If no one else shares an understanding of your vocalization, it cannot be called a language, which by definition is a form of communication. If no communication occurs, you just have sounds, regardless of how carefully organized they are in your own mind. In the same way, unless others share your understanding of cultural symbols, practices, or ideas, it is not a culture.

Power Laden

Culture is not neutral. In terms of access to social power, economic resources, ritual prestige, or political control, people use cultural resources to achieve their goals, even if those goals disadvantage others. Early anthropologists, such as Edward B. Tylor, Bronisław Malinowski, and Alfred R. Radcliffe-Brown, tended to be more concerned with *statis*, or stability, than with cultural change. Thus, they were less likely to notice or highlight the inequalities or relative advantages within cultural contexts. However, as later anthropologists became more interested in social and cultural change, it became more obvious that cultures developed in ways that advantaged some, disadvantaged others, and always expressed the agency, or power, of people.

Integrated

Any aspect of culture relates, in some way, to other parts of that culture. As demonstrated by the example of the Kofyar, some missionaries have thought that changing religion or giving up certain rituals, foods, or drinks is a relatively simple thing. They have said that in converting to Christianity, people need only change certain behaviors without changing their culture overall. It is a mistake, however, to think that some aspects of culture can change without influencing other aspects of culture.

YOUR TURN

Culture in a Cup

Anthropologists use the culture concept to study all aspects of human life and culture. They may seek to understand extraordinary events such as death and marriage, or unusual experiences. They also study ordinary events such as traveling, talking, eating, and drinking.

It's your turn to use the culture concept to investigate the human experience. Get a drink and set it down in front of you. Any drink will do, even a glass of water.

Set a timer for three minutes. Give your full attention to the drink for three minutes. Begin as a participant observer: Stand apart from the drink and just look at it. Then use the rest of your senses: Touch it. Smell it. Drink it. Listen to it.

After the time is up, use the culture concept to analyze the drink.

- *Culture is learned.* How do people learn to interact with this drink?
- *Culture is dynamic.* How has this drink, or the cup, or the ways people enjoy it changed over time?
- *Culture is shared.* How is knowledge about the drink shared: within social groups, with children, or with newcomers?
- *Culture is power laden.* How does this drink display or perpetuate power dynamics in society or in the world? (Consider its ingredients, its cost, the groups in society who like it most, or groups who don't have access to it.)
- *Culture is integrated.* How does this drink fit with other parts of life such as family, religion, economy, education, or politics?

You may want to use some secondary sources (online articles or sources from your library) to learn about the history or composition of the drink. Combine that knowledge with your primary, ethnographic research (observations and interactions).

The culture concept is a powerful way to understand the human experience. We can love our neighbors better when we really pay attention to their lives and their social contexts, including even something as ordinary as having a drink.

Affirming this interdependence of culture does not mean that any culture is perfectly or completely integrated, however. Different individuals have different levels of knowledge and understanding, may agree or disagree with various aspects of their culture, and may be working for or against change. Changes are often unpredictable and complex, unfolding over many years and among different subgroups.

Seeing Culture

Culture is a broad concept. Anthropologists use additional concepts to guide them as they describe and analyze the way of life of a group of people. **Norms** are behaviors that are considered good, right, or normal by a group of people. Anthropologists observe norms in people's speech and actions. In Christian terms, ethical behavior fits not only with cultural norms but also with norms established by God and by those who have followed God in many different times and places. **Values** are ideas about right and wrong that are held by a group of people. Values are not directly observable, so anthropologists infer values from the observable parts of culture such as speech, actions, objects, and symbols. In Christian terms, morals are values that are rooted in God's character and in the Bible.

Culture may be material or nonmaterial. **Material culture** includes physical objects made or used by a group of people. Computers or pens are considered material culture because people invented them. A stick or a rock is also material culture insofar as people name them and use them. Even unaltered nature becomes culture when people name it and draw it into the human domain for appreciation or for use. **Nonmaterial culture** includes intangible elements of life such as beliefs and values.

In religion, we can see all these elements of culture. When people learn and share religion with new generations, they share beliefs values and norms with others. In a religious gathering, people express nonmaterial culture (beliefs and values) with material culture such as symbols, sacred books, buildings with significant architecture, prayer beads, robes or head coverings, and more. Religion teaches norms for behavior, some of which apply only within the religious space, and others that apply in all parts of life. Religion can join forces with general cultural norms, infusing them with divine origins and authority, or religion can offer alternative norms and values that contrast with those of the surrounding culture.

Culture as a Conversation

People often use metaphors to describe culture. Though each has its strengths, many of these popular metaphors for culture obscure an anthropological understanding. For instance, to make the point that culture is pervasive, largely unconscious, and intrinsic to our very humanity, some have portrayed people as fish swimming in the "water" of their culture. However, unlike the fish, which cannot change its water, humans can change their culture. Fish cannot say, "With all these ships coming through, I think it would work better for us fish to change the chemical composition of water from H_2O to something less dense so these boats will sink. Let's try that out and see if it catches on." But humans *can* devise ways of changing their culture. Discussions of culture must include agency and innovation—how individuals and groups respond and adapt within a cultural context, resulting in intentional and unintentional changes to the culture itself.

Christian missiologists have often favored the description of culture as a pair of glasses through which we see the world. Prospective missionaries must understand that cultures are not just different from one another but also that cultural assumptions profoundly affect how we perceive the world.[7] This metaphor connects to the worldview concept, a subject of close study by anthropologist-missiologist Paul Hiebert. His work on worldview has been an important contribution to missionary thought and practice in the past fifty years. However, this metaphor of culture as a way of seeing the world wrongly implies there are "Italian glasses" or "Korean glasses" that fit everyone of that description. There are variations *within* contexts, as well as variations over time. Second, the glasses image or the concept of a worldview perspective implies that culture is a kind of stable thing that an individual has, either inside their head or in front of their eyes, before interacting with the material and social world. But we know that the world itself turns back to shape our culture. For example, in US society, most people would recognize that cars are part of the culture. Owners often give them names and customize them, while the government builds neighborhoods and cities around the use of them. But did the United States come to value cars because of a worldview that valued cars, or did a love of cars follow the development of cars themselves? There is a dynamic interaction between the material world, social relations, and our worldview(s) that the glasses metaphor does not capture well.

Theologian H. Richard Niebuhr greatly influenced the way Christians think about engaging culture with his categories: Christ against culture, Christ of culture, Christ above culture, Christ and culture in paradox, and Christ transforming culture.[8] This may not seem like a metaphor, but it is. By typologizing the different ways Christians have interacted with social institutions and cultural norms in various times and places, Niebuhr made both Christianity and culture seem more concrete, helping Christians become aware of how they and their traditions tend to approach culture—with a stance of appreciation, rejection, or control—and to understand why other Christians see the issues differently.

As helpful as his work has been, however, the metaphor conceptualizes Christianity and culture as discrete entities—like balls on a pool table

7. Paul G. Hiebert, *Transforming Worldviews: An Anthropological Understanding of How People Change* (Baker Academic, 2008); Randy S. Woodley, *Mission and the Cultural Other: A Closer Look* (Cascade Books, 2022).

8. H. Richard Niebuhr, *Christ and Culture* (Harper & Row, 1975).

bouncing against each other in occasional interactions. Since Christianity is, by definition, the expression of the gospel in a cultural context, there is no such thing as a nonspecific, free-floating Christianity existing apart from the particular times and places in which it is expressed. The metaphor of "Christ and Culture" is misleading in that it encourages Christians to think of themselves as existing outside culture, with unencumbered choice as to how they interact with culture. Anthropologists emphasize that all people, and all religions, exist within cultures and are influenced by culture in ways they are often unable to perceive.

Our preferred metaphor is *culture as a conversation*. In real life, a conversation has many of the qualities of culture. For example, a conversation, like culture, is shared by at least two people. At the same time, a conversation is dynamic. In any conversation, individuals respond to one another and to the environment they are in, and their responses may change from moment to moment. Similarly, culture is dynamic. Just as people might make up a new word in the course of a conversation ("Dude, that was a great speech! Total ska-doosh!"), individuals can play with their culture to express something others understand in new ways. These cultural innovations may or may not catch on—or even be understood well—but they are always possible.

Body language, facial expression, tone of voice, and word choice are all critical aspects of communication. If you meet the president of the United States or prime minister of Thailand, you are probably going to use different words (or a distinct *social register* [see chap. 3]), a different tone of voice, and even different body language than if you were speaking to your roommate, mother, or neighbor. In any conversation, there are ways for one person to subtly communicate superiority (a tone of voice, a patronizing pat on the shoulder) or submission (avoiding eye contact, a meek body posture) without words. Power differentials may be conveyed by tone, pitch, or body language.

At the same time, all these choices—to be friendly, to convey superiority, to modify one's words to be more respectful, to choose certain words and avoid others—are constrained by the words, grammar, symbols, and shared assumptions existing prior to the conversation. Individuals may have a lot of freedom in how the conversation goes, but this creativity is both enabled and limited by the language and culture in which the conversation occurs. Just as some people are good conversationalists, some people are especially good at working with culture, meaning they know how to use the symbols, meanings, and practices of their culture to influence others, get what they want, and communicate effectively.

Thus, the metaphor of culture as conversation captures the learned, dynamic, shared, power laden, and integrated aspects of the culture concept.

Developing Anthro-Vision

In May 1992, Gillian Tett was a journalist with *The Financial Times* taking refuge from a civil war raging in the streets of Dushanbe, Tajikistan. Sharing her shelter in a drab hotel was Marcus, a colleague from *The Daily Telegraph*. As she and Marcus chatted, listening to the gunfire outside, he asked about her background. She shared that before becoming a journalist she earned a PhD in anthropology from Cambridge and that she wrote her dissertation on marriage rituals in the mountains of Tajikistan. "Marriage rituals?" exclaimed Marcus. "What the <bleep> is the point of *that*?"

His reaction did not surprise Tett. Many people see the topics of anthropology as obscure or irrelevant. What is the point of studying marriage rituals when literal life and death are happening outside? But what Tett learned from her research has become the basis of her work, first as a journalist and now as a global business consultant and editor in chief of *The Financial Times*. She learned that culture matters. It shapes everything we do, whether in the forests of the Amazon or the warehouses of Amazon.com, Inc. Learning to see how people are creating, shaping, and shaped by culture allows others to understand how to help, serve, and engage more effectively. She wrote a book called *Anthro-Vision* aimed at helping people in business and all of life to "see around corners, spot what is hidden in plain sight, and gain empathy for others and fresh insight on problems."[a]

Learning to see culture is particularly important in a world shaped by volatility, uncertainty, complexity, and ambiguity (or "VUCA," as Western military leaders say). Tett warns, "Tunnel vision is deadly. Your compass may be technically brilliant and tell you where to aim. But if you only focus on the dial, you may walk into a tree. We need lateral vision. That is what anthropology can impart: anthro-vision."

It's your turn: Consider a group (club, team, church, family) you know well. If you were to describe this group to a complete outsider who wanted to fit in, what would you tell them? What would that person need to know? What sort of "lateral vision" do you have in that setting that the outsider would not?

a. Quotations are from Gillian Tett, "Introducing the Other 'AI': Anthropology Intelligence," *Sapiens*, July 20, 2021, https://www.sapiens.org/culture/gillian-tett-anthro-vision-interview/. See also Gillian Tett, *Anthro-Vision: A New Way to See in Business and Life* (Avid Reader Press, 2021).

In culture, as in conversation, there is improvisation and innovation, pattern and predictability, all happening at once. Culture is not so much a *thing* that we *have* as it is an *activity* that we *do*.

Christians and Culture

In the incarnation, God took on flesh and came to live among people. Jesus grew up in a culture and shared life with people through language, food, family, and everyday tasks. He also challenged the culture with new values and norms, and he ultimately suffered death through culturally constructed legal processes and means of execution. Christians are called to follow Jesus in incarnating the good news in all the cultural settings where we live. This can't mean simply affirming or going along with everything in the culture, but it also can't mean rejecting our surroundings, trying to be "just Christians" without any culture. God's truth in Scripture and in Jesus is only and always revealed to us through specific cultural forms. We then use our own cultural forms to understand that revelation as text, teaching, and tradition. Sometimes, in an effort to dig deeply into the Word, we try to strip away the medium by which God communicates to us to get to the "pure message" underneath. But God gave us different cultures so that we could understand God more fully. Without culture, we have no language, no symbols, no revelation, and no community. In short, we need culture in order to learn to love and serve God.

As we learn to understand our own cultural context and those of others, we should be aware of the ways in which all these cultures fall short of reflecting God's character and priorities. As those creating and re-creating culture all the time, we do have the ability to change and adapt our own cultures in positive ways. The reality that all cultural contexts are twisted by sin should make us even more determined to understand our own and others' cultures. Through an anthropological view of culture, we can understand the contours of cultures better, which in turn makes us intentional about preserving or changing them.

In the book of Revelation, John provides a vision of the new Jerusalem, a city in which God rules over the diverse nations of the world, in which the kings bring their splendor before God (Rev. 21:24). Culture, and cultural diversity, will not be wiped away but will be redeemed. This suggests that culture, in all its present diversity, is not a problem to be overcome but a blessing that will be present for eternity. It only makes sense that Christians would learn to understand it now.

TERMS

armchair anthropologists: Early anthropologists who gathered data from travelogues and books rather than from their own direct research.

cultural relativism: The view that various cultural practices and beliefs are best understood in relation to their entire context.

cultural superiority: The belief that one culture is more enlightened, advanced, civilized, or intelligent than another.

culture: The total way of life of a group of people that is learned, dynamic, shared, power laden, and integrated.

epistemological relativism: The belief that the validity of knowledge itself is limited to the context in which it was produced.

ethnocentrism: The use of one's own culture to measure another's; putting one's own culture (*ethno*) at the center (*centrism*) of interpretation, typically devaluing the other culture.

historical particularism: An early anthropological theory that argues that each culture embodies a unique representation of its history and context.

material culture: Physical objects made or used by a group of people.

monogenesis: The view that all humans originate from a single creation of God.

moral relativism: The idea that something is only right or wrong according to context-specific criteria.

nonmaterial culture: Intangible elements of life such as beliefs and values.

norms: Behaviors that are considered good, right, or normal by a group of people.

polygenesis: The theory that various groups of humans appeared on earth or were created separately.

racism: The belief that humans are organized into race groupings that are different from one another in intelligence and worth.

tacit ethnocentrism: The assumption that one's own way of life is just normal, not cultural.

unilinear cultural evolution: An early anthropological theory that states all cultures evolve from simple to complex along a single trajectory of progress.

values: Ideas about right and wrong that are held by a group of people.

xenophobia: An intense, irrational antipathy toward people from other countries or cultures.

DISCUSSION QUESTIONS

1. Name one culture you have visited or studied in depth. Describe a cultural difference that you first interpreted in an ethnocentric way and then learned to view with cultural relativism.

2. Design an ethnic fair exhibit for your culture (or one of the cultures with which you identify). What items would you choose to represent your culture? Now think critically: In what ways does the ethnic fair accurately represent your culture? How does the ethnic fair approach misrepresent or oversimplify your culture?
3. Read Genesis 1–2. List elements of culture present before the fall. This includes symbols, language, marriage, economy, family, custom, law, and other elements of life. In your experience, have Christians tended to consider culture as part of God's good creation or as part of the fall? How might a view of culture as emerging from creation shape Christians' cultural engagement?

ANTHROPOLOGY AND SCRIPTURE

Culture: The Pattern of This World

> Therefore, I urge you, brothers and sisters, in view of God's mercy, to offer your bodies as a living sacrifice, holy and pleasing to God—this is your true and proper worship. Do not conform to the pattern of this world, but be transformed by the renewing of your mind. Then you will be able to test and approve what God's will is—his good, pleasing and perfect will. (Rom. 12:1–2)

Culture is the total way of life of a group of people that is learned, dynamic, shared, power laden, and integrated. It also could be called the pattern of this world, the way of life we learn to be conformed to through enculturation. This passage encourages us to become critical thinkers, especially with respect to our own culture. When the Holy Spirit renews our minds, we are better able to engage our culture critically, not simply living from its values without even recognizing it. This won't lift us out of culture, but it will move us toward living with wisdom and discernment, always testing what is good, pleasing, and perfect.

Culture as Part of God's Good Creation

> Then the Lord God said, "It is not good that the man should be alone; I will make him a helper as his partner." So out of the ground the Lord God formed every animal of the field and every bird of the air and brought them to the man to see what he would call them, and whatever the man called every living creature, that was its name. The man gave names to all cattle and to the birds of the air and to every animal of the field, but for the man there was not found

> a helper as his partner. So the Lord God caused a deep sleep to fall upon the man, and he slept; then he took one of his ribs and closed up its place with flesh. And the rib that the Lord God had taken from the man he made into a woman and brought her to the man. Then the man said,
>
> "This at last is bone of my bones
> and flesh of my flesh;
> this one shall be called Woman,
> for out of Man this one was taken."
>
> Therefore a man leaves his father and his mother and clings to his wife, and they become one flesh. (Gen. 2:18–24 NRSVue)

Genesis 1 and 2 describe God's creation before the fall. In the passage above, we see elements of social organization that, many hundreds of years later, anthropologists call culture. We see work as Adam names the animals, marriage in the relationship between Adam and Eve, and extended family (or kinship) relationships. Even in this depiction of a world with only two people, Adam and Eve needed culture: shared understandings and ways of life that would allow them to thrive as human beings. Genesis 3 describes the fall, and the impact of sin is pervasive in human culture from then up through the present. But God created culture as a context for human flourishing, and we may work toward its redemption and enjoy its goodness.

3

LANGUAGE

After studying this chapter, you should be able to do the following:

1. compare and contrast historical linguistics, descriptive linguistics, and sociolinguistics
2. explain the Sapir-Whorf hypothesis
3. describe how sociolinguists study culture, language, and society

CHAPTER OUTLINE

Introduction

> In the beginning was the Word, and the Word was with God, and the Word was God. He was in the beginning with God. All things came into being through him, and without him not one thing came into being. What has come into being in him was life, and the life was the light of all people. The light shines in the darkness, and the darkness did not overtake it. (John 1:1–5 NRSVue)

Jesus is the Word (*logos*). God created the world by speaking it into existence. At Pentecost, the Holy Spirit appeared as "tongues of fire" (Acts 2:3), enabling the apostles to speak in the multiple languages of the people assembled in Jerusalem. Throughout Scripture, language and images of language are central in how God reveals truth and moves in the world. **Language** is a system of verbal and nonverbal symbols used to communicate. A **symbol** is anything that stands for something else. The human capacity to communicate by creating representations and meanings is astounding. It is not an exaggeration to say language, like culture, is a fundamental element of human life. As they do with culture, anthropologists ask many questions about language. How different are the various languages of the world? Are some languages more developed or sophisticated, or just more suitable for particular activities? How and why do languages change? How are people using digital technologies, such as texting, memes, and videos, to make innovations in language?

In this chapter, we present three areas of linguistics: historical linguistics, descriptive linguistics, and sociolinguistics. Then we describe how the Sapir-Whorf hypothesis shapes the anthropological perspective on language. We conclude with a consideration of how linguistics provides profound insights for Christians in understanding Scripture and in sharing the gospel.

Historical Linguistics

Historical linguistics is the study of how languages develop and change over time, including how different languages are related to one another. European scholars first began to systematically study language by collecting writing samples from India, China, sub-Saharan Africa, and elsewhere and by exploring connections between various languages. Sir William Jones, a British scholar living in eighteenth-century India, noticed relationships between Sanskrit and classical Greek, Latin, and modern European languages. Sanskrit was no longer spoken in Jones's time, but a number of ancient Sanskrit texts had been preserved. By studying linguistic morphology—the patterns and structures of words in a language—Jones and other scholars connected different languages into language families. A **language family** is a group of languages that is thought to derive from a common ancestor language.

Each language family traces back to a **protolanguage**, a postulated ancient language from which all the members of a particular language family are thought to be derived. It seems that languages as diverse as Sanskrit, Swedish, Yiddish, and English share a protolanguage that linguists call Proto-Indo-European (see fig. 3.1). This language family probably emerged in the Caucasus region of Europe, north of Turkey, and spread in all directions, developing differences over time. Linguists use the comparative method to trace a language's family tree. The comparative method identifies related words, establishes sound correspondences, and identifies correspondences between words. Table 3.1 demonstrates how linguists might notice similar words, including references to similar animals and natural features, which indicate a connection in the past between languages and people that are, at present, very different from one another. For example, there is similarity between words such as the English "father" and the Bengali "patr" in English terms such as "paternity."

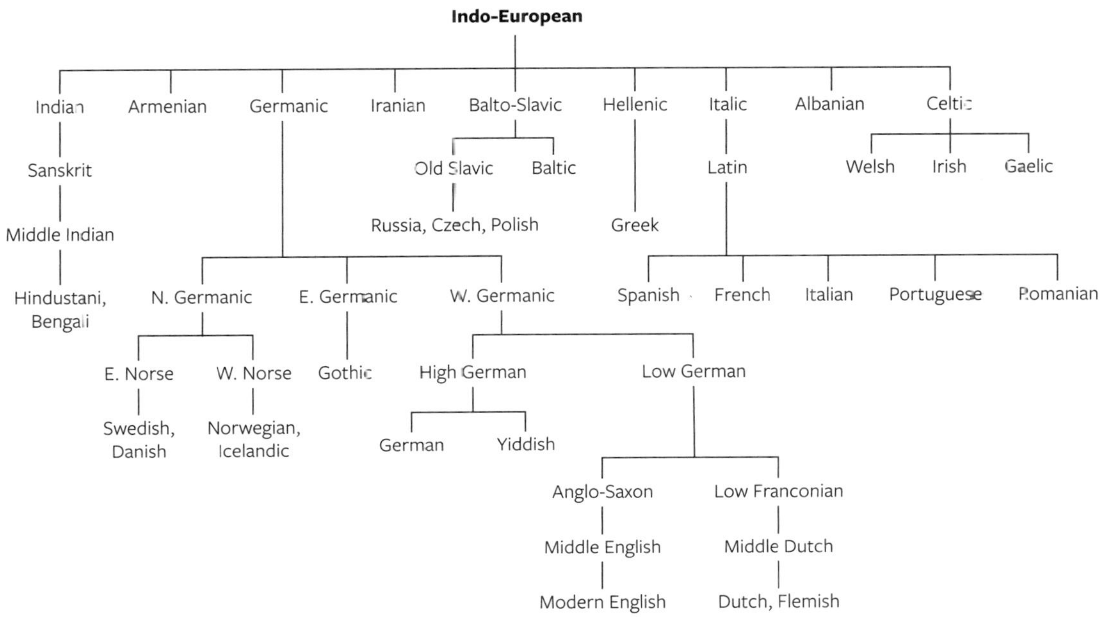

Figure 3.1. The Indo-European language family

Jones's work illustrates the principle that languages are constantly changing. Consider the following Bible passage in Old English: "forþam todæg eow ys hælend acenned. se is drihten crist on dauides ceastre."[1] Or search online for "listen to Old English" and see how many words are recognizable in a recording of this dialect. The grammar, syntax, and spelling (including letters no longer in use) are so different that no speaker of contemporary English could read it without training. The same passage taken from the Wycliffe translation approximately four hundred years later is a bit clearer to the modern eye but with unfamiliar spelling: "for a saueour is born to day to vs, þat is crist a lord in þe cite of dauid."[2] Even the King James translation of 1611 has many words spelled incorrectly by today's standards. "For vnto you is borne this day, in the citie of Dauid, a Sauiour, which is Christ the Lord."[3] Of course, there is nothing wrong with any of these versions. Each was written

1. Translation of Luke 2:11 in the Wessex Gospels, "Changes in the English Language," Bible Research, accessed July 20, 2025, http://www.bible-researcher.com/engchange.html.

2. Translation of Luke 2:11 in "Wycliffe Bible of 1382," Textus Receptus Bibles, May 12, 2024, https://www.textusreceptusbibles.com/Wycliffe. See H. Wheeler Robinson, *The Bible in Its Ancient and English Versions* (Praeger/Greenwood, 1970).

3. Translation of Luke 2:11 in *The Holy Bible: King James Version 1611 edition* (Thomas Nelson, 2010).

Table 3.1. Indo-European Word Correspondences

Word Category	European		Indo-Iranian	
	English	Swedish	Sanskrit	Bengali
kinship	mother	mor	mātár-	āmmā
	father	far	pitár-	pitr
animals	cow	ko	gáuh	gābhī
	mouse	mus	mūs-	musa
numbers	two	två	dvā (u)	du
	seven	sju	saptá	sapta
body parts	nose	näsa	nas-	nasika
	foot	fot	pada	psye

according to the linguistic standards of its time, and each represents different stages in the development of English.

This focus on language change over time, known as diachronic research, allowed scholars to consider how changes in social life, politics, and so forth were reflected in language. Today, many people who do historical linguistic research call it "philology," the study of societies through their texts. This distinguishes them from those doing descriptive linguistics, described below.

Descriptive Linguistics

After the initial development of historical linguistics, some scholars began to focus less on how languages change over time and more on how languages are patterned at a given moment in time (synchronic research). **Descriptive linguistics** is the study of a language as used by a particular group of people at a particular moment in time.

Descriptive linguistics is an extremely difficult field of study because language changes across time and geography, and because individuals constantly alter and innovate language. Descriptive linguistics may be viewed as building up from sounds to speech units to words to sentences to language in meaningful contexts, such as conversations.

Phonetics is the study of the production, transmission, and perception of speech sounds, including all possible sounds in all human languages. Any language in the world uses only a subset of the possible sounds humans

YOUR TURN

Talk to a Stranger

Humans have amazing abilities to create and share symbols as they communicate. People use language to strengthen social ties and to make new bonds by meeting new people. That new person could be a baby who needs to learn to speak the language of their group, or it could be a friend or colleague. Learning a new language is exciting and risky, and so is using a familiar language to meet someone new.

In the modern world, most of us encounter strangers every day. We may nod to a stranger in public to show that we see them. We may speak to a stranger to have a brief interaction or to make a bid for further interaction. By using language to connect, a stranger may become a classmate, a teammate, a neighbor, or even a friend.

Now, go and talk to a stranger. You could make small talk, or you could ask a stranger a big question about God or the meaning of life. Try to make the interaction last at least five minutes—or much longer if possible.

Take field notes on yourself, the other person, and the interaction. You could try taking notes as you go, though it is likely to be awkward (you're just practicing, so practice awkwardness!), or you could take notes right after the interaction ends. Notes must be taken during or immediately after a fieldwork episode, not hours or days later. Field notes describe the interaction as plainly as possible. Field notes do not interpret or evaluate the experience.

After you take notes, reflect on them. This could be later, even days later, than the fieldwork.

- How does it feel to approach a stranger?
- How is language used to make a connection?
- Was there a moment when a stranger felt less "strange"? What made you feel more familiar with a new person: a word, gesture, posture, or body movement?
- How does physical proximity matter?
- How does time matter? Does familiarity grow as time passes?

can make. The distinctive sounds in any particular language are known as the **phonemes** of that language. For example, the vowel sounds in the words "beat" and "bit" are two separate phonemes of English (represented in the International Phonetic Alphabet by the symbols /i/ and /ɪ/, respectively). Some languages include the former but not the latter in their phonemic inventory, and consequently, when learning English, speakers of such languages may conflate the two, giving "beat" and "bit" the same pronunciation.

Phonemes do not carry meaning on their own, but languages combine one or more phonemes to form a unit called a **morpheme**—a minimal unit comprising sound, meaning, and function. For example, the word "singing" consists of two morphemes, *sing* and *-ing*, each with a distinct sequence of

Tom Headland

Kenneth Pike served with Wycliffe Bible Translators and SIL International. Here, he is pictured with an Aguaruna man in Peru. In addition to writing many books and articles, Pike developed a method for learning, transcribing, and translating unwritten languages. His academic work left an enduring impact on linguistics, and his faith continues to inspire missionary service.

sounds and an associated meaning or function. Morphemes are minimal in the sense that they cannot be further subdivided without losing the connection between sound and meaning. Morphemes may be categorized as free, meaning they can occur in isolation as words (like *sing*, *dog*, or *happy*), or as bound, meaning they occur only in combination with other morphemes (like the prefixes *re-* and *un-*, or the suffixes *-ing*, *-ed*, and *-er*). Languages like Mandarin use separate words to convey meanings like past tense or plural number, rather than using prefixes and suffixes. Such languages are called analytic languages. Other languages, classified as synthetic, add prefixes, suffixes, or infixes (morphemes put inside another morpheme) to a stem to combine many different aspects of meaning into single words. In Spanish, for example, the verb form *hablamos* consists of a stem *habl* (a bound morpheme meaning "to talk") plus a suffix *-amos*, which conveys the first-person plural subject ("we"), present tense, and indicative mood.

Just as phonemes combine to form morphemes, and morphemes combine to form words, words are combined according to the rules of **syntax** to form larger units such as phrases and sentences. Syntactic conventions vary from language to language; for example, in English an adjective precedes the noun it modifies ("the *white* house"), while in Spanish adjectives typically follow nouns ("la casa *blanca*").

Syntax provides rules for the arrangement and order of words in sentences. The syntactic rules of any language may provide multiple options for how words can be ordered. In English, for instance, one might say, "The girl threw the ball," "The ball was thrown by the girl," or "By the girl the ball was thrown." Each communicates the same event but with different syntax.

The rules of morphology and those of syntax together are often referred to as the **grammar** of a language. Descriptive grammar aims to analyze and describe a language as it is used by a group of people. Prescriptive grammar specifies rules or conventions about how language *ought* to be used. In schools, language instruction is often focused on prescriptive grammar—the rules people ought to use, but often do not use, and may not even find familiar.

For example, the following sentence will make sense to a native English speaker: "I plan to consult a lawyer who I met in New York." Prescriptive grammar would find flaws; official rules in English state that the word "who" is for subjects, while the word "whom" should be used for direct objects. Descriptive grammar would describe how this usage is understood by speakers of the language and is considered by most people to be normal language, representing an example of how grammar and word use change over time. Similarly, the phrase "I ain't got no time for that" is prescriptively incorrect but descriptively appropriate because it has a clear meaning and is commonly used in many dialects of American English.

Semantics is the study of literal linguistic meanings, including the meanings of individual words (lexical semantics) and the meanings of complex phrases (compositional semantics). **Pragmatics** is the study of linguistic meaning in context. Pragmatics explains how a sentence such as "That's great!" to be interpreted as something other than its literal meaning (semantics)—for example, when uttered sarcastically. Pragmatics also accounts for why a question such as "Could you turn up the heat?" isn't typically seeking a yes/no answer (even though the literal form appears to be) but instead is a polite command or request. Linguists who study pragmatics may attend to communicative elements such as **paralanguage**, which includes the tone, volume, or vocalization of speech that can change a phrase like "That's great" into a sarcastic expression meaning "That's terrible." They may also look at **kinesics**, which includes body language like gestures, expressions, postures, or even eye movements that can change the meaning of words.

All of these aspects of language—phonology, morphology, syntax, semantics, and pragmatics—are adaptable and continually changing. Oral languages tend to change faster than those with literate traditions because writing helps preserve consistency over time. **Official languages**, those sanctioned by a ruling body and defined and protected by powerful interests such as royal courts, governmental institutions, or universities, tend to change more slowly than those used by populations that are not as strongly tied to the state, such as rural and poorer groups.

Sociolinguistics

In the 1960s, linguist William Labov became interested in social influences on language. His work was part of the founding of sociolinguistics as a subdiscipline of anthropology, one that addresses the mutual influences between culture and language.[4] He observed that American racism perpetuated the segregation of Black people distinctively. Additionally, racism influenced speakers of standard American English to devalue African American Vernacular English (AAVE) as an improper and less sophisticated way of speaking English. Labov and his students argued that AAVE is a legitimate dialect with its own coherent grammar, syntax, and lexicon (vocabulary). Negative perceptions of AAVE are grounded in social judgments, not in the inherent qualities of the language.

Sociolinguists often apply their research in social settings with the goal of improving human relationships by enhancing communication. They support Indigenous language revitalization efforts. They study how language functions in digital environments. They also support linguistic diversity on a global scale and analyze the dynamics of globally dominant languages such as English, Mandarin Chinese, and Arabic.

With their focus on language and culture in mutual interaction, sociolinguists are most interested in change, context, and culture, all of which are at play in arenas including social judgments of languages and dialects, multilingual societies, language contact, and globalization. **Sociolinguistics** highlights contextual issues like ethnic stratification, social inequality, and political representation. When historical linguists study similar issues, they acknowledge context but focus more on changes in and relationships between the languages themselves. Descriptive linguists explore the relationship of language design and cultural context, but often with less emphasis on change, political context, or social power.

4. William Labov, *Language in the Inner City: Studies in the Black English Vernacular* (University of Pennsylvania Press, 1973).

Language Hierarchies

Although the Philippines was colonized by Spain for four hundred years, Spanish overseers had a policy of *not* allowing Filipinos to learn Spanish (in contrast to Spain's Latin American policy). When the United States assumed colonial control in 1898, English became the official language for education, government, and business. As the country prepared for independence, it created a national language based on Tagalog (first called Pilipino and later Filipino).

Today, the medium of instruction in public schools is supposed to be Filipino until high school and university, at which point most subjects are taught in English. This creates difficulties in areas where there are few fluent Filipino speakers. Throughout much of the island nation, people grow up speaking other languages. When they become teachers, it is much easier to teach children in the language everyone understands than to use a language everyone is learning. The imposition of Filipino (as well as English) has created some resentment among speakers of other languages.

Language hierarchy, the system by which some languages or dialects are ranked in political, economic, and social status, exists in many countries. Kenyans speak dozens of languages, but Swahili (indigenous to a small group on the coast) and the colonial language English are most prestigious. In India, more than eighteen languages are recognized as official regional or national languages, yet Hindi and English are the most prestigious.

Where hierarchies exist, those who are raised speaking the more prestigious languages, or who have the resources to learn favored languages fluently, gain social advantages.

It's your turn: In your daily life, listen for a word, a sound, or a dialect that is high or low in a language hierarchy. What is the word/sound/dialect? How did you learn that it is high or low in the language hierarchy? How is it used in media? What kinds of advantages or disadvantages may come to a person who speaks in this way?

Social Judgments of Languages and Dialects

Distinct but mutually intelligible forms of a single language are called **dialects**. English has many dialects, such as Jamaican, African American Vernacular, Southern American, Appalachian, Kenyan, Australian, and varieties of British, all of which maintain standardized rules of grammar, vocabulary, and pronunciation. In studying dialects, sociolinguists use formal linguistic skills to study language structure and use, and ethnographic skills to describe how power dynamics shape social judgments of various dialects.

In practice, however, the categorization of one language as a distinct language while another is called a dialect is often more of a social judgment, reflecting how a particular dialect or language is valued by speakers of another dialect/language. For example, in the Philippines there are eight major languages and dozens of regional languages. Yet in addition to the colonial language of English, Tagalog (now often called Filipino) emerged as the most prestigious Philippine language. As the language spoken in the areas around Manila (the capital of the Philippines), Tagalog/Filipino became the second official language of the country. Though the languages of the Philippines are related (the way Spanish and French are related), Tagalog speakers cannot understand those speaking Ilokano, Cebuano, or any of the other many languages of their nation. These are separate languages, yet most Filipinos refer to these less prestigious languages as "dialects."

Conversely, some fluent or native speakers of Spanish say they can understand Italian or Portuguese and even learn to speak those languages relatively easily. Yet Italian is never considered a dialect of Spanish (or the other way around). The difference has nothing to do with the languages of Spanish, Italian, Tagalog, or Ilokano; the difference is in the relationship of Spaniards to Italians as opposed to Tagalogs and Ilokanos. Spain recognizes Italy as a separate country with its own history and value. Tagalog and Ilokano, in contrast, have been placed in the same country because of colonialism. Today, Tagalogs, and particularly urban people in Manila, tend to look down on speakers of other languages as being provincial or backward. That the speakers of languages other than Tagalog have adopted the terminology of dialects for their own languages reflects how they have accepted the judgment that their languages are less worthy of respect than Tagalog and English. Use of the terms "language" or "dialect" is not due to features of the languages but is instead a consequence of politics and history. By placing a language into the category of dialect, it becomes easier to argue that it should not be taught in school or used in literature or news media, or even that it is a degraded form of a more "pure" language.

Language hierarchy can even portray certain languages as intrinsically superior to other languages. Many who live in former colonies, and now speak dialects of European languages, have come to view their version of the language as "lower" than the version spoken in the original country. Throughout Latin America, people often refer to the Spanish spoken in Spain as "pure" Spanish or "good" Spanish. Similarly, some have come to see globally powerful languages as intrinsically superior in specific ways. For example, some might argue that English is an intrinsically superior language for business or German is more suited to theology. Linguists, however, believe there is no such thing as superior or advanced languages. Some languages do have relatively larger **lexicons** (that is, all the morphemes of a language) compared to others. In the case of English (a language with an exceptionally large lexicon), this is due to the willingness of English speakers (particularly US Americans) to borrow words from other languages, alter pronunciations, and adopt them as English. Speakers of other languages may be less willing to adopt words from another language or may

James Marohn

have vocabularies developed more specifically around local concerns, but every language *can* express anything a speaker of that language wants to express.

For example, Ilokano, a language of the northern Philippines, has grown and changed to reflect the concerns of the speakers. Ilokano has many words to refer to rice. Rice to be used for seed is called *bunubun*. Cooked rice (about to be eaten) is *inapoy*. If you leave the pot on the stove too long, the burned layer at the bottom is *itip*. There are specific terms for rice that has been harvested but not threshed, rice that has been planted but with seeds yet unformed, cold rice left over from the day before, and so on. It would be unfair to think that English is an inferior language because of our lack of specificity when it comes to talking about rice. Rather, because of the less-than-central role of rice in the diets of English-speaking populations, the English language has not become as specific on the topic of rice as Ilokano has.

Multilingual Societies

While one language is not inherently better or worse than another, societies with numerous languages have political dynamics in which the use of the languages becomes hierarchically arranged. This demonstrates the power-laden nature of culture. Some languages may come to dominate spheres of life such as home and church, while other languages are used in school and politics.

In most countries today, multiple languages are spoken even where an official language is mandated by law. In the United States, although English is widely spoken and has been declared an official language in thirty-two states, Spanish is also widely spoken throughout the country, along with French in the Northeast, Norwegian in the Midwest, Gullah in several Eastern sea islands, and numerous other languages, particularly in areas where new immigrant populations are concentrated. Many other countries, including South Africa

Naomi Haynes studied how Pentecostal prayer shapes personhood in Zambia. Prayer is personal and spiritual, but it has a social dimension. Pentecostal prayer is both personal and collective, and a person who "prays hard" becomes an iconic representation of the community. Individual believers are, indeed, individuals, but they are also symbols of community. Anthropologists notice how, through language, even something as personal as prayer has a social life.

and India, have encompassed dozens or even hundreds of languages from their inception.

Some multilingual societies may have few multilingual individuals, as languages tend to be separated by region. Switzerland, for example, is a multilingual state where German, French, and Italian are spoken in different regions of the country.[5] Yet many individuals are monolingual (speaking only one language) in the language of their region. In other cases, such as the Philippines, where the official languages of English and Filipino are spoken alongside seven major and dozens of minor languages, most individuals are multilingual, often growing up speaking three or more languages daily.

Language Contact, Pidgins, and Creoles

When speakers of different languages come together in one place, they may develop a **creole**: a type of language formed when different languages combine. Haitian Creole is a combination of French and the West African languages spoken by people brought to the plantations of Hispaniola. The Creole of Louisiana is also a French-based language, but it draws on Native American languages, Spanish, and English. In other situations, instead of combining language influences, speakers in a multilingual context use a simplified form of one language (often a colonial language) as a common language across a region or group. The simplified language, known as **pidgin**, may become a second language for speakers of older, more complex languages or eventually replace those languages. Linguists working in Bible translation note that biblical Greek took on characteristics of a pidgin language, reducing its grammatical complexity as it became widely spoken among formerly non-Greek speakers of the ancient world.[6]

5. Romansh, a Romance language related to Latin, is also an official language of Switzerland, spoken by fewer than fifty thousand people in the southeast of the country. It does not have the same national status as the three primary languages.

6. Other linguists argue that the simplification of Greek was a distinct process from the formation of pidgin languages. The point here is how simplification of grammar tends to follow languages spreading across linguistically diverse populations. For a more detailed description of

Modern pidgin languages often developed because of colonial rule. In contrast, some societies have responded to political and linguistic domination through **linguistic nationalism.** Linguistic nationalism is the use of language to promote nationalist ideologies. One example is the Basque community of northern Spain and southwestern France. Members of this community have been struggling against Spanish and French rule for decades, sometimes violently. One potent symbol of identity has been their language, Euskara. Anthropologist Steve Ybarrola noted that when fascist Francisco Franco came to power in Spain, he made the speaking of Euskara (and other minority languages) illegal. Correspondingly, as the Basque nationalists of the region began to resist, they emphasized the centrality of speaking Euskara as the most significant marker of being or becoming Basque. Living among the Spanish within the border of the Spanish state, they insisted immigrants learn Basque to integrate into *their* (that is, Basque) society. As the nationalist movement developed, language played a central role, with some arguing that "the Basque language encourages distinct sentiments, values, and beliefs within a person."[7] In other words, speaking Euskara made you into a certain kind of person. In this way, emphasizing the Basque language—and inducing people to learn and speak it—sustained Basque identity.

When sociolinguists study social judgment, multilingual societies, and language contact, they look at contextual factors such as ethnic stratification, social inequality, and political representation to understand how language and culture affect each other. Linguistic anthropologist Jane Hill has studied how English speakers in the United States often speak Spanish in particular settings for reasons that diminish the social valuation of the Spanish language.[8] Using "mock Spanish," English speakers use Spanish in joking ways—such as throwing out a casual "Hasta la vista, baby!" when saying goodbye to a friend—spoken with a strong US English accent. Using Spanish in a "slangy way" has the (often unintentional) effect of making that language appear less important or less sophisticated than English. Since English speakers in the United States tend to be wealthier, in positions of power, and members of the majority, the use of mock Spanish can be a way that Spanish speakers themselves are made to feel less a part of the society or inferior to English speakers.

---

pidgin versus other forms of simplification, see Eugene Nida, *Language Structure and Translation: Essays by Eugene Nida* (Stanford University Press, 1975).

7. Steven Ybarrola, "Identity Matters: Christianity and Ethnic Identity in the Peninsular Basque Country," in *Power and Identity in the Global Church: Six Contemporary Cases*, ed. Brian Howell and Edwin Zehner (William Carey Library, 2009), 111.

8. Jane Hill, "Language, Race, and White Public Space," *American Anthropologist* 100, no. 3 (1999): 680–89.

Linguistic Diversity in a Globalized World

Globalization brings opportunities for supporting local languages, such as travel and communication technologies that support connections between native speakers, and ease of audio and video preservation of language. Globalization also creates strong pulls toward linguistic homogeneity. People see more economic opportunity in learning globally dominant languages such as English, Mandarin Chinese, Hindi, and Spanish. The National Science Foundation estimates that about 50 percent of the world's seven thousand languages are endangered.[9] Linguistic diversity is valuable because each language holds unique local knowledge and distinctive mental and cultural patterns. Languages are never static: They are born, they grow and change, and they die. The speed and intensity of globalization are unique, however, in the incentives to favor globally dominant languages over local ones.

Anthropologists study languages for scientific purposes, documenting human history and studying how history, ecology, and culture mutually influence languages. Sociolinguists work to preserve local languages by strategizing with native speakers on ways to pass language on to younger generations and to document and preserve a language. At the same time, sociolinguists work with communities who need to learn globally dominant languages in order to access available economic opportunities. In both cases, sociolinguists study the contextual factors, including politics, language hierarchies, and economic trends, to support local communities as they adapt to a rapidly changing context.

Theories of Language

Anthropologists also ponder the nature of language itself. Philosophers of language developed theories about what language in general really *is*. One of the most influential in the development of a theory of language was Swiss scholar Ferdinand de Saussure (1857–1913).

Structuralism

Like many scholars of his day, Saussure wanted to study human phenomena with the same rigor and methods as natural scientists studying the natural world. Language, he argued, could be studied by separating the human forms

9. "Documenting Endangered Languages," National Science Foundation, accessed February 6, 2026, https://www.nsf.gov/funding/opportunities/del-documenting-endangered-languages/12816/nsf18-580/.

of speech (what he called *parole*) from the underlying rules on which these utterances were based (the *langue*). *Parole* could change with each speaker, reflecting idiosyncratic pronunciation, kinesics (body language), or paralanguage. What did not vary, Saussure argued, were the rules—the structure—that organized the meanings of words in relationship to one another.

All languages share a basic structure of word pairs and oppositions in which the meaning of one word came from the meaning of its opposite. In English, the word "hot" makes sense only if the listener also knows the word "cold" (or "not hot"). A "stool" can only be identified in relation to what it is not—a chair, bench, sofa, and so forth. Because meanings are rooted in this oppositional structure, the sounds themselves (words or signs) of this system are arbitrary symbols with no necessary connection to the thing to which they refer. A "chair" in English is an "upuan" in Tagalog and a "chaise" in French, though each sound can refer to the same object in space. What gives chair/upuan/chaise a meaning is not the object but the sign in relation to other signs in the language. The principle of arbitrariness is a design feature of language, a feature common to all languages. This means language always has openness, allowing people to innovate to express new ideas or reference new objects.

Saussure's theory is called **structuralism**, a theory that would later be extended to the study of culture generally (see chaps. 8 and 11). For both language and culture, structuralist theory posits that each could be studied as a system of signs unto itself. For linguistic structuralists, the social life of the people speaking becomes important only as it reveals the underlying structure governing the language.

Noam Chomsky, a well-known US linguist, further developed this theory of language. He saw language as having two parts: surface structure and deep structure. The surface structure, corresponding to Saussure's notion of *parole*, is the language coming out of people's mouths. Spoken language provides the empirical data a scientist would use to unravel the "generative grammar," or deep structure—the rules determining what could and could not be said in the language. Linguists could even apply mathematical principles to determine the range of possible utterances a particular grammar would allow in a particular language. By comparing linguistic systems, Chomsky believed linguists could uncover principles of human thought generally.

Anthropologists began to use the idea of surface and deep structures to understand culture as well as language. But even as Chomsky was elaborating Saussure's theory, other linguistic anthropologists developed an alternate theory. Following the work of early US anthropologist Franz Boas, linguistic anthropologists like Dell Hymes, Edward Sapir, and Benjamin Whorf argued that the speech of real people was not simply a reflection of a deep

Code-Switching

Sociolinguist Dell Hymes noted that within any given speech community—any group of individuals who interact verbally on a regular basis—there are varieties of language. Some are regional dialects, accents and word choices related to geography, while others are social dialects. For example, the pronunciation of "park the car" ("pahk the cah") by someone living in south Boston differs from the British-sounding accent used by those inhabiting the Back Bay area of the city. **Social registers** introduce even more variety, such as when people adjust their speech to match the atmosphere of specific settings like sporting events, university lectures, or religious functions.

An individual's competency with various dialects and registers comprises their verbal repertoire. Some individuals are adept at **code-switching**, which is the practice of keeping particular forms of speech separate. Code-switching occurs when a person speaks one way in one setting (with friends and peers, for example) and a different way in another setting (in the classroom or on the job). Speaking quietly in church and loudly on an athletic field is simply adjusting social register, not code-switching. Code-switching involves shifts in vocabulary, accent, body language, and qualities of voice.

People code-switch for many reasons. Code-switching may establish solidarity with another person in a conversation or signal deeper understanding of another culture. Code-switching may also be a political act, whereby a speaker demonstrates loyalty to a social group, a policy, or a view. It can be used strategically to navigate situations in which a socially favored language is dominant. College students who are racial and ethnic minorities, international students, and missionary kids may use code-switching to establish solidarity or familiarity with others who might share life experiences or country of origin. They may code-switch for humor or to point out a distinctive trait of campus culture that most other students simply take for granted.

It's your turn: Compare language use in two different settings (for example, a gym, a classroom, a cafeteria, or a dorm). How do people alter their language to fit with the setting? Take notes on lexicon, paralanguage, and kinesics.

After you take field notes and leave the research setting, reflect on what you observed. What motivates people to alter language use? Is power at play in these settings? How?

structure. The performance of language and its use in culture influenced the culture itself.

The Sapir-Whorf Hypothesis

The **Sapir-Whorf hypothesis** posits that language shapes people's perceptions, thoughts, and views of reality. This notion of linguistic determinism contrasts with a static view of language as derivative of culture—merely a set of tools used to communicate. Edward Sapir, a student of Boas's at Columbia

University, studied Native American languages and became interested in the relationship between language and culture. His student, Benjamin Whorf, elaborated Sapir's ideas as he conducted fieldwork among the Hopi of the Southwestern United States. Whorf noticed that while English has many markers of time (such as present and past tense and markers of future intention), Hopi speakers expressed things as ongoing processes without clear linguistic categories of past, present, and future. Whorf concluded that where English speakers saw discrete units of time (today, tomorrow, five days), the Hopi saw an ongoing process (the day that is happening now, the time that is coming). Thus, where English speakers saw a break with a new beginning, the Hopi perceived actions as connected to the past and future. Whorf wrote, "One might say that Hopi society understands our proverb, 'Well begun is half done,' but not our 'Tomorrow is another day.'"[10]

The Sapir-Whorf hypothesis offers an intriguing idea about the relationship between language, society, perception, and reality. Advocates of the Sapir-Whorf hypothesis believe that by comparing societies, they will discover how linguistic categories and terms shape or even determine how individuals view the world.

Ethnosemantics (or ethnoscience) focuses on the culturally and linguistically specific ways people make sense of the world. Ethnosemantic research on language and perception does not support an extreme version of linguistic determinism, which suggests that language makes culture. Research on color categories, for example, shows that although some languages offer only two words for colors, they are almost always the same categories: one for colors in the blue-green-violet-white spectrum and another for the yellow-red-orange-black spectrum. Those with three categories pull out red as the third color (by whatever name), and so on, in a consistent pattern. This suggests that humans physically respond to the light spectrum in the same ways—they see the same things—although those with fewer linguistic categories will have less interest in differentiating between, say, shades of red, orange, and yellow.[11]

Even while physical perception does not seem determined by language, linguistic determinism pushed many anthropologists to argue that language, particularly the performance of language, was more than just a reflection of a deep grammar. Through attention to the social use of language and its cultural settings, these scholars supported the idea that language use, as it is

10. Benjamin Whorf, "The Relation of Habitual Thought and Behavior to Language," in *Anthropological Theory: An Introductory History*, ed. J. L. McGee and R. Warms, 8th ed. (Bloomsbury, 2024), 195. Whorf's article was originally published in 1941.

11. Brent Berlin and Paul Kay, *Basic Color Terms: Their Universality and Evolution* (University of California Press, 1969).

Names and Metaphors for God

What do we speak of when we say the word "God"? The Hebrew people of the Old Testament and observant Jews today do not speak the divine name. They may substitute *Adonai* ("my Lord") or *Elohim* ("God") for YHWH, the Hebrew convention for writing God's name. This taboo symbolizes respect for the sacred nature of God. It also reminds people of their tendency to make an idol out of a symbol. A symbol refers to God but is not God.

Scripture contains hundreds of names and metaphors for God. "King," for instance, emphasizes power and authority. Contemporary praise and worship music relies on "You," "Father," "Jesus," and "Lord," all of which emphasize relationship and intimacy.

Other names and images for God, though just as biblical as the familiar ones, fall into disuse. God's fury and power are highlighted when God is described as a woman in labor (Isa. 42:14), and God's protectiveness is emphasized when God is described as a hen (Matt. 23:37) or as a seamstress making clothes for Israel to wear (Neh. 9:21). Sociolinguistics helps us see how culture shapes our preferred words and metaphors for God and how repeated use of that language, in turn, shapes our understanding of God.

An ancient hymn asks, "What language shall I borrow" to thank and praise God?[a] Language simultaneously illuminates and constrains our understanding of God.

It's your turn: At a chapel or church service, record all the words used for God. After your fieldwork, reflect on what you learned. Which words were most commonly used? Were any words noticeably absent? How might this shape the spiritual lives of the people in this community?

a. St. Bernard of Clairvaux, "O Sacred Head Now Wounded."

modified and shaped in real social contexts, potentially shapes how people think and behave. In other words, culture is not just a reflection of language; culture *changes* language.

Language and Scripture

Anthropology can help us better understand what the Bible is and how to read it. God provided revelation through language, and the written Scriptures are central to our understandings of God. For Christians, an essential question about language and language theory concerns how we read and understand Scripture.

Many Christians refer to the Bible as "the Word of God," but when Scripture refers to the eternal Word, this points to Jesus, not the Bible (see John 1; Ps. 119:89). For this reason, the Bible, in a theological sense, is the *words* of God, while Jesus is the Word. Throughout Scripture, particularly in the

Psalms, there are references to God's word, referring to the Law and the Prophets (Ps. 119:9–11, 105). Jesus affirms the authority of these texts (Matt. 5:18), and the apostles of the early church stress the Scriptures as central to Christian life (2 Tim. 3:16–17; Heb. 4:12). At the same time, one of the most profound Scriptures about the Word is the one that opens this chapter from John 1:1: "In the beginning was the Word." The Word, in this case, is not the Bible but Jesus himself.

In its approach to language and authority, the Christian Bible is very different from the Muslim Qur'an. The traditional understanding of the Qur'an teaches that the angel Gabriel dictated the words in classical Arabic to the prophet Mohammed, who wrote them down verbatim. For this reason, most Muslims affirm the teaching that while the Qur'an may be translated into various languages, only the classical Arabic is authoritative. In contrast, the Bible's authority is not seen by Christians to be limited to a particular language. Even in the original writings there were different versions of Hebrew in the Old Testament. Jesus spoke Aramaic (another iteration of Hebrew), but his followers wrote his words in Greek. Most Christians throughout the centuries have never read the Bible in its original languages, yet they have come to a saving knowledge of Christ nonetheless. It is part of the beauty of Christianity and the character of God that the gospel can be spoken in any language, any culture, and any time. Through the Holy Spirit, it has the power to change lives.

Some theologians have also emphasized the importance of social and cultural context for the writers and readers of Scripture. Thus, contemporary evangelical theologians also draw insight from sociolinguistics. Stanley Grenz and John Franke, for example, refer to the "cultural-linguistic" approach to Scripture to understand the dynamic between what Scripture says and how it is read in context.[12] They emphasize how the meanings of Scripture are always linked to the text itself as well as to the *use* of them in context. The truth of Scripture is not limited to a code underneath the printed words but exists as the church *lives* according to Scripture.

Among the many manifestations of Christianity around the world, we can see how the Spirit works with cultural forms such as music, dance, speech, language, and more in forming the many expressions of the global church. Historic Christianity teaches that the truths God has revealed through Scripture can be understood in any time and place, through any language. Thus, while these truths are not dependent on context, cultural contexts still matter.

12. Stanley Grenz and John Franke, *Beyond Foundationalism: Shaping Theology in a Postmodern Context* (Westminster John Knox, 2001).

As God's people live out the Scriptures and learn from the Holy Spirit, God continues to reveal the riches of God's revelation in the texts of the Bible. In terms of sociolinguistics, this happens when God's people interact with the text, discovering and making meaning as they read and talk and worship together.

TERMS

code-switching: The practice of shifting between different forms of speech or different languages, using one in one setting (e.g., with friends or peers) and another in another setting (e.g., in the classroom or on the job).

creole: A type of language formed when speakers of different languages combine their languages.

descriptive linguistics: The study of specific features of individual languages, such as patterns of grammar and sounds, as they are actually used by a given language community.

dialect: A distinct but intelligible form of a single language.

grammar: Rules governing the use of morphemes and syntax.

historical linguistics: The study of how languages develop and change over time and how different languages are related to one another.

kinesics: Body language; the ways in which gestures, expressions, postures, and eye movements change the meaning of words.

language: A system of verbal and nonverbal symbols used to communicate. A language may be analytic (using separate words for grammatical features such as past tense) or synthetic (in which prefixes, suffixes, or infixes are used for grammar features).

language family: A group of languages that derive from a common ancestor language.

language hierarchy: The system by which some languages or dialects are ranked in political, economic, and social status.

lexicon: All the morphemes of a particular language.

morpheme: A minimal unit comprising sound, meaning, and function; may be free (containing meaning apart from other morphemes) or bound (functioning only as part of another morpheme).

official language: Language sanctioned by a ruling body.

paralanguage: The tone, volume, or vocalization of speech.

phonemes: The sounds available in any particular language.

phonetics: The study of the production, transmission, and perception of speech sounds, including all possible sounds in all human languages.

pidgin: Language formed when speakers in a multilingual context use a simplified form of one language (often a colonial language) as a common language across a region or group.

pragmatics: The study of linguistic meaning in context.

protolanguage: The ancient language from which all the members of a particular language family are derived.

Sapir-Whorf hypothesis: A hypothesis that posits that language shapes people's perceptions, thoughts, and views of reality.

semantics: The study of literal linguistic meanings, including the meanings of individual words (lexical semantics) and the meanings of complex phrases (compositional semantics).

social register: A way of speaking that adjusts to match the atmosphere of a specific situation.

sociolinguistics: The study of how language is used by people in society.

structuralism: A theory of language developed by Ferdinand de Saussure that posits language is an arbitrary collection of signs arranged according to rules of opposition.

symbol: Something that stands for something else.

syntax: Rules for the arrangement and order of words in sentences.

DISCUSSION QUESTIONS

1. Choose a common phrase, such as "That's great!" or "I love you" or "Come here!" Say the same phrase three different ways to produce different meanings. Use kinesics and paralanguage to alter the meaning of the words.
2. If you were to develop a career in linguistics, would you rather work in historical linguistics, descriptive linguistics, or sociolinguistics? Offer an idea for a research project you could conduct in the field you choose.
3. Tell a story about a time when you observed one language or dialect being valued over another. How were these social judgments communicated, and what impact did they have?

ANTHROPOLOGY AND SCRIPTURE

Language and the Image of God

> In the beginning God created the heavens and the earth. Now the earth was formless and empty, darkness was over the surface of the deep, and the Spirit of God was hovering over the waters. And God said, "Let there be light," and there was light. (Gen. 1:1–3)

The phrase "And God said" introduces each day of creation in Genesis 1. God spoke light, darkness, water, ground, and all living things into existence. The power of language, seen in God's creation of the world, is also reflected in the image of God that is present in each person. Humans use language in powerful ways to create and shape human culture. Cruel or hateful words can destroy a relationship. Affirming words shouted by a coach to a player in a game can generate ambition, energy, and strength that wouldn't otherwise be present.

The ability to communicate with language and our reliance on language for culture transmission are distinctive characteristics of humans that set us apart from all other created beings. Language is one important way in which we bear the image of God. We can give thanks for the many ways in which language—each language in particular, and the general capacity to make and share language—is a blessing for and from the people of God.

Jacob's Multilayered Language

> Jacob went close to his father Isaac, who touched him and said, "The voice is the voice of Jacob, but the hands are the hands of Esau." He did not recognize him, for his hands were hairy like those of his brother Esau; so he proceeded to bless him. (Gen. 27:22–23)

Genesis 27 records the story of Jacob and Esau. In one episode, Jacob disguises himself as Esau, dressing and speaking like his brother. Jacob cons their father, Isaac, into giving him the blessing that was intended for Esau.

Sociolinguistics offers tools for interpreting the many layers of communication at play in this story. The words spoken, both the trick and the blessing, were just one layer of language. Language is also present in kinesics, the body language Jacob used when he covered his hands and neck with goatskins so they would seem hairy like Esau's. Jacob relied on paralanguage to alter the tone and quality of his voice to sound more like Esau. He used a kiss as a symbol to convey loyalty and truthfulness, a symbolic strategy that supported his deception.

True to his name, which means "supplanter," Jacob manipulated all the major elements of human communication—words, body language, vocal style, and symbols—to get what he wanted. Interpreting the story with the use of linguistic tools illuminates the relationships in the story and explores the dynamics of truth-telling and deception that people still employ today.

4

RACE, ETHNICITY, AND CLASS

After reading this chapter, you should be able to do the following:

1. understand how anthropologists analyze social structure and inequality
2. define race, ethnicity, class, and caste
3. explain how race, ethnicity, class, and caste structure and perpetuate social inequality
4. appreciate ways Christians can work to improve social structures

Introduction

Films, songs, books, and plays frequently feature underdogs who pull themselves up by the bootstraps, work hard, and become a success. News stories—and ministry newsletters as well—sometimes feature a disadvantaged child who aspires to become a superstar athlete, a captain of industry, or a doctor. Whether in real life or in fiction, we hope for the hero's success. These stories reinforce basic values of neoliberalism: that everyone is equal, that opportunity is there for the taking, and that anyone can make it to the top through talent and hard work (see chap. 6 for a detailed discussion of neoliberalism). Indeed, some individuals do skyrocket to the top despite beginning with less access to wealth, education, and power. But this is the exception rather than the rule. On a global scale, and within societies as well, growing inequality presents grave challenges to human well-being. For the vast majority of people, inequalities into which they are born cannot be overcome. The distance between the top and the bottom is growing, and instead of seeing opportunities open for all individuals to rise by virtue of their own hard work, groups of people seem fixed in place, closely tied to their circumstances of birth.

Social stratification is the organization of people into ranked groups, or hierarchies, based on particular characteristics. In addition to inequalities of wealth, hierarchies are often organized around cultural categories believed to be rooted in biology, history, or family—qualities over which individuals have little or no control. Social stratification is present in varying degrees in all societies. Even the most egalitarian bands make distinctions, if only temporarily, between individuals' skills in gathering, hunting, healing, or decision-making. In these societies, however, inequality does not result in some people having sufficient or luxurious resources while others live in desperate need. Social stratification is much more extreme and consequential for individuals' life chances in chiefdoms, kingdoms, and states (see chap. 7).

Social inequality refers to differential access to economic resources, political power, or social prestige that results from stratification. In some societies, inequalities are conscious and widely affirmed; this was the case in feudal medieval Europe, where royals, nobles, and serfs occupied distinct places in the social order. In other societies, social inequalities are officially prohibited, as in most democratic, constitutional states today where all citizens are equal under the law. Yet even when legal (*de jure*) inequalities may not exist and cultural ideologies favor equality and open opportunity, in practice (*de facto*) some people have less access to economic, political, and social power based on their social group.

This chapter starts with a discussion of social structure, exploring key concepts of status, role, stratification, and inequality. We then look at areas in which inequality is often expressed, specifically race, ethnicity, class, and caste. Finally, we consider Christian responses to social inequality.

Social Structure and Inequality

Social structure (also called **social organization**) refers to the ways people coordinate their lives in relation to one another at the level of society. Like culture (see chap. 2), social structure is often difficult to perceive, but, once grasped, it is a useful concept for anthropological inquiry. As Alfred Radcliffe-Brown noted of his own pioneering work, "Direct observation does reveal to us that . . . human beings are connected by a complex network of social relations."[1] In many democratic states, particularly those where individual accomplishments and identity are prized, ideologies of equal opportunity and individualism make social structure nearly invisible to those inside it. In

1. A. R. Radcliffe-Brown, *Structure and Function in Primitive Society* (1952; repr., The Free Press, 1965), 190.

the United States, for example, most are socialized to believe that the same opportunities are available to every individual. In reality, there is more to the stories of hard-worker-turned-superstar, or our own personal histories, than a hardworking individual succeeding in a neutral world.

Race, class, gender, religion, language, and citizenship are just a few important elements of social structure that influence an individual's life chances. Anthropology acknowledges the importance of individual motivation and effort in reaching goals. At the same time, an anthropological understanding of social structure highlights ways individuals always find themselves—through birth, institutional arrangements, or historical precedent—with advantages and disadvantages in life.

An anthropological perspective sees each person's life within a social context. In this way, social inequality does not refer just to how much someone has—that is, being rich or poor—but to differential access to valuable resources. Sociologist Max Weber (see chap. 11) identified three related areas of social stratification: **wealth**, or economic status; **power**, or the ability to influence others; and **prestige**, or the social affirmation and approval given to some members of society (see fig. 4.1).

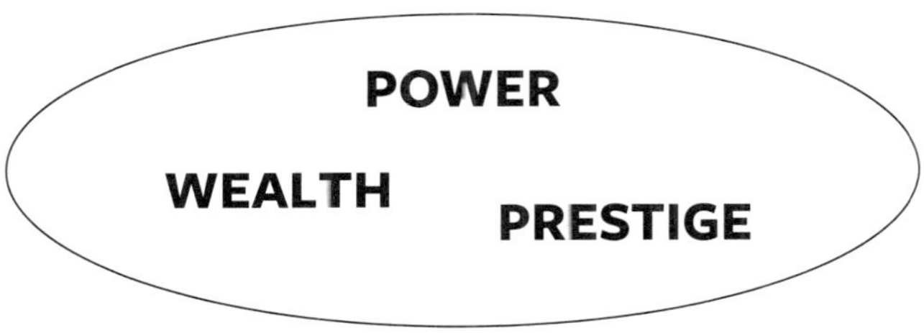

Figure 4.1. Three related areas of social stratification

These three areas of social stratification work together, such that wealth may bring power and prestige, or higher levels of prestige may provide access to wealth. For example, many university students around the world are "poor"; that is, they do not have a lot of disposable income (wealth). At the same time, simply by being university students, they have access to higher levels of prestige. When they graduate, they will generally have access to jobs with higher incomes. Through **cultural capital**—cultural knowledge, including linguistic skills—they will be able to navigate institutions in order to secure mortgages, access credit, or invest in financial markets.[2] For many college graduates, simply having a university degree (regardless of current income) will facilitate building a credit history, securing a loan to live in the

2. Pierre Bourdieu, *The Logic of Practice* (Stanford University Press, 1990).

neighborhood of their choice, getting their children into better schools, and giving their children relatively more access to wealth and prestige. Gaining in these areas often leads to power, or the ability to have influence. If an individual is already from a more powerful racial or ethnic group, these all combine to magnify social inequality, often continuing patterns of social stratification into the next generation.

Most societies organize individuals into groups that experience unequal access to power, wealth, and prestige, though it becomes more pronounced in communities integrated into states, kingdoms, and chiefdoms than in tribes and bands. Within every society, differences in age, gender, race, ethnicity, and other categories become social statuses arranged in hierarchical systems. Yet social stratification is not a consequence of difference alone; it forms around the ways those differences are given relative value in society.

Status

Status refers to any position a person may occupy in a social structure. Status may be achieved or ascribed. An **achieved status** is one that a person chooses or becomes associated with because of behaviors or skills. Occupations, political affiliations, and marital status, for example, are achieved statuses because people aren't simply born into them; they must make choices or learn skills for their status to be socially recognized. An **ascribed status** is given to an individual through no choice or action of their own; it is granted by circumstances of birth. Examples of ascribed status are son, Southerner, or female. Although an ascribed status can be changed in some circumstances, these are understood to be statuses derived from something over which most people have no control. Statuses may be linked—for example, a person cannot be a surgeon without also being a college graduate—or they may be independent.

In large-scale societies, each person has multiple statuses, some of which change throughout their lives. Often one status dominates in a given setting, such as being a child at home and a student at school. A **master status** is one that is considered most important across settings. For the leader of a chiefdom, for instance, the fact that he is the chief would likely be more fundamental to his identity than his being an uncle or neighbor. A master status can be frustrating when, for example, others insist on prioritizing a person's racial, gender, or disability status over other dimensions of identity that the person may wish to assert in a situation.

Even ascribed statuses that may seem permanent can be altered by culture and context. In some patrilineal cultures (see chap. 8), when a daughter marries, she is no longer part of the family into which she was born (her natal family). In the Hebrew Scriptures, in Ruth's declaration of allegiance to her mother-in-law, Naomi, she proclaimed herself no longer a Moabite. This was an affirmation that upon marriage she had relinquished her previously ascribed status and had become an Israelite (see Ruth 1:16–17).[3]

When a cluster of statuses is organized around a common focus, such as education, law, or art, it functions as an **institution**. A political institution, for instance, involves achieved statuses such as voter, president, or lobbyist, and ascribed statuses such as citizen or noncitizen.

Statuses are usually ranked, and in institutional settings, hierarchy is built into the system. For example, professors, students, administrators, office assistants, and custodians are statuses organized hierarchically in a university. All may be respected, but some are granted more resources, social recognition, and influence. In society at large, people may deny that status hierarchies exist, yet in practice people experience and understand some statuses as more advantageous than others. When viewed on a macro-level, statuses correlate with varying degrees of access to employment, education, security, health care, and more. For example, although social institutions may officially affirm the equality of men and women, status hierarchies are revealed in such linguistic expressions as "Take it like a man" or "Man up." In US English, it is rarely an insult to suggest someone is doing something "like a man." But accusing someone of doing anything "like a girl" or a "woman" (to say nothing of specifically gendered curse words) is a common insult directed at both men and women. However, to "be one of the boys" is a compliment given to a woman who is friendly and at ease with groups of men. To tell a man he's like "one of the girls" would seem odd, at best, and likely insulting.

Intersectionality refers to the ways the social meanings of one status play into the experience and meanings of others. For example, my (Brian's) ascribed statuses include man, Euro-American, able-bodied, and US citizen. In some contexts, the fact of my maleness, or my whiteness, or my citizenship will be the thing that is most relevant to how I am perceived in my context. However, even where one of those statuses is most significant, the others also matter.

Role

A **role** prescribes behaviors for those who occupy a particular status. Some statuses, especially those defined by institutions, have clear roles. Students, for instance, are to enter the classroom, sit at desks, take notes, ask questions, and

3. Although it is true that people in Judea referred to her as a Moabite when she returned with Naomi, they were reflecting what we would call ethnicity rather than her social status, which was as the wife/widow of Mahlon, from the clan of Elimelek.

send many gifts and notes of appreciation to their professors. (Okay, maybe just a few gifts.) Other statuses, such as child, grandmother, or urbanite, may have vague or variable roles within a society, but nonetheless, stereotypes suggest shared understandings of roles associated with these statuses. Roles offer cultural expectations for people to behave in accordance with their status.

Roles contribute to the organization of society by reducing ambiguity or confusion as to who does what. When social organization changes abruptly, people may become distressed and even violent when role expectations change. The Civil Rights Movement in the United States, for example, changed roles for Black Americans as well as White Americans. Whether based in paternalism and charity, or violence and superiority, race role expectations held by White people of the pre-Civil Rights era were no longer valid. The role expectation for Black Americans to be subservient, undereducated, and politically and socially marginalized also changed. People of all races in the United States had to reorganize their understanding of the roles associated with racial statuses.

Though individuals everywhere have multiple statuses at once, in large-scale societies the number of statuses increases, often becoming more distinct (separating work from family, for example) and more rigidly stratified. People experience **role conflict** when the expectations for one role collide with those of another role. A student may experience role conflict when they are expected to do homework for five classes (the student role), be home for important events (the child role), and be constantly responsive to texts and emails from

YOUR TURN

The Student Role

Anthropologists look at real people in their local contexts. From the local and the specific, they build an understanding of broader social structures ranging from regional to national to global. Every person is held in place by social structures that shape their life opportunities and outcomes.

The social structure is composed of social institutions that place people into statuses with associated roles. Looking at your own life in this way can illuminate how an individual life connects with society as a whole.

Look at your own life. (If you'd rather look at someone else's life, conduct an interview with a college or university student.) "Student" is an achieved status. List and briefly describe at least five role expectations that come with this status. When do you experience role conflict? When do you experience role strain?

work (the employee role). **Role strain** refers to tension experienced within a role—for example, when the student role becomes overwhelming.

Because social structure is invisible, it is difficult to precisely interpret the ways in which an individual's experience is shaped by social forces that produce inequality. Anthropology doesn't settle the question once and for all, but it provides important concepts like social structure, status, and role that help cultivate clearer perception, and clarity in communication, about how society influences individual experience.

The following sections present several categories—race, ethnicity, class, and caste—that are particularly important in understanding the way social structure encodes inequalities. Gender and sexuality are important as well and are the focus of the next chapter.

Race

Race is a cultural category that divides humanity into groups based on selected phenotypical (appearance) differences. Racial categories and their meanings change over time. But it is not only racial categories and meanings that change over time; race itself is a cultural construction that hasn't always existed, doesn't exist in all societies, and changes over time in race-based societies. The physical features used to identify races are arbitrary in terms of their biological or genetic value. Biologically speaking, there is no more reason to group people according to hair texture, skin color, or eye shape than by any other biological feature.

Humans do vary from one another owing to geography, culture, and gene pools (available mates), but genetic differences are tiny in comparison to genetic similarity across the species. Even more importantly, some differences are infused with social meaning while others are not. Geographer Jared Diamond notes that many human populations have biological distinctions by which they could be grouped.[4] For example, lactose intolerance is extremely frequent among the Japanese and most Native American groups. Ninety-nine percent of people in these groups cannot digest milk without taking a supplement. On the other hand, among the Fulani, a West African pastoral society, and among Swedish people as well, there is virtually *no* lactose intolerance. Lactose intolerance is a biological reality and makes a meaningful difference in people's lives, yet it is not considered a racial trait. Instead of having one race of Black people, one of White, and another of

4. Jared Diamond, "Race without Color," in *Applying Cultural Anthropology: An Introductory Reader*, 5th ed., ed. Aaron Podolefsky and Peter Brown (Mayfield, 2001), 107–14.

Anthropologists and Race

As early anthropologists encountered human diversity, many relied on their contemporary cultural sensibilities about the need for slavery, the inferiority of enslaved people, and the supposedly civilized and superior status of European societies. They didn't see how this ethnocentrism influenced their scientific work, so racial science "proved" the legitimacy of the very stereotypes and prejudices that were believed in the first place.

Franz Boas (1858–1942) was an early American anthropologist who challenged race theory. He studied biological changes in Europeans who immigrated to the United States and showed that dramatic biological change can occur as a result of culture and diet. Some anthropologists followed Boasian theory and sought to disprove racial theories, but many continued to believe in race theory.

Today the American Association of Biological Anthropologists' "Statement on Race and Racism" expresses the profession's main point of view. It states:

> Race does not provide an accurate representation of human biological variation. It was never accurate in the past, and it remains inaccurate when referencing contemporary human populations. Humans are not divided biologically into distinct continental types or racial genetic clusters. Instead, the Western concept of race must be understood as a classification system that emerged from, and in support of, European colonialism, oppression, and discrimination. It thus does not have its roots in biological reality, but in policies of discrimination. Because of that, over the last five centuries, race has become a social reality that structures societies and how we experience the world. In this regard, race is real, as is racism, and both have real biological consequences.[a]

It's your turn: Listen for a comment in a classroom or social setting that mentions race, or find a comment on race made by a public figure (entertainer, politician, academic) in the media. Does the comment fit or not fit with an anthropological perspective on race?

a. "Statement on Race and Racism," American Association of Biological Anthropologists, accessed February 14, 2026, https://bioanth.org/about/aaba-statement-on-race-racism/.

Asian, it would make as much sense to say that one race of people are the Milk People, comprising the very dark-skinned African Fulani and the blond, blue-eyed Swedes, while the other race is the Lactose Intolerant, made up of Japanese and Native Americans.

Racial categories are described as neutral scientific categories that simply reflect real biological and genetic human differences, but this is not true. The biological claim is really the ideological justification for racial categories that support particular systems of economic and political inequality.

The Creation of Racial Categories

During the colonial period, when European countries began controlling the resources and populations of places in Africa, Asia, and Latin America, the development of plantation systems and immigration made it advantageous for those in power (landowners, European rulers) to prevent laborers and slaves from banding together. In the early days of the plantation systems in the Caribbean and North America, poor White people from Europe and poor Black people from Africa worked together, often marrying and living in the same communities.[5]

As these populations grew, European settlers and landowners wanted to keep poor European servants on their side while keeping Africans under control as permanent labor. The idea of racial difference and racial superiority provided European colonialists with a seemingly natural and solid justification for keeping Africans enslaved while preventing poor European servants from finding common cause with poor African laborers. These processes are seen in historical documents such as journals, plantation records, and church records that began referring to people by color.

Scientists were influenced by these emerging popular sensibilities and encoded them in the seemingly objective and neutral language of science. Contemporary categories of race began in scientific classification systems emerging in Europe in the eighteenth century. Scientists such as Carl Linnaeus, who devised the Latin naming system used by scientists today, thought categories that applied to butterflies and birds (phylum, genus, and so forth) could be applied to human beings as well. These scholars used many ways to classify human beings, but they did not agree on which characteristics (cranial capacity? height? body hair?) were most important, nor on how many racial categories there ought to be. Economic systems that developed during colonialism were the reason that the physical features of skin color and hair texture, along with notions of national heritage, coalesced in modern understandings of race.

Despite claims that they are permanent and scientific descriptions of actual human differences, race categories vary dramatically across societies. A person labeled "colored" in South Africa could be "White" in the United States. A "White" person in parts of South America could be "Black" in the United States. People in some countries, such as Brazil, identify members of the same nuclear family as different "races" (called *tipos*) depending on skin tones, hair texture, and eye color.

Despite the commitment to racial separation in the United States, some groups "changed race" over time. Some European immigrant populations of the early twentieth century, such as Jewish and Irish people, were not

5. Indigenous people were used as laborers also, but European diseases killed the vast majority of them, leaving the colonialists in need of a permanent source of labor. See Thomas Gossett, *Race: The History of an Idea in America*, 2nd ed. (Oxford University Press, 1997); Audrey Smedley and Brian Smedley, *Race in North America: Origin and Evolution of a Worldview*, 4th ed. (Routledge, 2019).

considered White. Later, as these groups assimilated culturally and as White groups felt more threatened by newer immigrants from places such as Puerto Rico or China, Jewish and Irish people "became White."[6] New categories have emerged as well, such as Asian and Latinx.

Race and Inequality

The Thomas Theorem states a foundational social principle: "If men define situations as real, they are real in their consequences."[7] Social construction makes race "real," even if the supposed biological divisions are not. Because people believe race is real, it exists as a powerful social category that continues to structure social inequalities.

Throughout the world, people use racial categories to explain, if not justify, social inequality. Genetic heritage is assumed to determine intelligence, criminality, personality, and preferences. Seemingly objective measures such as IQ tests, and popular opinions expressed in media or online, are used to make race-based arguments about superiority and inferiority. Some people believe supposedly positive stereotypes of racial minorities (such as "Asian people are good at math" or "Black people are superior athletes"). Though they seem positive, these racial stereotypes minimize the accomplishments of individuals by suggesting they had an innate group advantage. Even medical research sometimes still uses racial groups (e.g., White and Asian women are more likely to develop osteoporosis) rather than breaking out more fine-grained data around economic, social, or political realities. Racial oversimplification makes it more difficult for public health workers to identify environmental, economic, and social roots of disease.[8]

Yet it is true that race correlates with social problems such as poverty, unemployment, violence, and imprisonment. In the United States, though the majority of poor people are White, disproportionately high percentages of Black and Hispanic people are poor. People from several racial minority groups, especially men, are overrepresented in prison. The

6. See, for example, Noel Ignatiev, *How the Irish Became White* (Routledge, 2012).

7. William I. Thomas and Dorothy Swaine Thomas, *The Child in America: Behavior Problems and Programs* (Alfred Knopf, 1928), 571–72.

8. Characteristics such as athletic ability and mathematical talent do have biological components. Biological anthropologists argue that some populations have advantages, particularly in specific athletic tasks such as sprints, high jumps, or marathons. Attributing these abilities to racial categories such as "Black," however, rather than to much smaller population groups, grossly distorts the variation of specific populations. For more discussion about athletics and race, see the American Anthropological Association's web-based curriculum, *Understanding Race*, https://understandingrace.org/.

Is Colorblindness the Answer?

When my wife and I (Brian) moved to Wheaton, Illinois, we left a part of St. Louis that was mostly Black and Latino for a neighborhood that was predominantly White. For my Filipino wife, Marissa, this often meant she was now the only person of color at a church gathering or neighborhood event.

When talking with new friends in the community, Marissa would sometimes mention that it was difficult being the only brown face in the room. In an effort to comfort her, some well-meaning friends would make remarks like, "Oh, I don't even think of you as Filipino! You're just like me," or, "Don't worry, Marissa. I don't even see color; I just think of you as one of my friends!"

While these comments were well-intentioned, they were not comforting. First, they were dismissive of my wife's feelings about her own identity. Second, they reflected some problematic views of race, ethnicity, and difference. Built into the idea that "You're just like me" was an implication that "Your race is not a problem for me, and I think of you as 'normal' or White." Saying that Marissa is just "one of my friends," and that they don't "see color," also suggests that Whiteness is the norm that she fits. Her Filipino ethnicity and physical identity are irrelevant or trivial, parts of her that should not be noticed or talked about. It suggested that what these neighbors valued were the ways she was like them, but that they were less interested in what made her different.

Colorblindness, or the denial of race as a relevant category of identity, is often a way that people try to emphasize sameness and unity. But it also ignores the experiences of racial minorities, downplays the continued relevance of race in society (or even the value of cultural differences), and obscures the forms of inequality that are still attached to race.

The most helpful responses my wife received were from people, including many White neighbors, who would listen to her, acknowledge her perceptions, seek to understand her experiences, and sympathize with the feeling that sometimes it is tiring to be the only person of color in the room. We can celebrate unity and commonality while still recognizing that race does shape how we experience the world and that our differences, even the socially constructed kind that have been part of social inequalities, can play a role in how God redeems diversity in the created order.

It's your turn: How can we respond to comments about race or ethnicity that are well-intended but wrong? When have you seen a helpful response? When have you seen a poor response?

likelihood of going to a substandard school, living in an under-resourced or environmentally degraded neighborhood, or experiencing abusive behavior from the police rises dramatically for some racial minority groups in the United States. Race does shape life opportunities, but this is the outcome of social and political processes rather than a necessary outcome of genetics.

Because the ideology of race has supported the separation of individuals, families, and communities, some racial groups have developed their own cultural traditions. Ways of speaking, artistic expressions, worship practices, educational styles, naming of children, and other cultural phenomena related to non-White races are often stigmatized as inferior or low-class. Members of these communities receive the message that if they want to fully participate in social life and have equal access to social resources, they should repudiate the well-established and rich cultural traditions that have developed among those racial groups. Today, as racial categories are deconstructed and critiqued, people face the unique challenge of maintaining valued cultural practices and beliefs even while they reject the racial classifications that once organized society.

Challenging racial hierarchies means repudiating race as a valid scientific category while valuing and celebrating the cultural diversity that has emerged from the shadow of racial ideology.

Ethnicity

Ethnicity is a category based on the sense of group affiliation derived from a distinct heritage or worldview as a people. Most ethnic identities are believed to be linked to heritage or bloodlines. At the same time, particular cultural features—language, religion, even occupation—may also be considered indispensable elements of an ethnic identity. The relative importance of cultural, biological, and historical criteria depends on the context.

What is the difference between race and ethnicity? In the United States, the federal government is a key institution that shapes the social construction of these categories. In 1990, the United States Census Bureau classified all US residents according to four racial categories: "Black," "White," "American Indian or Native Alaskan," and "Asian or Pacific Islander." In 2000, new categories made "Asian" its own group, put "Native Hawaiian" and "Other Pacific Islander" together, added "African American" to the category "Black," and included the option "Some Other Race." While these categories were meant to identify biological heritage, after choosing a race, each person was then asked to identify their ethnicity: "Hispanic or Latino," or "non-Hispanic or non-Latino." "Hispanic," the argument goes, refers to people who come from a Spanish-speaking country of Central or South America, and they may be of any racial group, including Asian.

In 2020, the United States Census Bureau first asked respondents to identify ethnicity as "Hispanic," "Latino," or "Spanish" heritage. If yes, they could choose "Mexican/Mexican," "American/Chicano," "Puerto Rican," "Cuban," or "Other" (with a blank to write in their country of origin). Then respondents were given five racial categories from which to choose one or more: "White," "Black or African American," "American Indian or Alaska Native," "Asian," and "Native Hawaiian or Other Pacific Islander." Within these race categories, people could indicate national or ethnic origins such as "German," "Irish," "Filipino," "Nigerian," or "Navajo."[9]

Anthropologist Eloise Hiebert Meneses notes that "in everyday conversations, people [in the United States] are inclined to use the terms *race* and *ethnicity* as functionally synonymous, with the former emphasizing biological connections within a group, and the latter, cultural connections within the same group."[10] As the previous section demonstrates, the biological features designated as races are cultural constructions themselves. Ethnic identities usually involve tangible practices such as a common language, relationship to a particular place, or common cultural practices. Ethnic identities tend to be more complex in their definitions than racial categories, being rooted in a wider variety of characteristics than simply physical appearance. However, anthropologists argue that, like race, ethnic categories are based on cultural markers by which members of one group distinguish themselves from others.

The Creation of Ethnic Categories

Some anthropologists argue that the desire for ethnic belonging is a basic human impulse. **Primordialism** is the view that ethnic identity is a naturally occurring and immutable feature of human life. Primordialist scholars stress that the experience of belonging to a group—knowing who is part of the group and who is not—is found among people all over the world.

In many societies, the term a group uses to refer to themselves can be translated into English as simply "the people" or "humans." The Waorani people of Ecuador are known to many North Americans (particularly Christians) through events related to the killing of five US missionaries in 1956.[11] At the time, these people were called the Auca Indians, but *Auca* is a Quechua word meaning "enemy" or "savage." The name used by the people themselves came

9. United States Census Bureau, "Measuring Racial and Ethnic Diversity for the 2020 Census," August 4, 2021, https://www.census.gov/newsroom/blogs/random-samplings/2021/08/measuring-racial-ethnic-diversity-2020-census.html.

10. Eloise Hiebert Meneses, "Science and the Myth of Biological Race," in *This Side of Heaven: Race, Ethnicity, and the Christian Faith*, ed. Robert J. Priest and Alvaro L. Nieves (Oxford University Press, 2007), 33–46.

11. The story of these men—Jim Elliot, Nate Saint, Ed McCully, Roger Youderian, and Pete Fleming—was told in a series of widely read *Life* magazine articles in the 1950s. Later, Elisabeth Elliot (Jim Elliot's widow) wrote a best-selling book recounting the incident and the years that followed. See Elisabeth Elliot, *Through Gates of Splendor* (Tyndale House, 1981). The story is fictionalized in the film *End of the Spear* (Twentieth Century Fox Home Entertainment, 2006).

A White Guy Considers His Ethnicity

As a European American, I (Brian) have ancestors from several European countries, specifically Wales, Ireland, and Germany. When asked my "ethnicity," I often give this multifaceted answer. Yet none of the cultural traditions of those countries are particularly meaningful to me in terms of my everyday life. In high school, I studied the German language to "get in touch with my roots." When visiting the United Kingdom, I made a special trip to Wales just so I could say I had been there. I have yet to make it to Ireland.

If I were to live in Germany, I could claim German citizenship on the basis of my heritage. However, I have no doubt that I would be considered a foreigner until I learned the German language and culture. Even after learning German, I would certainly have an accent that would give me away. My children could learn to speak German like natives, and they would be given citizenship through my family, but since they have a mother who is originally from Asia, I doubt they would ever be considered "ethnically German" in the same way I am.

Because his European ancestors came to the United States before the Civil War, my father likes to call himself, partly tongue in cheek, a "Native American." That doesn't seem quite the right ethnic label for people whose family originally emigrated from Europe. Yet claiming Irish, Welsh, or German as my ethnicity—without having the linguistic, cultural, or social knowledge to be accepted as a member of those communities—does not quite work either.

Sociologist Mary Waters describes how White Americans often choose ethnicities, picking from a number of European groups to which they are actually related or to which they just believe they are related. She notes that White Americans sometimes develop minor forms of attachment to their European ethnicities, as I did, and others develop strong ties to those places. Other White Americans affiliate most strongly with "American" (like my father), or with their racial identity of "White," abandoning their families' historic ties to Europe.[a]

If nothing else, my personal circumstances help me understand the complexity of racial, ethnic, and national labels in our country and around the world.

It's your turn: What is your story of ethnicity and/or race?

a. Mary Waters, *Ethnic Options: Choosing Identities in America* (University of California Press, 1990).

from their word for human (*wao*). In other words, while those around this group called them "the Savages," they referred to themselves as "the Humans." Similarly, prior to the arrival of the Spanish, the Navajo described themselves with the term "*Diné*," meaning human. Human beings have a deeply rooted propensity to create social boundaries, distinguishing "us" from "them," and considering "us" to be the more (or only) real humans.

These examples also demonstrate the political dimensions of ethnicity. By giving the Waorani the disparaging designation of "Auca," the Ecuadorian majority was able to justify oppressive policies and discrimination.

Anthropologists note that ethnic identities always have political and economic dimensions, often facilitating the exclusion of some from land, resources, or opportunities that belong to "us." **Instrumentalism** (or **constructivism**) describes how ethnicity changes with people's interests and context. Instrumentalist scholars counter the view that ethnic identity formation is a product of a universal human impulse. Instead, they emphasize the ways in which ethnic identities are created, shaped, and mobilized in response to economic and political circumstances.

Both primordialist and instrumentalist views acknowledge that ethnic identities are expressed and maintained through linguistic, cultural, and social markers. These markers—such as language, food, and clothing characteristic of a group—often have a long history. Even where unique languages disappear or distinctive clothing or foods are forgotten, people develop ways to distinguish themselves. The English tried at various points to assimilate the Scottish, forcing them to give up their distinct identity and to submit to English law and culture. The English were successful in virtually eliminating the Scottish language (few modern Scots speak Gaelic except those who have studied it in school). Scottish identity was not so easily squashed, however.

In the eighteenth century, politicians in Scotland, in the long tradition of resistance to English rule, promoted a distinctive type of clothing, the kilt. Prior to that point, the kilt was not widely worn by Scots living in the lowlands (that is, the majority of Scottish people) and likely looked quite different when worn by highland Scots. Historian Hugh Trevor-Roper credits the invention of the kilt to Thomas Rawlinson, an Englishman working in an iron-smelting furnace, who found the traditional tunic of the highland people a "cumbersome, inconvenient habit" and had a tailor cut it down for ease of use. Today, the kilt is seen as an example of historic Scottish identity, not the invention of an English metalworker or a tool of Scottish politicians for protesting oppressive English laws. Regardless of its history, it has become an indispensable symbol of Scottish identity that shapes an ongoing sense of shared history and culture.[12]

Ethnicity and Inequality

In some societies, ethnicity is seen as fairly unimportant for social organization. In relatively homogeneous societies like Korea or Armenia, more important differences within society include class or religion. Also, in

12. Hugh Trevor-Roper, *The Invention of Scotland: Myth and History* (Yale University Press, 2008).

multicultural societies with a dominant majority, ethnicity does not play a significant role in the way those in the majority think about themselves. For example, many White US Americans consider their ethnicity only in terms of a distant heritage, relevant on holidays or at family gatherings where key markers (foods, songs, clothing) are brought out in celebration. US Americans who identify as White are more likely to think of nationality and citizenship, rather than ethnicity, as key categories of belonging.

In other countries and cultures, ethnic identity is critical. Ethnic identity can become dramatically more or less important over the course of a single generation. At the end of the twentieth century, bloody ethnic conflict broke out between Serbs, Croats, and Bosnians living in the former Yugoslavia. This represented a dramatic shift from how they had interacted just three decades earlier. For centuries, neighbors of various ethnicities lived side by side, intermarried, and spoke the same language. When the central powers dissolved and national identity crumbled, ethnic identities determined who would live in specific areas, who would control the government, and how resources would be distributed.

New ethnic categories may emerge as a response to discrimination or the need for representation. The ethnic categories used in the US Census, "Hispanic/Latino" versus "non-Hispanic/non-Latino," are not based on an obvious sense of shared history or identity. Peruvians, Puerto Ricans, and Guatemalans may all speak Spanish, but they have very different cultures and histories. In the United States, however, these disparate people may discover common interests and political goals around such concerns as immigration law, education, and political representation. The label "Hispanic" therefore becomes a political resource as well as an ethnic category.

Just as racial categories became the basis for legal and everyday forms of discrimination, ethnicity has become a way to exclude some from access to resources or power. When new immigrant groups come to the United States, the established population of the country often stigmatizes the ethnic category of the newcomers. For instance, although they would later benefit from their ability to move into the "White" racial category, Irish and Italians at the turn of the twentieth century experienced discrimination. Because previous European immigrants resented their arrival, they were denied housing, employment, and educational opportunities on the basis of ethnicity. Today, people from Mexico, the African continent, and Central America often find themselves stigmatized because of accents or skin color. As a result, doctors, lawyers, and engineers from other countries may find themselves unable to get any but the most menial jobs after immigrating to the United States.

Class and Caste

Class (also called **social class**) is a cultural category describing how people are grouped according to their positions within the economy. Class systems are intrinsically hierarchical; membership in higher classes always provides privileged access to prestige, power, and wealth. Class systems may be more or less open, depending on the criteria by which a person is considered a member of a class. While social mobility is possible, the majority of people live, marry, worship, and socialize throughout their lives with members of the class in which they were raised. This is due both to the ways in which wealth provides access to political and social prestige, and to the cultural boundaries of class identity.

In societies in which class is particularly fixed, anthropologists use the term "**caste.**" A caste system assigns individuals to a position at birth, and mobility between castes is restricted. Such a system often prohibits people from marrying outside their caste and restricts caste members from working with, living near, or even touching members of other castes. The most well-known example of a caste system is in India, where caste membership is supported by Hinduism. Members of the highest caste, called Brahmins, are deemed superior, while those at the bottom, the Dalits or "untouchables," are deemed almost less than human.[13] Traditionally, members of castes would be restricted to the jobs of their caste. As the Indian economy has changed rapidly in recent years, some of these economic distinctions have begun to change. Yet many people, given their commitment to Hinduism and traditional Indian culture, maintain strong marriage and social preferences for those within their own caste or higher.[14]

Culture and Class

In highly stratified societies, class identity is not simply about having money. It is also vital for having the opportunity to learn the cultural norms that suggest membership in a particular social class. Classes are symbolically differentiated by patterns of speech, tastes and preferences, as well as religious affiliation.

13. The Dalits are considered so impure that technically they are not part of the caste system at all; they are Hindus born without a caste. For this reason, they can do things generally forbidden for Hindus, such as eating beef and touching dead animals. However, their "caste-lessness" effectively makes them the lowest category in the system, or the bottom caste.

14. Racial categories in the United States have worked as a caste system for many generations. Legal restrictions prevented marriage between people of different races; education, housing, and employment were segregated; and the economic opportunities available to Black people were socially and legally limited. See Isabel Wilkerson, *Caste: The Origins of Our Discontents* (Random House, 2020).

Eloise Meneses

Eloise Hiebert Meneses conducted fieldwork among market women of India, Dalit (untouchable) women who are poor and stigmatized. Meneses documents how fundamentalist Hinduism casts a vision for a national Hindu identity that incentivizes market women to practice dowry as a way of emulating higher castes. Women struggle to save a large amount of money to marry off their daughters with dowries, which only reinforces the existing social structure at great cost to themselves.

Even when individuals do not have a high income, by exhibiting symbols of class affiliation, they have a better chance of gaining access to money and power. For example, although many people in the United States consider class to be almost entirely based on income, studies have demonstrated that how people speak often influences others' assumptions about their background, intelligence, and education. In the 1960s, linguist William Labov compared the speech of employees in three New York department stores—Saks, Macy's, and S. Klein (which has since closed)—catering to the upper, middle, and lower classes, respectively. Measuring specific indicators, such as the pronunciation of the final "r" in the word "floor," he found disparities between the employees. Labov concluded that the upper-class store hired only people with the accents associated with the higher class for the image and clientele they sought.[15]

Sociologists and anthropologists both study the degree of mobility in various societies, looking at variables such as education, race, religion, sex, and income. Anthropologists particularly attend to the element of culture, as well as the ways people learn to be part of a class. Consider how people interact with art. While anyone can go to an art museum, many people do

15. William Labov, *Social Stratification of English in New York City* (Center for Applied Linguistics, 1966).

not know what to do there. They may wonder why a giant canvas covered in multicolored squares should be called art or what makes a Renoir different from a Van Gogh. Those who have learned what anthropologist Pierre Bourdieu called "the code" can talk about why abstract art (that is to say, *some* abstract art) is hanging in the museum even though it seems any four-year-old could paint it. Moreover, they have learned how to stand, move through the museum, and mutter appreciative phrases at just the right time. Those who do not know these habits ("codes") often see it all as a matter of personal taste. They may leave the museum saying, "I'm just not into that fancy stuff." Bourdieu argued that enjoyment of art is learned as a part of reflecting and reinforcing social class rather than simply personal preference. The same is true, of course, for learning how to appreciate a NASCAR race or a country music concert, but those forms tend to be more open and can be learned in more informal and accessible settings and do not require access to privileged places (e.g., elite schools or art studios). The ability to function as a member of higher classes is learned and taught in institutional settings that are often restricted by income or social network, reinforcing the boundaries of class.

Some societies, even though they are more equitable in resource distribution, may be considered less open because class mobility is limited. The United States, which is relatively open in terms of class mobility, is far more inequitable in the distribution of resources than many other countries in which class mobility is strictly limited. Because the symbolic boundaries of class are relatively less rigid and more easily adopted in the United States—as opposed to Japan, with its centuries-old traditions of nobility and royalty—the class system in the United States is considered more open despite greater inequalities of wealth.

Christian Responses to Inequality

An anthropological understanding of social organization helps Christians to perceive the invisible structures that shape our social lives and to make more informed decisions about how to be a blessing to others on both the individual level and the structural level. Racial categories, for example, were not created by God. When the apostle Paul writes that Christians should not "conform to the pattern of this world" (Rom. 12:2), we can see racial categorization as one such pattern.[16] But not all social structure will pass away in the new

16. Jenell Paris, "Race: Critical Thinking and Transformative Possibilities," in *This Side of Heaven: Race, Ethnicity, and Christian Faith*, ed. Robert J. Priest and Alvaro L. Nieves (Oxford University Press, 2007), 19–32.

heaven and new earth. In Revelation, John describes "every nation, tribe, people and language" worshiping God before the throne (Rev. 7:9). Thus, ethnic identity and nationality are things God preserves in the redeemed world and are therefore an aspect of human diversity we can embrace, though we reject the ways these identities have become twisted by sin, such as through violence or hierarchy.

In his vision of the new heaven and new earth, John writes about a place without suffering (Rev. 21:4), where nations are united in peace (21:24), economic resources are available to all (22:2), and everyone lives under the reign of God. Until that time, the Scriptures call on God's people to serve Christ by serving "the least of these" (Matt. 25:45), and to do what we can to redress oppression and injustice.

Christians have, of course, disagreed about what redemption means. Some have argued that Jesus would have us overthrow the systems perpetuating inequality in society. Liberation theology emphasizes the role of the church in directly confronting the structural roots of inequality and oppression. Others, citing Paul's injunction for Christians to be subject to earthly rulers and Jesus's unwillingness to lead a revolution against the Romans, believe Christians should work within current systems for reform. Sometimes known as "incarnational" or "missional" theology, this approach emphasizes the need for wealthy or privileged Christians to identify with the poor and marginalized. Others, such as Mennonites and other Anabaptists, have traditionally encouraged Christians to develop separate social lives and structures, challenging injustice by refusing to participate in social systems that foster injustice.

However we read the Scriptures, there is no doubt that the church has often been shamefully slow to challenge systems of inequality. In 1963, in response to a call from several White ministers to work only through legal means and abandon his protests, Martin Luther King Jr. wrote the following in his famous "Letter from Birmingham Jail":

> I have heard numerous southern religious leaders admonish their worshipers to comply with a desegregation decision because it is the law, but I have longed to hear white ministers declare: "Follow this decree because integration is morally right and because the Negro is your brother." In the midst of blatant injustices inflicted upon the Negro, I have watched white churchmen stand on the sideline and mouth pious irrelevancies and sanctimonious trivialities. In the midst of a mighty struggle to rid our nation of racial and economic injustice, I have heard many ministers say: "Those are social issues, with which the gospel has no real concern." And I have watched many churches commit themselves to a

completely other-worldly religion which makes a strange, un-Biblical distinction between body and soul, between the sacred and the secular.[17]

Billy Graham, who integrated his crusades when many told him he should not, regretted that he did not address inequality in the United States sooner. When asked what he might have done differently in his life, Graham replied, "I wish I had gotten more education. If I could have, I would have gotten a PhD in anthropology, to understand the race situation in this country better."[18] Both King and Graham saw that understanding and confronting the cultural and social dimensions of inequality are important for living out the second-greatest commandment: to love our neighbor as ourselves.

TERMS

achieved status: A status that a person chooses or becomes associated with because of their behaviors or skills.

ascribed status: A status given to an individual through no choice or action of their own; it is a status granted by circumstances of birth.

caste: A tightly bounded social group based on family background. Caste systems assign individuals to a position at birth, and mobility between castes is restricted.

class (or **social class**)**:** A cultural category describing how people are grouped according to their positions within the economy.

cultural capital: Cultural knowledge, including linguistic skills.

ethnicity: A category based on the sense of group affiliation derived from a distinct heritage or worldview as a "people."

institution: A cluster of statuses organized around a common focus, such as education, law, or art.

instrumentalism (or **constructivism**)**:** The idea that ethnicity changes with people's interests and context.

intersectionality: A concept of how multiple identities interact in shaping a person's experience.

17. King's famous letter has been reprinted many times. One source is Martin Luther King Jr., "Letter from Birmingham Jail," in *Philosophical Questions: East and West*, ed. Bina Gupta and Jitendra Nath Mohanty (Rowman & Littlefield, 2000), 274–87.

18. Billy Graham, in an interview with *Parade* magazine, October 20, 1986, 6.

master status: The status that tends to be most important in shaping a person's life.

power: The ability to influence others.

prestige: The social affirmation and approval given to some members of society.

primordialism: The view that ethnic identity, like race, is a naturally occurring and immutable feature of human life.

race: A cultural category that divides humanity into subgroups based on particular phenotypical (appearance) differences.

role: A prescribed set of behaviors for those who occupy a particular status.

role conflict: The stress that occurs when the behavioral expectations from various roles come into play simultaneously.

role strain: The stress that occurs when the expectations of a single role become overwhelming.

social inequality: The differential access to economic resources, political power, or social prestige that results from social stratification.

social stratification: The organization of people into ranked groups or hierarchies based on particular characteristics.

social structure (or **social organization**)**:** The ways people coordinate their lives in relation to one another at the level of society.

status: Any position a person may occupy in a social structure.

wealth: Economic status, or access to economic resources.

DISCUSSION QUESTIONS

1. Where do you see social inequality in your society? Where do you see it across the globe? How does it affect people's lives?
2. What is your ethnicity? What is your race? Is one of these easier to define than the other? Why might that be?
3. When have you seen Christians respond to social inequality, racism, or ethnic harm in a way that you admired? How did this admirable response reflect the commandment to love our neighbors as ourselves?

ANTHROPOLOGY AND SCRIPTURE

Who Are We in Christ?

> In Christ Jesus you are all children of God through faith. As many of you as were baptized into Christ have clothed yourselves with Christ. There is no longer Jew or Greek; there is no longer slave or free; there is no longer male and female, for all of you are one in Christ Jesus. And if you belong to Christ, then you are Abraham's offspring, heirs according to the promise. (Gal. 3:26–29 NRSVue)

In this passage, Paul addresses three dimensions of social structure: gender, ethnicity, and social class. He encourages the Galatian believers to view themselves with a new perspective. Believers should not rely on the social hierarchies of their culture, which prioritized men over women, free persons over slaves, and (among some believers) Jews over Greeks. Instead, they should see themselves as Abraham's seed, all heirs to the promise given to Abraham. This passage doesn't speak directly to race because race wasn't a concept in the culture at the time. Interestingly, however, the metaphor of Abraham's seed calls forth a consideration of descent and lineage. In Christ, we are all part of the same family, so racial concerns about genetic purity are no longer valid.

This passage doesn't erase all distinction between men and women, slaves and free persons, or different cultures. That is as ridiculous as it is impossible, and it would ignore the suffering of those in the lower ranks of each hierarchy. Instead, the new perspective empowers people to see each other for who they really are: children of God in the lineage of Abraham. This fresh view may encourage new forms of love and mission that would address the inequalities in society that demean those who deserve better because they are part of God's family.

Real Worship

> Then you shall call, and the LORD will answer;
>   you shall cry for help, and he will say, "Here I am."
> If you remove the yoke from among you,
>   the pointing of the finger, the speaking of evil,
> if you offer your food to the hungry
>   and satisfy the needs of the afflicted,
> then your light shall rise in the darkness
>   and your gloom be like the noonday. (Isa. 58:9–10 NRSVue)

In this passage, the prophet Isaiah addresses the Israelites harshly. The Israelites had been fasting—but also exploiting their workers. They had been praying—but continuing to quarrel and fight. With their words they said they were seeking God's will, but with their actions they showed that all they really wanted was to advance their own self-interest.

Isaiah encourages them to discover the true meaning of fasting and praying. Throughout this chapter in Isaiah, the prophet declares that real worship isn't just a day or an hour set aside for personal devotion. Real worship includes loosening the chains of injustice (v. 6), sharing food with the hungry (v. 7), providing shelter to the homeless (v. 7), and, at the very least, caring for those within your own family and religious group (v. 7). In other words, God's people are to acknowledge and address the social and economic inequalities around them. Only by addressing such inequalities can the people come to God in spirit and truth. These are the worship practices that will bring true healing and blessing because they will infuse conventional worship practices, such as prayer and fasting, with real meaning.

5

SEX, GENDER, AND SEXUALITY

After studying this chapter, you should be able to do the following:

1. define sex, gender, and sexuality
2. appreciate how anthropologists study sex, gender, and sexuality
3. explain how gender and sexuality connect with systems of globalization and social inequality
4. understand how anthropological perspectives on sex, gender, and sexuality can be helpful for the church

CHAPTER OUTLINE

Introduction

> Then God said, "Let us make humans in our image, according to our likeness, and let them have dominion over the fish of the sea and over the birds of the air and over the cattle and over all the wild animals of the earth and over every creeping thing that creeps upon the earth."
>
> So God created humans in his image,
> in the image of God he created them;
> male and female he created them.
> (Gen. 1:26–27 NRSVue)

Genesis presents the creation of humanity as male and female as part of God's good design. Humans even bear God's image. In the same passage, God gives humans the capacity for culture and a special relationship with creation. From the very beginning, sex, gender, and sexuality have been a part of human life.

After humans rebelled against God and brought sin into the world, sex, gender, and sexuality came to reflect both good and broken elements (Gen. 3:14–24). Theologian Beth Felker Jones explains that as humans turned from God "we see what sin does to our relationships, bodies, and sex."[1] In all parts of life, we see evidence of God's good creation and also of the fall.

In many parts of the world today, gender and sexuality are contested in policies, stances on issues, and even words. This is certainly true in the United States, where transgender identity, same-sex marriage, and changing norms around marriage and sexuality figure into important political, social, and religious conversations. Globally, conversations about sexuality and gender have become part of virtually every church community, and generational changes continue to bring these issues into sharp relief.

Anthropologists have always studied gender and sexuality, if only by noting that men's and women's lives are different. This area of study became more developed in the mid-twentieth century when prominent women anthropologists such as Margaret Mead, Laura Bohannon, and Marilyn Strathern documented how gender, marriage, gender roles, and sexuality were practiced and expressed in diverse ways.[2] This countered a disciplinary bias that treated male experiences as "normal" or "simply human." Women in the field could see that women's experiences of cultural life were often very different from men's. Attention to gender differences prompted anthropologists to pay more attention to men's experience as gender-specific as well, and masculinity studies grew in the field. Appreciation of gendered differences in social and cultural life led other anthropologists to look at sexuality as a cultural phenomenon, because the ways people experience attraction and erotic love are also shaped by culture.

The anthropological perspective can help Christians understand the creative and dynamic nature of these phenomena and how they play out around the world. Christians will continue to draw varying conclusions on important issues, and accepting such pluralism within the church is an additional challenge alongside navigating changes in society. Christians can exercise both an anthropological perspective and a biblical perspective to understand the deeper dynamics of these issues as well as faithful policy responses. Through prayer and in community, we can discern what faithful presence requires in cultures that are changing rapidly.

In this chapter, we first describe how anthropologists approach sex, gender, and sexuality as elements of culture. We connect these topics with moral

1. Beth Felker Jones, *Faithful: A Theology of Sex* (Zondervan, 2015), 31.

2. Margaret Mead, *Sex and Temperament in Three Primitive Societies* (1935; repr. Harper Perennial, 2001); Laura Bohannan, "Dahomean Marriage: A Revaluation," *Africa* 19, no. 4 (1949): 273–87; Marilyn Strathern, *The Gender of the Gift: Problems with Women and Problems with Society in Melanesia* (University of California Press, 1988).

"Eunuchs for the Sake of the Kingdom of Heaven"

From the Genesis narrative through the tribes of Abraham, the kingdom era, exile, and the New Testament period, the Bible praises marriage, reproduction, and family. People of these cultures recognized, however, that not all individuals will marry and reproduce, and not all bodies are male or female. Biblical scholars have found several cultural concepts that include people who don't fit the normative categories. The "barren woman" is a category that highlights some women's inability to biologically reproduce and marks them as different and associates them with shame. Hermaphrodites and androgynes were sometimes classified as men, if warranted by their external genitalia. The "eunuch" was a culturally familiar category, referring to males with malformed or removed genitalia, such that they could no longer be considered "men."[a]

In a discussion of marriage and divorce, Jesus offered a difficult teaching: "Not everyone can accept this teaching, but only those to whom it is given. For there are eunuchs who have been so from birth, and there are eunuchs who have been made eunuchs by others, and there are eunuchs who have made themselves eunuchs for the sake of the kingdom of heaven. Let anyone accept this who can" (Matt. 19:11–12 NRSVue). Scholars dispute what this teaching means, but it certainly points to the social and spiritual value of the eunuch, a category like "barren woman" that was a mark of deficiency and associated with shame. Moreover, Jesus de-emphasized the biological purpose of sex as determining a person's worth, whether by assuming a patriarchal role in a family (for men) or producing offspring (for women). He proclaims that all people, including eunuchs made so by any means, are valued by God.[b]

It's your turn: Are there any biblical teachings about sex, gender, or sexuality that you find difficult? What is the teaching? Why is it difficult?

a. Megan DeFranza, *Sex Difference in Christian Theology: Male, Female, and Intersex in the Image of God* (Eerdmans, 2015).

b. Biblical scholars and theologians work with ancient materials to understand what concepts and stories might have meant to original audiences. This work often relies on archaeology.

concerns of inequality, well-being for men as well as for women, and diversity of genders and sexualities. Finally, we offer some ways that an anthropological perspective can contribute to Christian thinking and discernment about areas of life that are both foundational for human thriving and also contested.

Sex and Gender

Sex refers to the biological attributes that distinguish males, females, and intersex individuals. Sex is based on chromosomes, hormones, and reproductive anatomy. **Gender** refers to socially constructed norms, roles, and identities for girls, women, boys, men, transgender people, nonbinary people, and more. The term "**sexual dimorphism**" refers to the fact that an organism comes in two sexes that are necessary for the species' reproduction. But for humans, male and female is about much more than just reproduction. Gender is the meaning humans give to sex differences. Societies develop values and norms for how men and women *ought* to look, behave, speak, and dress. Some people conform to norms, some rebel against them, and others defy or reinvent labels, categories, and expectations.

Gender norms vary widely. For example, in many European societies it has long been assumed that because women's bodies give birth, women are more skilled and interested in caring for children. Conversely, because men's bodies do not gestate or feed babies, men naturally are less inclined toward childcare. In many North American communities, then, it's considered "natural" to see more women in the church nursery or working as elementary school teachers.

Among the Ikalahan of the Philippines, however, traditional "women's work" included the maintaining of gardens that were sometimes a kilometer or more from the village. Men, due to their physical strength, were needed to protect the village, so men stayed closer to home. It was thought "natural" that they would care for young children. Older children might do some of the childcare, particularly sons who did not go to the gardens, and mothers would occasionally take children to the garden, especially young children who were still nursing. But because fathers were most often the adults in the village, they were considered best-suited to provide childcare.

In the past, sex was defined as "just" biology. In contrast, gender was seen as entirely cultural, composed of the social meanings given to biology. These definitions portray biology as totally separate from culture. Yet humans experience biology in cultural terms, and biology both empowers and constrains what is possible in culture (for example, biology limits our ability to socially construct a society in which people live for two hundred years). Nature does exist, in and of itself, but humans feel, think, interpret, and speak of biology with language in cultural context.

All definitions of sex and gender carry biases. Some Christians refuse to use the term "gender" because they see biological sex as intrinsically and properly grounding family and society in a two-sex order. Others separate sex and gender as a way of highlighting variations in **masculinity** and **femininity** across cultures. Using "sex" and "gender" as distinct terms also recognizes that in people's sense of self and social roles, "male" doesn't always match to "man," and "female" doesn't always match to "woman." Making meaning is a weighty responsibility God gave to humans, as seen in Genesis 2:19.[3]

3. See Amy Peeler, *Women and the Gender of God* (Eerdmans, 2022); Fellipe do Vale, *Gender as Love: A Theological Account of Human Identity, Embodied Desire, and Our Social Worlds* (Baker Academic, 2023).

Intersex refers to people whose bodies have variations of sex characteristics, variations that develop for numerous reasons. It is estimated that between 0.5–1.7 percent of the global population have bodies that do not reflect clear male or female characteristics.[4] Bodies that are born or that develop in this way may be stigmatized or accepted. These differences may be recognized but unacknowledged, or given a name, and that name may change over time. In US society, "hermaphrodite" is now seen as an outdated term. However, both medical professionals and intersex individuals themselves disagree over which alternative term is more suitable, "disorders of sex development" or "intersex." One designation indicates something gone wrong in development and the other indicates a norm. Words matter: for how people see themselves, how they are treated by others, and how these biological traits are handled in medical research and treatment.

Since the inception of fieldwork, anthropologists have documented how cultures name and include persons whose sex, sexuality, or gender are different from the majority. In more recent decades, they explore how such persons experience their own lives in society. The Bugis, an ethnic group on the peninsula of Sulawesi in Indonesia, provide an example. People born with ambiguous genitalia in this society often grow up to become *bissu* (transgender shamans). The Bugis blend local beliefs with Islam to understand God as beyond gender. Therefore, humans who do not seem to fit the male/female binary are viewed as more like God/Allah and therefore as better positioned to develop spiritual insight or ability.[5] The *bissu* play a role in blessing marriage and fertility, the very parts of social life from which they might otherwise be excluded. Similarly, if a person grows to have a personality or sense of self that does not "fit" their biology, they may adopt another gender identity. Masculine females are *calalai*, while feminine males are *calabai*. A feminine woman (what in the United States might be called a "cisgender woman") is called *makkunrai*, and a masculine man ("cisgender man") is *oroane*. Each of these five is considered a distinct gender and has a different place in the social order (see more under "Gender Variation" below).

4. Intersex conditions may affect anywhere from four million to more than one hundred million people worldwide. Because definitions vary, statistics are not collected consistently, and stigma likely reduces reported totals, statistics on intersex prevalence are imprecise. The 1.7 percent estimate is widely cited as a reputable estimate. World Population Review, "Intersex People by Country, 2026," accessed February 7, 2026, https://worldpopulationreview.com/country-rankings/intersex-people-by-country.

5. Sharyn Graham Davies, *Challenging Gender Norms: Five Genders Among the Bugis in Indonesia* (Thomson Higher Education, 2007).

Gender and Inequality

The United Nations' Gender Inequality Index measures gender inequality, which ultimately connects with human well-being. The index measures reproductive health, empowerment, and labor market participation. It reports severe inequality across the 159 nations measured as well as some positive trends over time.[6] Gender equality is one important sustainable development goal that the United Nations hopes to achieve. Most goals affect men and women alike, such as ending poverty and hunger, improving education, and ensuring clean water and sanitation.[7]

Decades before such global thinking was common, anthropologist Margaret Mead's 1949 book *Male and Female: A Study of the Sexes in a Changing World* offered anthropological insight to American readers interested in creating change in their own society.[8] Mead studied several cultures in the Pacific, sometimes on her own and sometimes with a male research partner who could establish deeper rapport with male informants. Based on her fieldwork, she argued that gender traits commonly taken as natural—such as affection in parenting, capacity for nurture, ambition, or styles of childhood play—are culturally produced; that is, in various cultures, supposedly gendered traits are sometimes held by women, sometimes by men, and sometimes by both genders. A look at cultures around the world shows that gender roles and expectations aren't simply natural or biological. People play a vital role in assigning meaning to biological attributes.

By the mid-twentieth century, anthropologists became increasingly aware of how gender inequality diminishes well-being both for women and men, and they also found male bias within the field of anthropology. For example, early-twentieth-century anthropologist Bronisław Malinowski described the **kula ring** exchange system, a pattern of exchange practiced around the chain of Trobriand Islands.[9] Men in the Trobriand Islands exchange armbands and shell necklaces across islands. These items are not valuable in and of themselves, but the exchange solidifies relationships and strengthens the regional economy. Decades later, Annette Weiner traveled to the Trobriand Islands to

6. Isis Gutiérrez-Martínez, Samina M. Saifuddin, and Rana Haq, "The United Nations Gender Inequality Index," in *Handbook on Diversity and Inclusion Indices: A Research Compendium*, ed. Eddy S. Ng, Christina L. Stamper, Alain Klarsfeld, and Yu (Jade) Han (Edward Elgar, 2021), 83–100.

7. United Nations, "17 Goals to Transform Our World," United Nations Sustainable Development Goals, accessed February 7, 2026, un.org/sustainabledevelopment.

8. Margaret Mead, *Male and Female: A Study of the Sexes in a Changing World* (William Morrow, 1949).

9. Bronislaw Malinowski, "Kula: The Circulating Exchange of Valuables in the Archipelagoes of Eastern New Guinea," *Man* 20 (1920): 97–105.

study tourism but was surprised to see a complex system of exchange among women as well, which involved banana leaf bunches and grass skirts. Malinowski had noticed only men's economic behavior. Weiner's ethnography, *Women of Value, Men of Renown*, argued that ignoring women's experiences left anthropological understanding of this culture lacking a full and complete picture of how all Trobriand Islanders understood exchange and cosmology.[10]

Anthropologists also explore whether there are any societies marked by equality between men and women, why male dominance happens at all, and how women express power in private and public domains. Most societies are marked by gender inequality, but in a few interesting cases, men and women are seen as near equals. Kirk Endicott and Karen Endicott conducted ethnography among the Batek of Malaysia and concluded that, prior to the era of globalization, Batek men and women had equal access to resources, prestige, and power, and not only did people not inflict violence on one another, but violence was nearly unimaginable. They concluded that the Batek lived in a niche that provided both food security and a balance of individual self-governance and family interdependence; these favorable contextual factors contributed to equality and nonviolence.[11]

More typically, cultural configurations of sex and gender result in economic and social inequality. Religion can strengthen existing norms, challenge them, or offer alternatives. Major world religions regulate gender expression, promoting virtues such as modesty for women and honor for men. Modern Christianity offers competing norms of headship and submission—or mutuality and equality. Similarly, in Islam, the wearing of a hijab may be interpreted as mutual responsibility (the woman wears a hijab, and the man lowers his gaze), as oppression of women, as a necessary restraint of men's sexuality, or as a personal choice that, when freely chosen, is liberating.[12]

In the United States, the notion that women are more emotional than men—and thus less likely to use reason in decision-making—has historically led to the marginalization of women in political and economic spheres. In Indonesia, however, it is thought that men are the more passionate and emotional gender.[13] Men are seen as more likely to lose control of their emotions

10. Annette B. Weiner, *Women of Value, Men of Renown: New Perspectives in Trobriand Exchange* (University of Texas Press, 1976).

11. Kirk Endicott and Karen Endicott, *The Headman Was a Woman: The Gender Egalitarian Batak of Malaysia* (Waveland Press, 2008); Maria Lepowsky, *Fruit of the Motherland: Gender in an Egalitarian Society* (Columbia University Press, 1993).

12. See, for example, Anjum Alvi, "Concealment and Revealment: The Muslim Veil in Context," *Current Anthropology* 54, no. 2 (2013): 177–99.

13. Suzanne A. Brenner, "Why Women Rule the Roost: Rethinking Javanese Ideologies of Gender and Self-Control," in *Bewitching Women, Pious Men: Gender and Body Politics in*

and to be tempted by gambling, alcohol, and sex. It follows, then, that women should control family finances. Men control the public sphere, including religion and politics, where values of spiritual strength and social status are considered important. But, absent the stereotype of women as emotional, Indonesians have elected a woman to be prime minister and generally accept women in high-ranking positions.

Christian churches today are marked by disagreement over sexuality and gender roles and what love, truth, justice, and grace mean in practice. We will likely navigate these disagreements for generations to come. As we do, anthropological insight can inform our arguments with data and allow other ways of life to inform our ideas of what is universal, necessary, or natural. We can take a global, cross-cultural perspective on what human thriving requires and what diminishes it.

Gender Socialization

Humans everywhere are taught how to properly live as men, women, and other genders in their own cultures. The process of learning how to act according to the gender norms of society is called **gender socialization**.

Socialization begins in the family, with direct contact between caretakers (usually parents) and infants. Socialization continues in schooling, peer relationships, workplaces, and through media. In a famous study, infants were randomly assigned gender-specific clothing (blue or pink). Adults treated the babies differently depending on the baby's supposed gender. Adults talked more to, used more eye contact with, and had closer facial proximity with infants thought to be girls. They were more physical with those thought to be boys. In the Western context, these responses fit with cultural assumptions that girls are more emotional, verbal, and relational, and that boys are more physical. Adults communicate gender norms to infants and children, often in subtle and unconscious ways.[14]

Gender ideals are often expressed in shared stories. In the United States, stories expressing ideals of masculinity often involve men on heroic quests, including larger-than-life characters like Paul Bunyan, the Lone Ranger, or Marvel Comics superheroes. They show an idealized man as stoic, physically strong, adept at violence, and in control. Western folktales depicting women—Cinderella, Sleeping Beauty, Rapunzel—have traditionally made

---

Southeast Asia, ed. Aihwa Ong and Michael G. Peletz (University of California Press, 1995), 19–50.

14. Marilyn Stern and Katherine Hildebrandt Karraker, "Sex Stereotyping of Infants: A Review of Gender Labeling Studies," *Sex Roles* 20 (1989): 501–22.

Mari Mendez

A young Mexican woman being presented at her quinceañera.

physical beauty a virtue and depict the main character needing rescue and wanting relationship. Contemporary media portray subversions and fusions of these norms, but the traditional stereotypes are still recognizable.

Ideals of womanhood or manhood are expressed in rituals as well, particularly rites of passage that mark the transition from childhood to adulthood (for more on ritual, see chap. 9). The **quinceañera** is a ritual marking the passage of a girl from childhood to adulthood that is popular in Mexico, other Latin American countries, and in Hispanic communities in the United States. The quinceañera ("age fifteen") is marked by symbols of ideal womanhood as the girl is arrayed like a bride, symbolizing beauty and purity. She may be escorted by a young man known as the *chambelán*, or by her father or godfather, reinforcing the importance of male protection. In many ceremonies, especially in Mexico, La Virgen de Guadalupe is portrayed, reinforcing the importance of motherhood. This ritual has continued through many generations, changing in style but continuous in its emphasis on family unity.

Media is another powerful and prevalent source of gender socialization. Men and women use media images as reference points for body image and beauty. Influencers have successfully monetized their message, so in addition to recommending that men be strong, self-sufficient, or dominant, or that women be beautiful, independent, or available for relationship, they also convey that wealth goes along with successful masculinity or femininity.

I (Jenell) conducted media research on Christian advertisements. I looked at hundreds of Christian magazines, websites, college catalogs, and other commercial literature, coding the images for Christian ideals of masculinity and femininity. I found that Christian advertisements commonly portray women as relational and emotional, happy in relationships with other people or lonely without them. They commonly rely on motifs of princesses, wives, and mothers. In this way, I observed, American Christianity communicates ideals of Christian womanhood.[15] Men, on the other hand, were more often portrayed as solitary figures portraying strength, leadership, and individual dependence on God (as opposed to within a community of believers or a family). Men were associated with motifs of warriors and were involved in active pursuits such as athletics or organizational leadership. The prevalence with which these images appear—and the relative rarity of images depicting women handling responsibility well, or men in nurturing relationships, or individuals who do not neatly fit the "man" and "woman" categories—reveals the process of cultural socialization by which people are taught to conform to particular ideals.

Men and Masculinity

What is it to be a man? Some elements of manhood are universal while others are culturally specific. How do people learn what it means to be a "good man," a "real man," a "bad man," or a "failed man"? Anthropologist Matthew Guttman describes the breadth of **masculinity studies** within anthropology. These studies consider the "social renegotiations regarding gender and sexuality; what gender equality might look like; institutional violence, including war; and the relationship of men and masculinity to other social institutions such as religion, education, and the state."[16]

In reviewing data from the United States and the United Kingdom, Richard Reeves found that men now lag behind women in educational attainment, many indicators of physical and mental health, relational vitality, and overall life satisfaction.[17] Research challenges the notion that patriarchy produces happiness or even power for most men. An imbalanced society creates imbalance for everyone. Even those who are supposedly "on top" of the power structure face serious challenges that flow from that very system of advantage.

15. Jenell Williams Paris, "Gender Messages in Christian Media and Advertising," CBE International, August 1, 2009, https://www.cbeinternational.org/resource/gender-christian-media-and-advertising/.

16. Matthew Gutmann, "Remarking the Unmarked: An Anthropology of Masculinity Redux," *Annual Review of Anthropology* 52, no. 1 (October 23, 2023): 55–72.

17. Richard V. Reeves, *Of Boys and Men: Why the Modern Male Is Struggling, Why It Matters, and What to Do About It* (Brookings Institute Press, 2024).

YOUR TURN

Interview a Man

Ethnographic interviews are often very casual, even conversational, though the anthropologist puts a lot of effort into planning them. Interviews can also be more formal, with a structured set of questions.

Nearly everyone has an opinion about how men are doing these days or how men ought to dress, speak, and behave. Anthropologists go deeper than popular opinion. They go to the people being talked about, and they listen.

Interview a man about some of the important ideas in this chapter. The man can be any age and from any culture. Before defaulting to a man you already know well, think about all the men in your daily life. Is there someone you'd like to learn about—a pastor, professor, employer, or classmate? Is there a man you haven't even met yet but who seems interesting and approachable? If you are a man, you might want to interview someone different from you in some significant way (age, race, cultural background) to learn how his experiences diverge or converge with yours.

First, identify a few topics for your interview. They could be masculinity, men's struggles, the transition into manhood, fatherhood, marriage, dating, appearance, opinions about online influencers, or something else.

Next, generate a list of at least eight questions for each topic. You may or may not use all the questions. It's more important that you listen closely than that you get through all your questions. You can generate new questions on the spot. You can let the interview go in a direction you hadn't expected.

Take notes as you conduct the interview. Your professor may ask you to write a summary or to share what you learned with a small group.

Gender and sexuality are complex, controversial, and rapidly changing topics. Anthropologists approach these kinds of topics by focusing on real people in real-world settings. How are men doing? Start to find out by listening to one of them.

Men face serious challenges *as men*. Research on nearly four thousand men from the United States, Canada, and Mexico ranging in age from eighteen to thirty described the primary cultural messages boys and young men learn about manhood. The dominant cultural messages teach that a "real man" is self-sufficient, hypersexual, tough, and adheres to rigid gender roles for men and women. The more that men in the survey held to these beliefs, the more likely they were to be lonely, unsatisfied, and to engage in risky or addictive behaviors.[18] In other words, striving for hypermasculinity can make a guy miserable.

Globalization has created new challenges for men in many developing countries. Daniel Jordan Smith did fieldwork in Nigeria analyzing how financial

18. Brian Heilman, Gary Barker, and Alexander Harrison, *The Man Box: A Study on Being a Young Man in the US, UK, and Mexico* (Equimundo & Unilever, 2017).

displays of wealth allowed a man to gain a reputation as a "good man."[19] In this setting, a son is expected to provide an elaborate funeral for his father. This displays both the father's and son's success as a man. A funeral is incredibly expensive, requiring purchase of a coffin and burial plot, food for hundreds of people, and gifts for certain guests. A man's reputation is lowered when he cannot afford all of this. He may be seen as a child into his thirties or forties, which limits opportunities for employment, marriage, and leadership. Expectations that were once attainable for subsistence farmers in rural villages have become impossible. With the growth of industrial capitalism, urbanization, and vast wealth inequalities, expectations have increased but in most cases earning potential has not.

Gender Variation

Some varieties of gender challenge two-gender systems that reflect biological dimorphism. Like the Bugis discussed earlier, many cultures have more than two categories for gender. In the Philippines, biological males who dress as women are ***bakla***. While the term "*bakla*" translates into English as "transvestite," "cross-dresser," or "transwoman," those translations don't fully capture the meaning. *Bakla* have existed in many Philippine towns and cities for centuries. They may wear everyday women's clothing, but frequently *bakla* dress in glamorous or flamboyant clothing. Some *bakla* mix typically masculine clothing with long fingernails, a feminine hairstyle, and makeup. Many, if not most, Filipino television shows feature a *bakla* character, typically a flamboyant, fast-talking, sarcastic jokester in a role meant for comic relief. *Bakla* are assumed to be involved in same-sex relationships, although there is a category of "gay man" in the Philippines that is not the same as *bakla*. Gay men are understood through the lens of traditional masculinity. Many Filipinos call the *bakla* a "third gender." Like the five gender categories of the Bugis, the third category of *bakla* is seen as necessary for those who are born with this nature.[20]

Christians have always accepted some degree of gender variation according to local cultural and historic customs. For instance, in 1 Corinthians, Paul required women to wear head coverings and have long hair, while men should not cover their heads while praying or wear long hair (11:14–15). Some

19. Daniel Jordan Smith, *To Be a Man Is Not a One-Day Job: Masculinity, Money, and Intimacy in Nigeria* (University of Chicago Press, 2017).

20. Similar categories exist in Thailand (*kathoey*), India (*hijra*), Indonesia (*waray*), and in many traditional North American Indigenous groups (generally rendered in English as "two-spirit"). These gender categories are typically thought to be related not to being intersex but rather to a personality or even a spiritual state of an individual such that while the body may be male, the "heart" or "soul" of the person is female.

Brian Howell

A *bakla* in a civic parade.

Christians today continue these practices, but most Christians agree that these are not essential expressions of respect and piety. Gendered presentation of the head (and specific hairstyles) is not a requirement for Christians in all times and places. Ideas such as a **third gender**, a gender spectrum, or even a post-gender society are more foundationally challenging than hairstyles or gendered symbols of respect. Christians can study Scripture for ways that believers in the past have engaged disagreements related to gender, and they can study anthropology to see how believers in societies with vastly different gender configurations have lived faithful lives.

Sexuality

Sexuality refers to ways human beings experience the erotic dimension of human life. Christians are often immediately concerned with the moral dimensions of sexuality, and anthropological fieldwork does not offer an answer. Anthropologists document the variety of sexual lifeways in the human experience. They analyze sexuality in a holistic, integrated framework that connects with culture as a whole. The existence of variety, or of a new sexual form or label, does not answer the important question of God's intent for human sexuality. The anthropological perspective contributes real-world insight and global views that often round out the quest for truth with empathy and mercy.

Culture influences even that which seems natural, including sex categories, gender roles, and sexuality. Sexuality has public and cultural dimensions; for example, laws prohibit certain behaviors and even relationships, and media

How Can Christians Respond to a Changing Culture?

Christians sometimes want to preserve good aspects of society. Other times they want to promote change. Sometimes Christians agree on what "the good life" looks like. Sometimes they don't.

Christian anthropologists have offered research-based insight and wisdom to the church on many important topics. Their insights are grounded in real-world experience with the people who are most impacted. Katrina Greene studied women's opportunities in economic development in South Africa.[a] Eloise Hiebert Meneses delved into the lives of "untouchable" (Dalit) market women in India.[b] Robert J. Priest surveyed Christian colleges and universities, looking at how their policies articulate and promote a sexual ethic that connects with marriage. He also studied gender roles and dynamics in missionary families.[c]

Christian anthropologist Vince Gil holds a PhD in medical and psychological anthropology, with two postdocs in clinical sexual sciences and in public health / sexual diseases. He is also a clergyperson. Through speaking and training and writing, he supports Christian communities in working through issues that cause division and confusion. In *A Christian's Guide Through the Gender Revolution*, Gil takes on the topics of gender, cisgender, transgender, and intersex.[d] He supports individuals and families in their relationships, and he educates people who want to learn about both science and theology.

Vince Gil

Vince Gil introducing rapid HIV testing and training to a provincial hospital in Yunnan, China. Medical anthropologists are often co-trained in medicine or public health and are thus capable of providing cross-cultural medical technology training.

It's your turn: Choose the heading in this chapter that interests you the most. What is a question you'd like to ask about this topic? How might an anthropologist conduct fieldwork in your area of interest? How might a Christian anthropologist make connections with biblical study and theology?

a. For a summary of Greene's current research, see Charlotte McKinley, "How Black Female B&B and Guesthouse Entrepreneurs Impact Economic Empowerment in South Africa," *Biola News*, May 25, 2023, www.biola.edu/blogs/biola-news/2023.

b. Eloise Hiebert Meneses, *Love and Revolutions: Market Women and Social Change in India* (University Press of America, 2007).

c. Robert J. Priest, "Faith Integration and the Outrageous Ethic of Sex Only in Male-Female Marriage: Towards an Anthropology of Sex and Marriage for the Christian Community," *On Knowing Humanity* 6, no. 1 (2022): 1–41.

d. Vince Gil, *A Christian's Guide Through the Gender Revolution: Gender, Cisgender, Transgender, and Intersex* (Wipf & Stock, 2020). See also the Faith and Sex Science website at www.drvincegil.com/faith-and-sex-science.

sets expectations for what is beautiful, handsome, or sexy. In the West, it was previously assumed that men were more visually stimulated and felt stronger sexual urges; therefore, women were expected to dress and behave in ways that would constrain men's sexuality. Today, women's sexuality is also often asserted as strong and expressive, and the presumption of heterosexual partners of different genders in a relationship no longer holds. In many conservative Islamic countries, male and female sexuality is regulated through cultural institutions such as **purdah**—the seclusion of women from public view—and restrictive clothing such as the **burqa**, a long garment covering the entire body, even the eyes. This expresses a cultural logic of male sexuality that says temptation is rooted in men's exposure to unrelated women. It also links to a (contested) interpretation of Islamic virtues of honor, modesty, and respect.

Katerina Friesen

Young girls poised for their entrance to the annual "Little Miss Santa Fe" competition. Talent shows and beauty competitions for girls of all ages are extremely popular in the Philippines. *Baklas*, a third gender in the Philippines, usually organize and run these pageants (one is standing behind the girls on the far-right side of the photo).

In other cultural contexts, some people assume that women's sexuality needs to be controlled. This is often the motive for **female circumcision** or **female genital mutilation** (FGM). FGM is most common among Islamic communities in northern and sub-Saharan Africa. Techniques vary, but it involves the removal or closure of part or all of a girl's genitalia. The idea is that reducing the possibility of pleasure limits a girl's sexuality, and consequently her virginity will be preserved for a good marriage.

Even physical responses to sexual stimuli are culturally conditioned. The example of the Wodaabe challenges the common notion that relationships are sparked by men enjoying the sight of beautiful women. The Wodaabe are nomadic cattle herders in Niger, Cameroon, Nigeria, and the Central African Republic. They make marriage arrangements at annual clan gatherings. Young men adorn themselves with makeup and feathers and sing and dance for marriageable women who judge the men's appearance and skill. The male beauty ideal includes elaborate accessories, white eyes and teeth, and height. Women are socialized to appreciate male beauty, and men are socialized to dress and act in ways that will catch a woman's eye.

Anthropologists study many aspects of sexuality, including the formation of sexual minority neighborhoods in cities, how kinship works for LGBTQ+ individuals, and how the concept of heterosexuality has developed over time.[21] With the growth of the internet and portable electronics, the production and consumption of sexually explicit materials has become a major influence in how many people are socialized into sexuality. Though the stereotype of males as visually oriented suggests that men are the primary consumers of pornography, research conducted in the United States by the Barna group reveals that more than half of women twenty-five and under reported consuming pornography, with more than one-third saying they did so at least monthly.[22]

Like gender, sexuality is a topic that has been important to some anthropologists since the discipline's inception. The **two-spirit**, for example, was a social status documented in over one hundred Native American cultures, including Navajo, Zuni, Cheyenne, and Crow. The two-spirit person dressed as the other gender and performed the work of that gender or both genders. This person often was seen as embodying both male and female essence and was gifted in healing or spiritual roles. The sexuality of a two-spirit person varied by culture. While Indigenous societies have different terms for this social role, today some have reclaimed two-spirit as an Indigenous social status.[23]

Many cultures don't recognize sexual identities; that is, people do not build social statuses or identities around sexual desire. Cultures depicted in the Bible put gender first (man, woman, father, mother, husband, wife), and sexuality happened within these statuses. People in biblical cultures did not develop sexual identity statuses that they used to form social groups with others of shared identity. North American concepts such as straight, gay, lesbian, and so forth are **sexual identity** categories, which create social categories based on sexual desires. On a global level, categories, labels, and identities are being actively negotiated, and they are changing rapidly. This isn't mere semantics; to identify as "gay" is to identify with a global social category rather than

21. See, for example, Ulrika Dahl and Jacqui Gabb, "Trends in Contemporary Queer Kinship and Family Research," *Lambda Nordica* 24, no. 2–3 (2019): 209–37; Tatiana Vargas Condori, "LGBTQ+ Spaces in the Urban Evolution of the City of El Alto: An Ethnography of a Popular and Dissident Bar," *Bolivian Studies Journal* (2025): 149–74; Jenell Paris, *The End of Sexual Identity: Why Sex Is Too Important to Define Who We Are* (InterVarsity, 2011).

22. Barna Group, *The Porn Phenomenon: The Impact of Pornography in the Digital Age* (Barna Group, 2016).

23. Some North American scholars or activists now use "2SLGBTQAI+," with the initial *2S* signifying the "two-spirit" designation. These categories are dynamic and reflective of cultural and political debates rather than settled scholarly or social convention.

categories from one's local culture.[24] Similarly, to prioritize "LGBTQ+" over "homosexual" is to reposition identity away from the sex act and toward affiliation and participation with a social group.

Anthropological Contributions to the Church

The apostle Paul enjoined the Corinthian Christians to "flee from sexual immorality." He asked them, "Do you not know that your bodies are temples of the Holy Spirit, who is in you, whom you have received from God? You are not your own; you were bought at a price. Therefore honor God with your bodies" (1 Cor. 6:19–20 NRSVue). The human body matters to God. This passage compares the human body to the temple, the dwelling place of God. At the same time, human bodies are the medium through which culture and society are made and experienced. Sexuality is a powerful part of our embodiment that affects every aspect of human life: communities, family members, children, politics, economics, and more. Sexuality can be structured by society and lived out by people in ways that lead to flourishing or to diminishment.

Both anthropology and Christianity are concerned for human well-being, although the ground from which these traditions build their understanding differs significantly. As a secular discipline, anthropological ethics is based in human rights that prioritize bodily safety, freedom from oppression and violence, and nonharm or nonexploitation in relationships. Even when cultural practices threaten human well-being, anthropologists still use cultural relativism to understand the insider's point of view, but moral considerations are not discarded. Sometimes such an approach can develop a deeper and more accurate interpretation of cultural practices that may have been misinterpreted. Other times, fieldwork fosters strategic interventions; consider, for example, how much more effective an intervention in sex trafficking can be when it is based in an accurate understanding of the meanings, values, and motivations of those involved.[25]

Christians often ask a fair question: Does studying and documenting human sexual practices in all their diversity encourage a view of all sexualities and sexual practices as morally equivalent? How can anthropological studies

24. See, for example, Tom Boellstorff, *The Gay Archipelago: Sexuality and Nation in Indonesia* (Princeton University Press, 2005).

25. See, for example, Elżbieta M. Goździak, "Human Trafficking in a Time of Crisis," *Anthropology News* 57, no. 11 (November 25, 2016): 128–32, https://anthrosource.onlinelibrary.wiley.com/doi/abs/10.1111/AN.220.

that take no moral stance help Christians to understand God's good purposes in sexual practice? Christians see sexuality as embedded in God's purposes for humanity, so concerns rooted in human rights only begin to scratch the surface of all that we might say about the good life, which includes gender and sexuality.

Gender is part of God's original creation. Note, however, that while **gender status** is described as part of the pre-fall creation, distinct **gender roles** are not described until after the fall, as part of what is often called the curse of Genesis 3. Some have taken this description of how the woman and the man will relate to each other after the fall as being normative—that is, how men and women *should* relate. Whereas traditional views of women's and men's spheres in twentieth-century Western cultures cast women as mothers and men as breadwinners, women in Scripture are commended for pursuing economic activity (Prov. 31), theological education (Luke 10:42), and exercising leadership skills (Judg. 4:4), as well as for their roles as wives and mothers. Likewise, men are encouraged to display humility in marriage (Eph. 5:33) and long-suffering patience (Hosea 3:1–3) in addition to carrying out more typically masculine roles of economic provision or political leadership. Both men and women are depicted as serving faithfully in a wide variety of roles. Regardless of how individual Christians interpret passages about men's and women's roles and place in the church, it is clear there is to be no oppression or inequality in how Christians treat one another (Gal. 3:28; Col. 3:11).

Anthropology helps Christians to see how Scripture reflects social and cultural contexts. This, in turn, can help us apply scriptural truths more faithfully in our diverse cultural contexts. It can often be difficult for modern readers of the Bible to see how their own cultural assumptions shape their understanding of Scripture. It is important to continue studying key biblical themes and passages, and it is becoming increasingly important to learn about conflict within religion. Even while disagreement remains, we can work together to develop modes of discourse and relationship that can help preserve Christian unity even during conflict. Perhaps distinctively Christian cultural practices such as patience in robust and difficult conversation, relationship across deep difference, and worship as an expression of unity could deepen the faith as this generation (and likely the next several generations) works toward transformation and resolution of these difficulties.

TERMS

bakla: A gender status in the Philippines that involves a natal man dressed as a woman.

burqa: A long garment that covers every part of a woman's body, including her eyes.

female circumcision (or **female genital mutilation** [FGM]): A cultural practice that involves removal of part or all of a girl's genitalia and may involve the surgical closure of her vagina until she is married.

gender: The meaning humans give to sex differences.

gender role: A set of expectations regarding proper behavior and appearance for a particular gender.

gender socialization: The process of learning how to act according to the gender norms of a culture.

gender status: A position a person can occupy in the social order that is directly related to maleness or femaleness. Gender status is usually ascribed. The most common English-language gender statuses are girl, boy, woman, and man.

intersex: People whose bodies have variations of sex characteristics, around 1 percent of most populations.

kula ring: An exchange system around the chain of Trobriand Islands.

masculinity/femininity: Specific behaviors, traits, and characteristics ascribed to humans based on male/female gender categories.

masculinity studies: Research on men with a focus on how gender relates to their experience of the world.

purdah: The seclusion of women from public view.

quinceañera: A popular Catholic tradition of Mexico involving a ritual passage of a girl from childhood to adulthood.

sex: The biological attributes that distinguish males, females, and intersex individuals.

sexual dimorphism: The biological binary of male and female as physical conditions.

sexual identity: An element of some cultures; the intentional sense of having a sexual desire around which social identity is built.

sexuality: The erotic domain of life: sexual thoughts, feelings, and behaviors.

third gender: A gender other than man or woman.

two-spirit: A Native American social status in which a person dresses as the other gender and performs the work of the opposite gender or both genders.

DISCUSSION QUESTIONS

1. What is one important element of gender socialization in your upbringing? This could be something you were taught or something you observed about how women or men ought to be.
2. Tell a story about a time you encountered a gender norm (a status or role) that was different from the gender norms of your background. This could be in a different culture or within your own society. How did you recognize it as different? How did you respond to the difference?
3. In your opinion, what is the most important thing Christians should do as they address difficult issues of gender and sexuality in church and society? How could anthropological concepts or perspectives be helpful?

ANTHROPOLOGY AND SCRIPTURE

The Proverbs 31 Woman

> Charm is deceitful and beauty is vain,
> but a woman who fears the Lord is to be praised.
> Give her a share in the fruit of her hands,
> and let her works praise her in the city gates.
> (Prov. 31:30–31 NRSVue)

The activities of the Proverbs 31 woman exceed those prescribed by her gender socialization. It is certainly true that she is praised for her work in the domestic sphere, pleasing her children and her husband with her diligence and care. She wears beautiful clothes and earns her husband's trust. Yet in addition to these domestic skills, which all married women were expected to develop, she also works in the public sphere. She "perceives that her merchandise is profitable" (v. 18)—meaning she produces and sells for the marketplace. She buys real estate ("she considers a field and buys it," v. 16) and works in agriculture ("with the fruit of her hands she plants a vineyard," v. 16). Especially for cultures that prescribe a narrow social role for women, Proverbs 31 provides an example of femininity that includes a wide range of women's gifts and abilities. As a woman of strength and social standing ("strength and dignity are her clothing," v. 25) who is not principally known for her appearance ("beauty is vain, " v. 30), the Proverbs 31 woman is known for her wisdom and even her abilities as a teacher ("she opens her mouth with wisdom, and the teaching of kindness is on her tongue," v. 26). She is not afraid of aging but looks forward to her standing as an elder in the community ("she laughs at the time to come," v. 25). She is well-known as a generous person who cares for the poor in her community.

How do those in your Christian community tend to talk about the Proverbs 31 woman? What do they emphasize? Is she an exemplar just for women, or for both women and men? Which aspects of her character or activities are most inspiring or thought-provoking for you?

Is It Well to Remain Unmarried?

> To the unmarried and the widows I say that it is well for them to remain unmarried as I am. But if they are not practicing self-control, they should marry. For it is better to marry than to be aflame with passion. (1 Cor. 7:8–9 NRSVue)

Marital status is often a contributor to social inequality in the church. In New Testament times, widows were vulnerable to poverty, particularly widows without sons. For women, financial stability required them to be linked to a man in marriage. Today, in some parts of the world, being single makes a person more vulnerable to being pitied or excluded from certain activities (like family activities or married-only groups), and a single person may also be more vulnerable to poverty or neglect as they age. For many men and women, the nuclear family is important for financial stability. Paul encourages Christians to make the church into a community that truly supports all believers. Within the church, believers should provide social and material support to each other in such profound ways that though the widow and the single person lack spouses, they still have family. In this way, the church becomes a beacon to society and a blessing to believers. How do you see the church in your context serving as family for widows, orphans, or unmarried people? In what ways can we all be more faithful in supporting one another and exalting all members of the body of Christ?

6

ECONOMICS

After studying this chapter, you should be able to do the following:

1. distinguish between different systems of production
2. distinguish between different systems of exchange
3. analyze the interplay between economics and social life
4. appreciate the variety of economic systems described in Scripture

CHAPTER OUTLINE

Introduction

Côte d'Ivoire is a top cocoa producer in the world, yet many cocoa farmers have never tasted chocolate. A Dutch film correspondent asked cocoa farmer N'da Alphonse what happens to his crop after it is sold. "Frankly, I do not know what one makes from cocoa beans," he replied. "I'm just trying to earn a living with growing cocoa. They make good food from them, but I've never seen that. I do not know if it's true." The correspondent then pulled a chocolate bar from his pocket and offered a piece to Mr. Alphonse. For the first time in his life, the farmer tasted the literal fruit of his labor. He was surprised by its sweetness.[1]

In the contemporary global economy this scenario is unsurprising. Workers who are essential for chocolate production often cannot afford to purchase it. At the time Mr. Alphonse was interviewed, a chocolate bar cost about US $2.50, but a farmer's daily earnings would be about US $9. A farmer providing for his

1. "Cocoa Farmers Taste Chocolate for the First Time," posted September 7, 2014, by Viral Gig, YouTube, 6 min., 11 sec., https://www.youtube.com/watch?v=bCyDJAh1fi4.

family can't afford to spend 30 percent of a day's income on a treat. Despite their hard work, cocoa farmers have no access to land ownership or capital. They are largely at the mercy of a system over which they have little control.

Economy shapes all aspects of life: time, work, food, leisure, housing, and even values and expectations. Virtually all of us participate in a global system of production, exchange, and consumption. Millions of people are intimately involved in producing goods and services they may never have the opportunity to consume, while others consume goods and services with little idea of how they are made. This global system fosters great inequalities hitched to historic injustices of the modern era.

Economic anthropologists analyze how economic systems provide, and fail to provide, for people's material and social needs. They are especially interested in the ways these economic processes shape everyday life. Many economic anthropologists see **alienation** as a fundamental economic problem: People are disconnected from the fruits of their labor and experience deep disconnections between the work of their hands and the desires of their hearts. This term originates in the work of Karl Marx but has come to be applied to many circumstances in which human work becomes separated from choice, personal fulfillment, and flourishing. Christian theology ties this problem to a disconnection between God and the fruit of his labor, which is humanity. This root separation plays out in the economic lives of humans in the beginning of Genesis. The garden provided abundantly, but with sin came the "curse" of toil and pain in labor. The message of redemption is for individual souls, of course, but culture will also be redeemed. The curse of work becomes the blessing of service (Rev. 22:3), and wealth is no longer hoarded by the few but is freely available to all (Rev. 21:21).

In this chapter, we describe how anthropologists study the social organization of production and exchange. We explore ways that economic anthropologists look at the current global economy and its influence on culture and society. We conclude with a discussion of how economic anthropology can inspire deeper understanding of biblical contexts and how Christians can engage today's globalized economies.

Systems of Production

Systems of production describe how cultures produce food, which is a fundamental need. Systems of production also make more than just food and provide for more than just needs (e.g., global supply chains also produce and distribute luxury goods). In the 1960s, anthropologist Elman Service

Table 6.1. Modes of Subsistence

Subsistence System	Definition	Examples in This Chapter
Foraging	A subsistence strategy based on gathering plants that grow wild in the environment and hunting available animals	Ju/'hoansi
Horticulture	A subsistence strategy in which people cultivate varieties of wild or domesticated crops, primarily for their own use, using relatively little technology	Ikalahan
Pastoralism	A subsistence strategy based on the use of domesticated herd animals	Maasai Nuer Samburu Dukha
Agriculture	A subsistence strategy that requires constant and intensive use of permanent fields for plant cultivation	Latin American plantations Southeast Asian plantations

developed a four-part typology of modes of subsistence: foraging, horticulture, pastoralism, and agriculture.[2] This typology continues to be useful for gaining a global view of the variety of ways humans make a living (see table 6.1). At the time it was developed, many people believed that cultures advanced through these stages over time, but this isn't accurate. People are adaptive and strategic. As conditions change, a culture may retain a mode of subsistence, blend two or three, or alter its base strategy. This typology was developed before globalization, so when anthropologists use these categories today, they must consider how a local economy intersects with global capitalism.

Foraging (or **hunting and gathering**) involves gathering plants that grow wild in the environment and hunting available animals. This may not seem like production because it does not involve plant domestication or animal husbandry, but **production** refers to any human action intended to convert resources in the environment into something that can be used or consumed. Therefore, foraging is production because it involves knowledge, skill, intention, and effort by humans as they bring natural resources into the human domain for use.

2. Elman Service, *Primitive Social Organization: An Evolutionary Perspective*, 2nd ed. (Random House, 1971).

Foraging has been a primary **subsistence strategy** throughout human history, with people relying on a consistent supply of plants, nuts, and berries, and occasional supplies of meat. Adam and Eve in the garden of Eden are portrayed as foragers; God gave them plants, trees, and fruit for food. God said, "See, I have given you every plant yielding seed that is upon the face of all the earth and every tree with seed in its fruit; you shall have them for food. And to every beast of the earth and to every bird of the air and to everything that creeps on the earth, everything that has the breath of life, I have given every green plant for food" (Gen. 1:29–30 NRSVue).

Around the world, most foragers gain more calories from gathering than from hunting. The Ju/'hoansi, for instance, historically lived as foragers in the southern African desert areas of Botswana, Namibia, and South Africa. Just as most of the Ju/'hoansi people today mix foraging, pastoralism, agriculture, and employment in cash economies, contemporary US Americans and other largely urban people may use forms of foraging (mushroom hunting or picking wild blackberries) as a way to augment their diet and consume foods that may be expensive, rare, or simply plentiful.

Katerina Friesen

Ikalahan Farmer Noemi Beilan harvesting *lya* (ginger) at her family's swidden farm. Most of the ginger crop is used at home, but some of her ginger is sold at market for a small profit.

Horticulturalism is the practice of cultivating a variety of crops using relatively less input of energy in terms of technology or labor than is taken out in the form of calories. Like foraging, this **subsistence farming** usually involves group participation in production, often with a strong division of labor between sexes. Compared to many foraging societies, horticulturalists generally have less flexibility between men's and women's roles and a larger community size due to a more settled lifestyle.

Since virtually everyone in a horticultural society has a role in food production, it might seem that a society like the United States, where less than 2 percent of the population is directly engaged in farming, is a much more efficient producer of food. Surprisingly, it takes a lot more energy (through fossil fuels, manufacturing, and chemical industries) to produce a calorie of food in the United States than in horticultural systems. For example, each family among the Ikalahan, an upland group in the high Gran Cordillera mountains of Northern Luzon in the Philippines, traditionally maintains a garden that supplies most of their food. They practice **swidden farming** (or **shifting cultivation** or **slash-and-burn**), a relatively efficient method when considered from the perspective of energy-in versus energy-out. Garden plots, which may be several kilometers from home, are cleared from the forest as the farmers cut down trees and brush and conduct a controlled burn on the land. The farmers may plant a variety of crops, from the staple sweet potato called an *obi*, growing low to the ground, to corn and beans (which can climb the corn). Around the edges of the field, particularly on the low edge of the slope, the family grows tiger grass, a tall, broad-bladed grass that controls erosion and provides fibers for weaving brooms, baskets, and other household goods. By **multicropping**, the family can meet a variety of nutritional and domestic needs while providing a balance among the crops that maximizes land fertility.

Pastoralism is a subsistence system based on the use of domesticated herd animals. Animals are used for a wide variety of purposes, such as transportation, trading, plowing, meat consumption, and dairy provision, and for

A young Samburu herdsman tends his family's cattle.

iStockphoto.com/brittak

making cultural artifacts from wool, hair, skin, bone, and horn. Herd animals, such as cattle in East Africa, sheep or goats in central Asia, camels in North Africa, and llama and alpaca in South America, are important for both the economic and social lives of pastoralists.

Just as horticulturalism requires ecological resources (predictable rainfall or other accessible water, domesticable plants, sufficient and fertile land), pastoralism has requirements as well. For instance, East Africa and Central Asia have many animals that can be herded, milked, and bred relatively easily, while South America has wild ancestors of the llama and alpaca, which were well-suited for cold mountainous regions. North America, on the other hand, had no domesticated herd animals prior to the introduction of European horses and cattle. Buffalo did not herd well, and bears were hard to milk.

Agriculture is a subsistence system that requires constant and intensive use of permanent fields for plant cultivation. By "intensive use," anthropologists mean agricultural techniques that directly replenish the nutrients in the soil, producing marginally higher crop yields. Techniques of intensification include the use of the plow, irrigation, fertilization, mechanization, and the application of greater human labor in increasingly specialized tasks. Much of the time, a portion of a crop—and sometimes the vast majority of it—is sold at

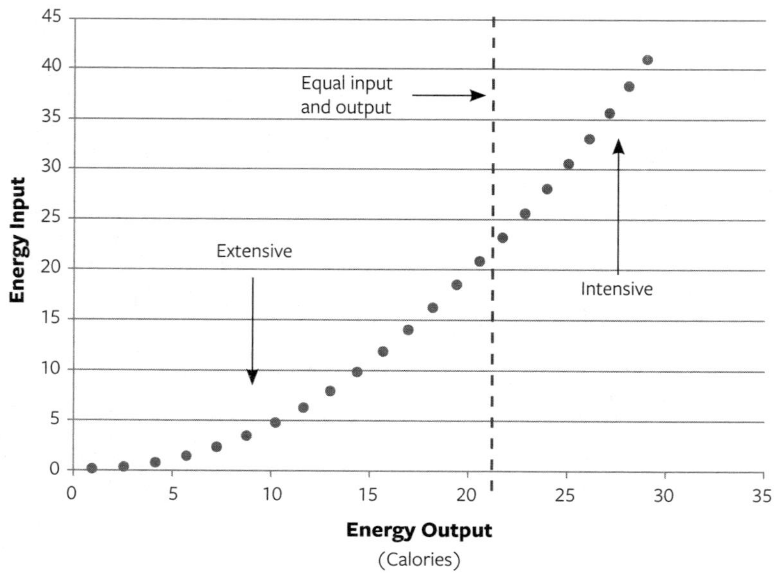

Figure 6.1. Extensive and intensive agriculture

market. Agricultural systems support the specialization and stratification of society, whereby some become producers for many, allowing nonproducers to focus on other tasks (see fig. 6.1). The cocoa farms where N'da Alphonse and his team work reflect an agricultural system engaging in monocropping and cash cropping.

Today, it is rare to find a community where only one economic strategy is employed. Most people practice **economic articulation**, in which multiple strategies are combined. A Kawelka person in the highlands of Papua New Guinea may get the bulk of her calories from her garden (*horticulture*), while also keeping pigs as an important economic and social resource (*pastoralism*), and growing a cash crop or working on a nearby plantation growing coffee or tobacco (*agriculture*) to obtain cash for the market economy. Similarly, contemporary US Americans may get most of their calories from food purchased in the supermarket (*industrial agriculture*) but may also have a garden at home (*horticulture*), go hunting or fishing in certain seasons (*foraging*), or even raise some chickens to obtain eggs (*pastoralism*). But in each case, there are social configurations that are associated with these various economic strategies. The dominant strategy will have its own cultural logic that has a profound effect on the social structure and cultural frameworks.

Economics and Social Structure

Economy intersects with cultural values and practices in profound ways. In fact, economic systems even shape people's values. Anthropologists who take a political economy perspective on culture see economic life as the foundation of culture. They would consider many, or even all, of social life, values, and beliefs to be driven by the ways economic life is organized.

Consider ways of life that many US Americans consider legitimate or normal. A person graduates from high school and then attends college or job training or starts working full time. The person hopes to become economically independent, even seeing this as a mark of full adulthood. They hope to secure their own housing (establishing *neolocality*, see chap. 8) and may build a nuclear family of their own. They may even move hundreds or thousands of miles away from their parents or extended family for education or career advancement. Not everyone does this, of course, but it is an easily recognizable cultural ideal for adulthood. The dominant social values reinforce ideals such as "respect," "success," or "wealth" to make this lifeway seem even more valuable.

Interestingly, hunter-gatherers may use somewhat similar strategies, though their traditional lives rely on foraging, not market capitalism. Like contemporary US Americans, Ju/'hoansi people living in traditional foraging communities also will frequently leave their parents or other relatives, taking their nuclear family and "fissioning" the community for the sake of economic opportunity elsewhere (e.g., better foraging resources). For both the Ju/'hoansi and contemporary US Americans (and many others around the globe) there is a logic to keeping one's strongest kinship bonds to a small group that can be moved easily in response to changing ecological/economic conditions. For most horticultural or pastoral communities, however, the extended family is absolutely required for the economic viability of the household. There you see people emphasizing the importance of staying physically close to one's wider kinship network. Multigenerational families in one household may be the norm, with all the joy and stress that sort of arrangement includes.

A political economy perspective emphasizes that economy matters—a lot. It shapes how people get what they need to survive, and, beyond that, economy shapes major social institutions and cultural values. Christian anthropologists see a compatible theme in Scripture, in concern for the poor, the widow, the orphan, and all vulnerable people. It's important that people be able to get what they need to survive in the here and now. Paul envisioned a good society where individuals desired only what they needed, where people could learn to be content in all circumstances (Phil. 4).

Systems of Exchange

Subsistence and economic systems are linked to **systems of exchange**, which are social processes whereby people give and receive goods and services. Anthropologists use three major categories to classify systems of exchange: reciprocity, redistribution, and markets (see table 6.2).

Reciprocity is an exchange system based on gifting. In his classic work *Stone Age Economics*, anthropologist Marshall Sahlins argues that there are three basic forms of reciprocity: generalized, balanced, and negative.[3]

Generalized reciprocity refers to gift exchanges with no precise accounting of value and no precise expectation for type or time of return. It was the dominant exchange system for most of human history, when people lived in foraging societies. There are no set rules. Everyone gives and receives as they are able, with a great deal of personal freedom and choice. Behavior is regulated mostly with informal sanctions such as teasing, complaining,

3. Marshall Sahlins, *Stone Age Economics* (Aldine-Atherton, 1972).

Table 6.2. Exchange Systems

Reciprocity	Redistribution	Markets
• Generalized • Balanced • Negative	• Taxation • Potlatch	• Buying and selling

and gossiping when imbalances are perceived. Distribution may be managed by kin relationships, indebtedness from past exchanges, or need. Generalized circulation of goods among members of a group helps to spread the risk of shortage and creates bonds between the members of the group.

Today, for those living in contemporary market systems, generalized reciprocity is normally confined to the private sphere. In the United States, generalized reciprocity is practiced within small groups, particularly within families. It would be unusual for a child to reach maturity—say, for example, their eighteenth birthday—only for the parents to turn around and demand repayment for all the meals, laundry, toys, and other expenses involved in raising the child. Of course, many families have an expectation that each member will contribute to the family's well-being, but this is usually based on physical strength, age, and aptitude. There is no explicit or precise expectation for repayment of food consumed or services rendered. Likely, there is often hope that children will respond to their caretakers by being good members of the family (however that is defined). When children are grown, they may express gratitude by visiting, calling, or giving gifts. Similarly, a group of friends may loan each other money, "spot" someone for a purchase ("I'll buy your frozen yogurt today, and you can buy me a churro next week"), or otherwise give time or money with the expectation that, over time, things will generally even out. If one of the members of the friend group becomes known as the one person who always "forgets" her money or is constantly asking for "a few bucks" to get by, others may use complaining, teasing, or gossiping to pressure the person to change their behavior.

Balanced reciprocity is a form of exchange in which the exchange is immediate, or within a relatively short amount of time, and answered or repaid in a way that is considered roughly equivalent—with or without the use of money. Balanced reciprocity may or may not involve ongoing relationships between the partners, but it does involve a moral order that considers more than merely the use or material qualities of the thing being given and received.

As with generalized reciprocity, the expectation of balance can create important links of indebtedness. For most contemporary US Americans, gift giving typically follows a form of balanced reciprocity. For example, you may choose a gift for a friend based on your sense of closeness with them. If, after several birthdays or other occasions, that friend does not reciprocate at all, or gives gifts that are much less valuable (giving a card after receiving concert tickets), you may begin to question the relationship. We expect, informally, balanced exchange as a symbol of mutuality in the relationship. The "free gift" may seem to be an ultimate act of generosity or altruism, but balanced reciprocity suggests that accepting gifts incurs an obligation to reciprocate.

Negative reciprocity involves exchanges in which one or both parties seek to receive more than they give. This may be as blatant as stealing, lying, or conning someone into an unequal exchange. In small-scale societies, negative reciprocity is less frequent because society requires positive, ongoing relationships. Even when practiced with strangers or enemies, negative reciprocity often creates conflict, but sometimes the short-term gain is considered worth the trouble. The used-car salesperson might lie or apply pressure tactics to convince someone to pay more for a car than it's worth. If there are many potential car buyers out there, he might not be concerned about the negative reaction from one particular customer.[4]

Redistribution involves a centralized authority collecting goods and services from a group of people and redistributing them. The most famous example was the Potlatch, a ceremony of Pacific Northwest Native American groups (e.g., the Kwakiutl). Clan leaders would gather large amounts of valuable goods to give as gifts to rival leaders. Giving a large gift signaled a leader's ability to mobilize resources and would place the receiver in a subordinate position until the gift was repaid. For the receiver to shed the shame of having received an embarrassingly large gift, he would have to give an even *larger* gift, creating an ongoing process of exchange. The leader would distribute among his clan the goods he had received, which might include valuable commodities, animals, or even people.

In Melanesian societies, where gift-based redistributive economies used to be widespread, the leader (known as a Big Man or, in rare cases, a Big Woman) would repay clan members who had given resources for earlier gifts distributed by that leader. As leaders accumulated resources for a gift, they gathered surpluses and redistributed them, making it impossible for one person or group to control so much that other groups would be left wanting. The economic standing of community members, while temporarily unbalanced, was thus leveled out over time.

In large-scale contemporary societies, taxation is the most prevalent form of redistribution. A political authority imposes a tax and then redistributes

4. Technically speaking, the sale of a car is not an example of reciprocity; it is a market exchange. However, the tradition of buying a car often involves trust and confidence on the part of the consumer, and the price of the car is typically negotiated—at least partly—based on the testimony and skill of the car salesperson. In this way, it is one of the few examples of a common situation that illustrates negative reciprocity in contemporary US life.

or spends the money in ways that, ideally, contribute to the common good. When redistribution reduces social inequality, it is called a **leveling mechanism**, though redistribution may also increase social inequality by rewarding those faithful to the power structure.

A **market economy** is a system of exchange in which people provide labor for money, which can then be exchanged for goods and services. The value of goods and services is precisely accounted with money, and exchanges are typically precise and impersonal. Paying cash for an item at the store, for instance,

Kinship as Survival Strategy

In the late 1960s, Carol Stack, a young White anthropologist, started her fieldwork in a low-income urban setting in the Midwest, where she studied Black families' survival strategies. In *All Our Kin: Strategies for Survival in a Black Community*, Stack described how people make it in a money-based market economy when they don't have very much money.

Stack observed complex networks of sharing and swapping between individuals and families. As exchange relationships became closer and more enmeshed, people extended their kinship networks. A neighbor could become an "aunt," a classmate a "cousin," and a fellow church member a "mom." These domestic networks solidified relationships of exchange that helped everyone access food, money, childcare, shelter, and other necessities. Stack concluded that the urban poor become generous not out of altruism but out of necessity. "In times of need, the only predictable resources that can be drawn upon are their own children and parents, and the fund of kin and friends obligated to them."[a]

Nearly thirty years after Carol Stack, I (Jenell) began my fieldwork in a similar setting: an urban neighborhood of low-income Black Americans. I saw that reciprocity-based survival strategies were still alive and well. Initially, I thought of myself as a "have" working and ministering among "have-nots." I was a financially independent young adult working my way through graduate school. I quickly learned that in the eyes of many of my Black neighbors, I was the one who was poor. I had no husband and no parents, siblings, aunts, or cousins within the vicinity. I had no one to back me up when times were hard. In various difficult circumstances, I learned to lean on others and was grateful for neighbors who welcomed me into their lives as fictive kin. I received meals, information, companionship, prayer, and a variety of material goods, and then was obligated to give similar things in return—not with any precise accounting but according to the rhythm of ongoing relationships of mutuality.

It's your turn: Who are your fictive kin? You might have a loved one who you call "aunt" or "cousin," even though they aren't biologically related to you. You might have a mentor or a pastor who is "like one of the family." Connect with one of your fictive kin in a meaningful way. Give a gift. Receive a gift. Give or ask for advice. Offer an expression of love or gratitude. What did you do? How did it reinforce the bond of fictive kinship?

a. Carol Stack, *All Our Kin: Strategies for Survival in a Black Community* (Harper & Row, 1974), 107.

is a precise exchange that results in no ongoing relationship between customer and cashier. Markets can exist within any system of subsistence, as they are designed to deal with the distribution and exchange of resources, however those resources are produced. The image of a literal marketplace—a physical location where people come together to exchange goods—is a metaphor for the diffuse workings of the contemporary global economy.

Economic Globalization and Cultural Change

In the early years of anthropology, anthropologists often conducted fieldwork in communities where production and exchange were relatively limited to a local ecological and social context. Even then, however, the anthropologist might have to make an effort to find the most remote and least modernized group in a region. Colonial expansion brought money, markets, and modern capitalism around the world long before early anthropologists began doing fieldwork in the areas where their colonial ties allowed access.

Historically, many large political states, from the Zulu nation in southern Africa to the Mongols of northern China, have used their strong numbers, economic organization, and political structures to invade and control other territories for economic gain. Yet the scale and scope of European colonialism has had an indelible impact on economic systems and social life globally.

In the modern era, various European nations established comprehensive plans for controlling vast areas of Africa, Asia, and Latin America. They wanted a supply of raw materials to support industrializing economies. They wanted empires to establish national political power. Because of their technological capacity to extract resources from the lands they controlled, European colonialism led to greater economic entanglement and cultural change than earlier instances of colonialism. For example, the British colonial regime encouraged thousands of people from their own countries to settle in the colonial territories of North America. In other places, the only Europeans to live in colonized territories were colonial administrators. This was the Portuguese approach in Brazil and Southeast Asia, the Spanish agenda in the Philippines, and the French strategy in West Africa. These Europeans used local people to govern on behalf of the colonial regime. Whether or not settler colonialism was utilized, the goals were largely economic: to develop wealth and access raw materials and labor for the colonial empire.

The anthropological perspective highlights how the economy shapes social and cultural life. Colonialism created a global market. Altering local economic systems led to changes in kinship, gender roles, and systems of authority—in other words, all aspects of culture. Local economies came under greater influence of long-distance merchants and the economic interests of distant empires. Local cultures adapted, developing new norms, values, beliefs, and practices.

In fieldwork, anthropologists carefully document and analyze local contexts. They also develop theories that explain the global processes that provoke changes in local contexts. Several theories from the field of economics are particularly helpful.

World-systems theory explains how the consolidation of European and North American empires brought local systems of subsistence and organizational production strategies into a global market.[5] Market dominance eliminates or sidelines local economics and cultures that rely on reciprocity or redistribution for regional economic sustainability. This had been predicted by political economists Adam Smith and Karl Marx. They predicted that the organization of production would move from those systems embedded in local kinship and households (foraging, horticulture, pastoralism) and into systems of currency, trade, and impersonal distribution. The globe would no longer contain diverse economies with different logics, values, and practices. Instead, nations would compete in an economic game of common rules, goals, and strategies.

In this world system, core nations benefit tremendously, while other nations are destined to remain excluded from economic growth. World-systems theory argues that even after political empires end, the economies they developed will persist. Core nations (the wealthiest) exploit other nations in extraction of raw materials, unfair labor practices and supply chains, and vast inequalities in consumption patterns. Semi-periphery nations are middle-wealth nations, and periphery are the poorest nations. In this global division of labor, wealthier nations bring industries in farming, fishing, and mining to these peripheral countries to extract raw materials. Local people derive wages but little else as resources are sent to the consumer nations to be processed. The core nations consume the goods, often processed in nations of the semi-periphery, while core-nation citizens engage in service industries such as finance, insurance, and health care. Some of the most skilled workers in the semi-periphery and periphery nations are drawn into the core via immigration, leaving the poorer nations even less able to contribute more than raw materials or manual labor to the global economy.

Modernization theory took a more optimistic view of the global economy. **Modernization theory** teaches that all societies move through stages of

5. Immanuel Wallerstein, *The Modern World-System: Capitalist Agriculture and the Origins of the European World-Economy in the Sixteenth Century* (Academic Press, 1974).

economic, political, and cultural development toward becoming industrialized, democratic, and "modern" societies. In this view, colonized societies were improving as they became more economically and politically complex and interdependent. The colonial rule of Western countries was necessary, it was argued, to move the "backward" economies of Asia, Africa, and Latin America through the stages of development Europe had experienced. This is an optimistic (and ethnocentric) view similar to unilinear evolutionary approaches to culture (see chap. 2). Modernization theory undergirds theories of international development that see poorer nations as fundamentally in need of intellectual or moral "progress."

Dependency theory offers a contrasting view of the global economy. Advanced by scholars such as Andre Gunder Frank, **dependency theory** argues that nations do not necessarily move from agricultural to industrial economies, and from less wealth to greater wealth, as global trade grows. Instead, some states become dependent on other states. Global capitalism creates permanent relationships of economic dependence between industrial and nonindustrial nations. Dependency theory explicitly challenged some of the assumptions of modernization theory. Modernization theory suggested that colonial relationships invariably benefited the colonized. Dependency theory argues that the system of global capital created poverty and underdevelopment through relationships of dependency and the creation of inequality.

Today, anthropologists often use the concept of neoliberalism to analyze the cultural dimensions of the global economy. Liberalism is the political assertion of individual human rights, the morality of political freedom, and the rights of people to self-determination. **Neoliberalism** is the extension of these political values into the economic and social realms. Neoliberal political values promote free-market capitalism, less regulation, and the privatization of services often provided by government, such as utilities, public services, and criminal justice. These values rest on a vision of the global economy thriving when capitalism has more freedom from government regulation. Champions of neoliberalism argue that this view provides more autonomy and freedom for people in all areas of their lives. Critics of neoliberalism point out that many seemingly "free" markets are subject to powerful global/international forces and institutions, such as the World Bank and International Monetary Fund, multinational corporations, and financiers who operate through multiple countries and institutions, often with little or no accountability. The ability, and perceived legitimacy, of national governments to control or "interfere" in economic processes becomes limited, labor movements are weakened, and economic decision-making often lies in the hands of corporate boards or unelected global organizations.

Katrina Greene

Katrina Greene (second from the left) is in Vrygrond, an informal settlement outside of Steenberg in Cape Town, South Africa. In such settlements, people live in self-constructed houses made of corrugated iron, tin, and scrap metals. Katrina is with fieldwork participants attending an *Ambhaso*. The *Ambhaso* is a combination of a bridal shower and and an engagement party. Invited guests bring gifts for the groom and bride (second from the right) and celebrate the couple's engagement.

Neoliberalism is political, economic, and cultural. Its political values guide economic policies that have tremendous influence on national and local cultures. When neoliberal assumptions are applied to other areas of cultural life, it transforms education, health care, and even national security. When these areas of life are privatized, wealthier people may provide for themselves, while poorer people cannot. In national security, private firms may even wage war, as when "security contractors" were hired to fight in Afghanistan or Iraq.[6]

Culture is holistic and integrated. What happens in the economy influences kinship, religion, politics, and all aspects of culture. Anthropologists studying neoliberalism in the world today have explored how people think about city planning in Scotland, tourism in the Dominican Republic, and conservation efforts in Indonesia.[7] Like all economic systems, neoliberalism not only organizes production; it is a powerful influence on the organization of social life generally.

6. See, for example, Peter W. Singer, "The Dark Truth about Blackwater," Brookings, October 2, 2007, https://www.brookings.edu/articles/the-dark-truth-about-blackwater/.

7. Christa Ballard Tooley, *Tenement Nation: Working-Class Cosmopolitanism in Edinburgh* (Indiana University Press, 2023); Steven Gregory, *The Devil Behind the Mirror: Globalization and Politics in the Dominican Republic* (University of California Press, 2014); Anna Lowenhaupt Tsing, *Friction: An Ethnography of Global Connection* (Princeton University Press, 2024).

Sustainability in a Neoliberal World

Even when studying the global dynamics of an economic system, anthropologists keep their focus on people. How do people sustain and adapt their cultures to changing economic conditions? How do they learn and share values, beliefs, and norms? Culture includes words and categories for understanding reality itself. Today, some anthropologists have adopted new frameworks for understanding the categories of nature and culture, human and nonhuman, and the epoch of life on earth in which we find ourselves.

The **Anthropocene** is a concept proposed to replace the Holocene as the earth's current geological epoch. The suffix "cene" refers to a geological age.[8] The prefix "anthropo" refers to human influence on the planet. As geologists debate whether this new name is warranted according to geological standards for naming epochs, scholars in other fields use it regularly. Aside from this negotiation, there is widespread agreement that we are living in a new environmental age, one in which human activity has profound negative influence on the planet. This influence includes the emission of billions of tons of carbon in the past two hundred years and subsequent changes to the global climate, as well as vast amounts of plastics (including microplastics), nuclear radiation, and PFAS ("forever chemicals") that can be found in the environment, biosphere, and even in human and animal bodies. Without question, these changes flow from the economic systems that require massive amounts of natural resources to be maintained and grown.

Many of these changes to the natural world (such as the creation or rerouting of rivers and lakes and the extensive built and cultivated environment) have allowed for human creativity and forms of flourishing that would not have been possible in the past. At the same time, the global economic system has created vast inequalities, altered the functions of the natural world in negative ways, and provided new challenges for human community.

Anthropologists conduct fieldwork to understand how people experience and adapt to this new economic, political, and ecological context. Anthropologist Patrick O'Hare used participant observation to understand the lives of people who pick through waste in Uruguay. From that firsthand, up-close experience, he interpreted the dynamics of waste processing in light of the global economy.[9]

8. The official body of geologic scientists ruled that the Holocene is ongoing and rejected the Anthropocene as an official designation. The conclusion was disputed by many other geologists, and, even in making their ruling, the scientists noted that there are good reasons for others, particularly social scientists, to use Anthropocene in describing our present world.

9. Patrick O'Hare, *Rubbish Belongs to the Poor: Hygienic Enclosure and the Waste Commons* (Pluto, 2022).

The vast volumes of trash thrown away each day have created an entire informal economy of workers who sort recyclable landfill materials. In Uruguay they are called *clasificadores* because they classify, or sort, trash. They perform an environmentally beneficial service while making a small living, yet they enjoy few of the rights and protections of other workers.

O'Hare documents a dramatic story of workers' resistance that illustrates neoliberalism in the Anthropocene. Using the notion of public health as a rationale, the Uruguayan government tried to ban workers from retrieving items from the trash mountains and rubbish bins. These workers protested, blocking streets and making their grievance public. O'Hare uses the concept of neoliberalism to explain this local situation. The national government used neoliberal logic of private property and individual ownership—even over trash. By this logic, the government was within its rights to prevent anyone from accessing the landfills and the garbage there. The workers, however, saw a trash mountain as a common good, like the pastures or water holes to which herders would have taken their animals in the past. Is a trash mountain a public good that should be accessible to all, or is it a private resource that should be used by owners for their own profit? Is a "mountain" created by human beings throwing away their garbage like a mountain that rises from tectonic plates and is therefore part of the landscape? Or is it a thing owned by those who threw the stuff away, or the owner of the land where the mountain was made (in this case, the Uruguayan government)? This was, O'Hare argued, a clash in the Anthropocene, in which a "mountain" becomes a site where people clash over different understandings of ownership, access, and the meaning of trash in the economy.

Anna Lowenhaupt Tsing followed neoliberalism in the Anthropocene through the story of the matsutake mushroom. She spent time with people at various points in the matsutake mushroom industry, using ethnographic methods to understand how humans and nonhumans come together in a world radically reshaped by human activity. Multispecies ethnographers explore the taken-for-granted lines between the "natural" world and the "cultural" or human world, lines that are changing during the Anthropocene.[10]

The matsutake mushroom grows in the "salvage" forests left behind by the logging and plantation industries. Amid fallen and rotting trees, in soil that has been stripped of whatever fertility it once had, the highly valued matsutake mushroom springs up. These mushrooms, most valued in high-end Japanese dining, are often the most expensive food, per pound, in the world. Mushroom hunters can make considerable money foraging these wild mushrooms. In

10. Anna Lowenhaupt Tsing, *The Mushroom at the End of the World: On the Possibility of Life in Capitalist Ruins* (Princeton University Press, 2015).

the United States, those most likely to be involved in such work are members of the Southeast Asian diaspora communities—Hmong, Mien, Vietnamese, Filipino, Cambodian—whose roots in mountainous and forested areas make them attuned to the opportunities such places provide and who often retain ties to Asia where the mushroom is sold.

Tsing points out that the economy of these mushrooms reveals the ways that we do not live in a world that is simply moving upward into "progress." Instead, we inhabit what she calls a "disruption economy," where a landscape that appeared to be "ruined" and wasted may be the source of riches for some and of danger or sadness for others. What are the sustainable means of living in a world where resources are needed for so many? What will emerge from land that is dramatically altered by human life?

God created this world "good" and gave humans a special caretaking responsibility. How does anthropology help us take up this responsibility? Anthropology helps us notice and understand some of the biggest problems

YOUR TURN

Financial Success

Subsistence is a cultural requirement. All humans need food, water, and shelter. All human groups work to provide for their own survival. But humans are meant to do more than merely survive. We are meant to flourish and enjoy God's created world. The question, then, is this: What does it mean to flourish in our globalized political economy? How do people define and experience "flourishing" or economic or financial success, and how does Christian faith matter?

Explore the idea of financial success in the context of Christian faith. Interview three people who are Christians. Ask something like, "As a Christian, how do you define financial success?" Remember, an ethnographic interview can be conversational. It may last just a few minutes or an hour. Be sure to let the person know that they are participating in an interview for an anthropology class. Take notes on what people say or, with their permission, record what they say. Remember to listen carefully and ask follow-up questions. While you can share your own ideas, you don't want this to become a debate! You want to understand what each person thinks and why.

Once you've talked with three people (ideally people who differ from each other significantly), analyze how Christian faith and financial success fit together for the people you interviewed.

- What Christian values or beliefs were expressed, if any?
- How do these values/beliefs shape how a person might engage with the structures and identities of their society (family/kinship, politics/power, status, gender, race)?
- In your opinion, do the values and ideas your interviewees express fit easily or uneasily with society's notions of "financial success"?

of our day. Because O'Hare spent time picking trash himself with the *clasificadores*, he came to understand connections between humans and nature in integrated and holistic ways, using the culture concept. He also learned how culture is power laden, seeing both the power of the state and the power of the people. Anthropology also helps us learn to care. Tsing used the anthropological perspective to see many different dimensions of a complex industry. This can reveal opportunities for meaningful action in all aspects of the economy, from sustainable production to distribution to consumption.

Economics and the Bible

We can gain new insight from the Bible by seeing economy as foundational in the many cultural contexts of various books of the Bible. Early in Genesis, before the fall, humans are depicted as having free access to everything in the garden of Eden. Although God gives the mandate to "care for" and "tend" the garden, production took the form of gathering (foraging) the products available in the garden (Gen. 1:26–30). The man and the woman are given the same task, thus there is no division of labor or inequality in access to resources. This description correlates with a foraging mode of production and a reciprocity-based system of exchange.

After the sin of humans, Adam was told to engage in horticulture or agriculture, which would be frequently frustrating and difficult. Eve would suffer by bearing children with pain and often experiencing disappointment in marriage. Genesis 3:14–19, often called "the curse," has been analyzed from many perspectives. Anthropology contributes a new layer of meaning, highlighting gender-based injustice: the labor-related misery that men experience in some horticultural and most agricultural systems of production, and the family-related inequality suffered by women once sexual divisions of labor are solidified in society.

Cain and Abel are described as practicing horticulture and pastoralism, respectively (Gen. 4:1–16). Cain, the horticulturalist, brings some fruits to God, while Abel, the pastoralist, brings "fat portions from some of the firstborn of his flock" (v. 4). Abel's offering is accepted while Cain's is rejected. The point of the passage is not to prioritize pastoralism over horticulture but to comment on the state of the heart and the nature of sacrifice (Heb. 11:4). From an anthropological perspective, the passage also demonstrates how social conflicts, even violent ones, can emerge when different subsistence systems collide.

Pastoralism and horticulture are present throughout the Old Testament. There are examples of **nomadic pastoralism** (e.g., Abraham moving from Ur with his flocks) and **transhumant pastoralism** (Joseph and his brother moving their father's herds to fields away from their home). Scholars of the Old Testament believe that for most of Israel's history, horticulturalism (subsistence farming) was the primary economic system.[11]

Agriculture is also described, particularly among Israel's neighbors. The kingdom of Egypt, through the predictable flooding of the Nile and the early use of technology (metallurgy) in production, was able to create large food surpluses to support centralized government and relatively large cities. Archaeological evidence has revealed agricultural economies in the ancient Babylonian and Assyrian Empires as well. The presence of large, grain-bearing grasses, predictable water, and fertile soils made the development of agriculture in these places the preferred system for those who wanted to consolidate political power.

By the time of Jesus, most of Israel was living in the Roman Empire, which relied on a complex economic system involving long-distance trade, coinage, and taxation. Economically speaking, the New Testament context is more like our contemporary context in that markets mediated exchange in an agriculture-based mode of subsistence—although their economic world was not capitalist or global, and the scope of their agricultural pursuits was smaller. Jesus makes several radical statements about how followers of God should value their material wealth and respond to social inequality. At the same time, Jesus doesn't endorse or condemn any subsistence or exchange system.

Some Christians of the early church lived, for some time, in an alternative economic arrangement in which they "held all things in common" (Acts 2:44 CSB), but by the end of the first century most Christians were engaged in mainstream economic activities. The apostle Paul affirmed and encouraged this when he wrote to the people that they should seek to "lead a quiet life" and "work with [their] hands" (1 Thess. 4:11). He likewise told people that they should work to have something to share with those in need (Eph. 4:28).

Anthropologists view subsistence and exchange systems as adaptive; people create and shape systems that ensure human survival in accord with their ecological and historical environments. God calls people to be generous and thankful no matter how they sustain themselves. From the beginning, God placed humanity in a symbolic relationship with the environment, declaring that it was more than simply a resource for our benefit but that it also had a moral quality; it was pronounced "good." Whether God's people are foragers, horticulturalists, pastoralists, or agriculturalists, they should generously use resources for human flourishing, not aggrandizement of oneself or one's own group.

11. Charles Edward Carter and Carol L. Meyer, *Community, Identity and Ideology: Social Science Approaches to the Hebrew Bible* (Eisenbrauns, 1996), 11.

TERMS

agriculture: A subsistence system that requires constant and intensive use of permanent fields for plant cultivation.

alienation: A state of separation between people and the fruits of their productive labor.

Anthropocene: The unofficial geological age many scientists believe is the current age, replacing the Holocene. It denotes the profound impact of human activity on the earth and its climate and ecological systems.

balanced reciprocity: A form of exchange in which roughly equivalent goods or services are exchanged immediately or within a relatively short amount of time.

dependency theory: A theory of global economic organization in which some countries/regions become permanently dependent on others through unequal exchange.

economic articulation: Employing strategic use of several modes of subsistence at the same time.

economy: A system of production and exchange.

foraging (or **hunting and gathering**): A subsistence strategy based on gathering plants that grow wild in the environment and hunting available animals.

generalized reciprocity: A form of exchange involving gift giving with no precise accounting of value and no precise expectation for type or time of return.

horticulturalism: A subsistence strategy in which people cultivate varieties of wild or domesticated crops, primarily for their own use, using relatively little technology.

leveling mechanism: Redistribution processes that reduce social inequality.

market economy: A system of exchange in which people exchange their labor (physical, mental, creative, etc.) for money, which is then exchanged for goods and services.

modernization theory: A theory that all economies must pass through the same stages of development toward modernization.

multicropping: Growing a variety of plants in a single garden.

negative reciprocity: A form of exchange in which one or both parties seek to receive more than they give.

neoliberalism: A philosophy that emphasizes individual autonomy and freedom in social, economic, and political spheres.

nomadic pastoralism: A form of pastoralism that involves moving in response to food and water supply.

pastoralism: A subsistence strategy based on the use of domesticated herd animals.

production: Any human action intended to convert resources in the environment into food.

reciprocity: An exchange system based on gifting.

redistribution: A system of exchange in which a centralized authority collects goods and services from a group of people and redistributes them.

subsistence farming: Growing food exclusively, or at least primarily, for consumption by one's own family or group.

subsistence strategy: A culturally created means of securing food.

swidden farming (or **shifting cultivation**, or **slash-and-burn**)**:** A form of horticulture involving clearing and burning a section of forest for gardening, and after some time, moving on to a new forest space.

systems of exchange: Social processes by which people give and receive goods and services.

transhumant pastoralism: A form of pastoralism in which people move herds seasonally between high meadows in the summer and human settlements in the winter.

world-systems theory: An economic theory that analyzes global capitalism as a single interconnected system dividing regions into core, periphery, and semi-periphery locales.

DISCUSSION QUESTIONS

1. In your own society, how does the economy shape people's values? Where do you see evidence of this?
2. What was a gift you received that made you confused or uncomfortable? Why? Can you explain this in terms of generalized reciprocity, delayed reciprocity, or negative reciprocity?
3. How does Christian faith shape your ideas about economic success? In what ways might faith support mainstream ideas of success? In what ways might faith challenge prevailing expectations?

ANTHROPOLOGY AND SCRIPTURE

True Wealth

As for those who in the present age are rich, command them not to be haughty or to set their hopes on the uncertainty of riches but rather on God, who richly provides us with everything for our enjoyment. They are to do good, to be rich in good works, generous, and ready to share, thus storing up for themselves the treasure of a good foundation for the future, so that they may take hold of the life that really is life. (1 Tim. 6:17–19 NRSVue)

This passage takes on new meaning when read from the point of view of a forager. In foraging societies, people don't store up possessions, and economic inequality is minimal. For foragers, good works are a literal form of wealth. Good works, generosity, and sharing are all foundational elements of generalized reciprocity. Giving and receiving solidify society-wide bonds of obligation and generosity that extend for generations and across families. In this passage, Paul reminds us of God's message in Genesis 1: God has provided humans with everything they need. Reviving the economic strategies of sharing, generosity, and good works helps us rely less on hoarding wealth and more on our relationships with others.

Economic Dimensions of the Fall

To the woman he said,

> "I will make your pangs in childbirth exceedingly great;
> in pain you shall bring forth children,
> yet your desire shall be for your husband,
> and he shall rule over you."

And to the man he said,

> "Because you have listened to the voice of your wife
> have eaten of the tree
> about which I commanded you,
> 'You shall not eat of it,'
> cursed is the ground because of you;
> in toil you shall eat of it all the days of your life;
> thorns and thistles it shall bring forth for you;
> and you shall eat the plants of the field.
> By the sweat of your face
> you shall eat bread

until you return to the ground,
  for out of it you were taken;
you are dust,
  and to dust you shall return." (Gen. 3:16–19 NRSVue)

This is a description of how life would be for Adam and Eve, and their descendants, because of their sin. It is a far cry from the material abundance and relational happiness of the garden of Eden. In today's world, these verses describe the experience of foragers, pastoralists, and horticulturalists who are forced—by virtue of land restrictions, political decisions, and economic necessity—to enter the globalized market economy.

In many cases, women who enjoyed relative equality and harmony with men are made subservient as men work in the productive sphere and women are isolated in the domestic sphere without the income-generating opportunities that build social status. Men who shared the work of subsistence with their wives and children are now forced to labor in agriculture or cash-based economies, hard work that too often results in cycles of poverty and hunger. Women and men experience sin and brokenness in gender-related ways, with particular pain for women in family life and particular pain for men in their work. "The curse" as recorded in Genesis 3 is, in part, a commentary on economic hardship and its implications for men, women, and families in a fallen world.

7

AUTHORITY AND POWER

After studying this chapter, you should be able to do the following:

1. define political anthropology, authority, and power
2. distinguish between coercive, persuasive, and hegemonic power
3. understand systems of political organization with the typology of bands, tribes, chiefdoms and kingdoms, and states
4. appreciate the variety of ways in which Christians engage in politics

CHAPTER OUTLINE

Introduction

What does it mean to call something "political"? In contemporary US news reports, public figures—often politicians themselves—complain that accusations of wrongdoing or questions about their integrity are "politically motivated." These same politicians accuse their opponents of "playing politics." In advocating for their point of view, a political leader might say, "Now is not the time for politics to interfere with the good of the nation." It may seem odd that politicians complain about politics, but this understanding of politics reflects a broader, anthropological use of the word.

Anthropologists take a broad view of politics that includes elections, governments, and international relations as well as the ways in which people use and understand power and authority in their everyday lives. Anthropologists see politics happening when lawmakers gather to pass legislation, and when politicians attempt to influence others through informal means. Anthropologists look at both those in seats of power and the everyday people who live with the results of policy or governance. Anthropologists study politics as part of culture, using a holistic, ethnographically grounded perspective.

For nearly a century, politics has often been defined simply as who gets what, when, and how.[1] In a similar way, anthropology defines **politics** as the distribution, understanding, and use of power and influence in social groups. Political anthropologists study politics in this sense, and they also study the social and institutional organization of power and authority.

In this chapter, we explore **political anthropology**. First, we explain how anthropologists define and study power and authority. Then we describe how anthropologists model systems of political organization with the typology of bands, tribes, chiefdoms and kingdoms, and states. We conclude with a discussion of Christians and politics.

Power and Culture

People exercise **power** when they influence or control the behavior of others. What makes it possible for one person to get what they want while other people have little influence? Some individuals or groups have more authority than others; that is, people grant legitimacy to their words and actions. **Authority** is the right to exercise power. Attributes that make a person or institution persuasive, powerful, or authoritative reflect cultural understandings and social organization.

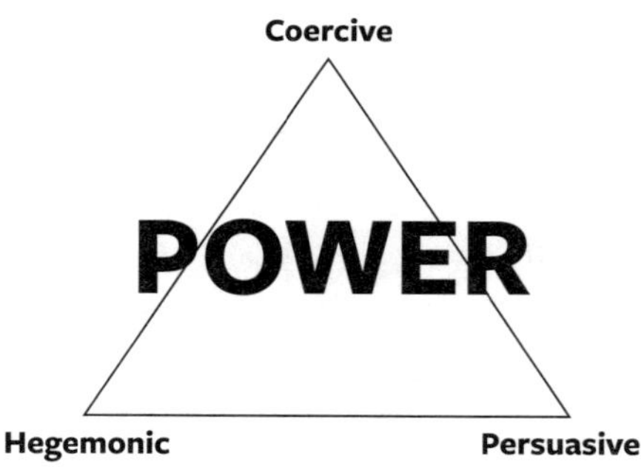

Figure 7.1. Power and culture

Power is an important theme in anthropology because power relations are present in all kinds of social interactions and cultural understandings. As described in chapter 4, power dynamics and inequality are fundamental to anthropological understandings of culture. There are three types of power that often work together: coercive, persuasive, and hegemonic (see fig. 7.1).

Coercive Power

Coercive power refers to the use or threat of force to make people or groups do things. Coercive power may be legitimate or illegitimate. A common understanding of coercion is a scenario in which an individual uses force illegitimately: A bully demands lunch money, or a robber steals a wallet at gunpoint. Coercion also occurs on a larger scale. War, genocide, and

1. See Harold Dwight Lasswell, *Politics: Who Gets What, When, How* (1936; repr., Literary Licensing, 2011).

brinksmanship (threatening war or mass destruction) are dramatic examples of coercive power. Whether these large-scale examples of coercion are considered illegitimate depends on the extent to which they are supported by cultural norms and social groups.

While examples of illegitimate coercive power are plentiful, coercive power may also be legitimate, buttressed by cultural norms, morality, or law. For example, throughout the world, parents and other adults occasionally force children to follow the adults' wishes; an adult may take a child's hand and lead them in a particular direction or carry a child who is protesting. A person may injure another by pushing them out of the way of a bus or a train, and the one injured would be grateful for the use of coercive force.

Likewise, legitimate uses of coercive power exist at higher levels, such as a state forcing its citizens to pay taxes or obey traffic laws by imprisoning them or seizing their property if they do not. In societies with formal legal systems (which is most societies these days), laws reflect and reinforce cultural norms about the legitimacy of coercive force. Citizens often accept coercive power as a trade-off in which they give control to the state in exchange for security, rule enforcement, and order. In other cases, such as with the death penalty or gun laws in the United States, citizens and governments negotiate about appropriate use of coercive power, with multiple views on the ethical implications taken into account.

Persuasive Power

Coercive power is fairly easy to identify and seems pervasive and often dramatic, yet persuasive power is even more common and often more effective. **Persuasive power** involves the use of words, relationships, and actions that influence others. Coercive power always brings the threat of retaliation and often disrupts relationships. Persuasive power, on the other hand, often depends on relationships for its operation and subsequently strengthens or creates relationships, even when a person is reluctantly or unhappily persuaded.

For example, throughout Melanesia, individuals can become leaders when they develop reputations for being able to bring people together for a common cause. Traditionally, that cause is a large gift-giving ceremony in which a Big Man (or sometimes a Big Woman) convinces relatives to contribute to a gift to be given to a rival group.[2] The Big Man convinces his group to

2. Milan Stanek and Florence Weiss, "'Big Man' and 'Big Woman' in the Village—Elite in the Town: The Iatmul, Papua New Guinea," in *Common Worlds and Single Lives: Constituting Knowledge in Pacific Societies*, ed. Verna Keck (Falgrave Macmillan, 1998), 309–28.

amass resources for the big gift, including pigs, shells, birds, foodstuff, and other valuable goods. The gift links the two groups because the rival group becomes indebted and obligated to respond with a gift of their own in the future (for more on reciprocity, see chap. 6). Members of the extended family that is giving the gift strengthen their social bond as they cooperate to pool their resources.[3] This process demands that leaders use persuasive power effectively. Not every individual will necessarily see that giving away their pigs, sweet potatoes, or sago palm flour will benefit either them or their immediate family. By employing rhetorical skill and negotiation tactics, some individuals in these groups emerge as particularly effective in convincing others to participate in these ceremonies.

Leaders must be very careful that they are not perceived as pushing a selfish agenda or gaining advantage at others' expense. Personal reputation often translates into wider, or future, social power. Members of the community begin to seek out those individuals before making plans about where to live or where to plant a garden. In these contexts, using coercive power may prove counterproductive. Even if a particular person has physical strength or can otherwise employ force, that person must also have the voluntary support of friends or relatives; otherwise, the leader may be toppled by others working together to resist.

Persuasive power is at play in all relationships. In a close friendship, one person may want to go to a movie while the other wants to take a walk. One grants authority to the other to prioritize one activity over the other. A mother or father wants to sleep, but the baby cries for attention. Babies have tremendous persuasive power! Power dynamics always carry destructive potential, yet they also create strong bonds between people. We express what we want and need, and others respond in a wide variety of ways.

Hegemonic Power

The third type of power is diffuse and difficult to identify. Hegemonic power is a pervasive, effective force of social control. "Hegemony" (he-ˈjə-mō-nē) means "control" or "domination." A hegemony may be literal; for example, the control of the National Socialists (Nazis) in Germany in the 1930s could be described as a political and military hegemony. In anthropology, however, **hegemonic power** (or **hegemony**) refers to the dominance of ideas or culture, such that the status quo is maintained.

3. John Barker, *Ancestral Lines: The Maisin of Papua New Guinea and the Fate of the Rainforest*, 2nd ed. (University of Toronto Press, 2016), 152–69. See also Ann Chowning, "Leadership in Melanesia," *Journal of Pacific History* 14, no. 2 (1979): 66–84.

Hegemony is a broad concept that includes political and military hegemonies (such as the Nazis), and hegemonic elements of culture such as dominant ideas or values, both good and bad. For example, during the Middle Ages, from approximately 600 to 1500 CE, hegemonic power helped stabilize European society and politics. European kings and queens had armies and other coercive means to control the population, but people rarely resisted monarchical control. Even the most inept or corrupt rulers rarely faced popular uprisings. This was largely due to a hegemonic idea known as "the divine right of kings." This notion purported that God established monarchs to rule; to challenge a monarch was to challenge God. The divine right of kings consolidated church, military, education, and family in a unified view that, regardless of how cruel, capricious, or even insane a particular monarch might be, resistance to the monarch would be wrong or even unthinkable.

Like all human constructs, hegemonies change and even disappear over time. While many European monarchies still exist, they must justify their existence as primarily cultural and historical institutions. They no longer wield military or political force in the name of divine right. In place of the divine right of kings, democratic ideas about individual rights and voting officials into office have become hegemonic.

To be successful, hegemonic power requires widely shared cultural beliefs. Institutions embody and entrench ideas and values supporting those in power. Italian political philosopher Antonio Gramsci (1891–1937) theorized about the social control of ideas as he sat in prison during the reign of fascist dictator Benito Mussolini.[4] Gramsci had been involved in workers' rights movements, organizing for now-common practices such as the forty-hour workweek, basic safety, and minimum pay. At the time, many people believed it was fate, or God's will, for some to be rich and most to be poor. Working for change was seen as a violation of the "natural order."

Gramsci argued that people accepted the social order not because it was God-ordained but because the ruling classes were controlling the values and thoughts of the masses. The government needed to change, but so did the way people thought about government. People needed to learn to expect government to serve the citizens, not just amass power for the political elite. In proposing new ways to think about society, Gramsci was fostering a **counter-hegemony**, an ideology or movement that challenges a reigning hegemony. At times, an alternative vision of society becomes a kind of hegemony of its own.

4. Antonio Gramsci, *Selections from the Prison Notebooks*, ed. and trans. Quintin Hoare and Geoffrey Nowell-Smith (International Publishers, 1971).

Eventually, many of Gramsci's ideas (and those of other like-minded thinkers) became widely accepted. Italian society changed. People thought about the role of government, human rights, and political power in new ways. Gramsci's ideas about how power works, particularly in complex industrial societies, are still influential in many academic disciplines.

Power in Action

Coercive power, persuasive power, and hegemonic power are often at play simultaneously. The line between persuasion and threat can be fuzzy, and the influence of hegemony is pervasive, often supporting the other two sorts of power. Whether coercive or persuasive, power can be enacted formally or informally, through official organizations or by an individual or group. Hegemonic practices and beliefs support the maintenance of existing power dynamics.

Coercive and persuasive power often mix when certain individuals have a recognized right to accomplish something but need the willing cooperation of others. When individuals or groups without organizational power want to make changes, they also rely on both coercive and persuasive power. People work to change systems and cultures at the level of ideas, expectations, and even theology. Whether they are working through officially recognized roles or not, they are challenging a hegemony.

Social sanctions are the responses, positive and negative, that people receive for their behavior. A sanction may be informal or formal. **Formal sanctions** are approved or delivered by official institutions. **Formal negative sanctions** include fines or other punishments meted out for breaking laws: If you get caught driving too fast, you will be fined. Organizations also establish **formal positive sanctions**, which are official rewards for socially desirable behavior. An example would be a promotion or a raise, being placed on the dean's list at a university, or receiving the Congressional Medal of Honor. Formal sanctions influence behavior with rewards and punishments.

Informal sanctions are pervasive and effective in everyday life. **Informal sanctions** are positive or negative actions or words intended to shape behavior, delivered by people in their everyday lives (not by organizations such as governments). As members of various groups—families, educational institutions, and churches—we sanction other members of the group. For example, in many undergraduate college settings, a student serves as a resident adviser or assistant (RA) and is responsible for enforcing dorm rules. The RA uses informal sanctions including verbal affirmations ("Great job!") and discouragements ("Knock it off, will ya?"). The RA shifts to formal sanctions when reporting behavior or issuing a fine. The hegemonic context normalizes rule-keeping; the university stresses the importance of rules for personal character and later professional success and even morality. In this, the education hegemony gains strength by intersecting with government and religion. Most RAs do not want to act as police officers; they want to build community, offer wise counsel, and enable the members of the dorm to get along well. Achieving these goals often involves convincing people that they should *want* to follow the rules for their own benefit and the benefit of others.

Members of the group can respond with their own mix of coercion and persuasion. On the dorm floor, there may be an official process for students to protest rules or consequences. Students may use these formal processes, or they may turn to informal negative sanctions such as talking about the RA behind their back, boycotting floor events, or complaining about the college. When students talk positively or encourage others to follow rules, they are using informal positive sanctions.

Formal and informal strategies used by students mirror ways in which people with little or no formal power assert agency. Labor contracts, for example, reflect a combination of coercive and organizational power. If a company fails to fulfill its contractual obligations, union members may sue or strike, using the threat of monetary loss to force the company to comply. Most workers throughout the world, however, have no formal arrangements to protect them against abuses by employers or political leaders.

Political anthropologist James Scott analyzed states, exploring reasons why states emerged, how states can improve the human condition, and how political systems punish those who do not conform to their hegemonic ideas.[5] Scott conducted fieldwork among Malaysian and Filipino peasants and workers in other parts of the world and found that among low-paid laborers, workers developed practices, beliefs, and ways of talking ("transcripts") that kept their sense of justice and their own best interests alive under repressive conditions. These "weapons of the weak" included practices such as working more slowly than usual, intentionally breaking machinery or equipment, underfilling bags of rice, or leaving some rice unharvested (which they might go back to get later and eat for themselves). In these ways, supposedly powerless people could exert power as a means to enhance their own survival. Even without subverting the overall system, they could exert pressure on dominant people or organizations to change.

5. James Scott, *Weapons of the Weak: Everyday Forms of Peasant Resistance* (Yale University Press, 1985); James Scott, *Seeing Like a State: How Certain Schemes to Improve the Human Condition Have Failed* (Yale University Press, 1998); James Scott, *Against the Grain: A Deep History of the Earliest States* (Yale University Press, 2017).

Christianity and Power

One of my (Jenell's) students had been raised in a Christian home, and while he knew abuses of power happened in churches, he thought Christianity was surely more good than bad. While studying the history of Christianity in a college course, he began to worry, "What if Christianity is nothing more than an institution that uses its power to dominate and control people?" Experiencing Christian faith in a local church is one thing. Analyzing it as a historic tradition is quite another. It can be hard for faithful Christians to take in all the power dynamics of a global religious tradition that has exerted great influence for centuries—for better and for worse.

The anthropology of Christianity is a subfield of cultural anthropology that examines this topic, among others. Anthropologists don't draw conclusions about any religion being "good" or "bad." They use the anthropological perspective to describe how power flows through organizations. They document how people grant and challenge authority. They track how beliefs and practices that are widely taken for granted remain stable over time and also how they change.

Religion scholar Derrick Lemons is the director of The Center for Theologically Engaged Anthropology at the University of Georgia. This organization bridges anthropology and theology. For example, ethnographies show that people everywhere want healing, wholeness, and good lives. Religion names and facilitates this existential desire in a special way. Christianity has concepts, beliefs, and practices that support the process of rupture and repair: sin, repentance, restoration, sanctification, redemption, and resurrection, to name just a few.[a]

The intersection of anthropology and theology sparks fascinating research. Lemons analyzed why prominent religious leaders backed Donald Trump's candidacy in the 2016 election, describing how theology, religion, politics, and social pressures work together.[b] Naomi Haynes conducted fieldwork among politicians, pastors, and cabinet members in Zambia to understand how Christian nationalism was being understood and supported in the country.[c] Jonathan Miles-Watson considered newly restored pilgrimage trails in County Durham (England) and explored how religious traditions use space to counterbalance trauma.[d]

Anthropological research doesn't provide pat answers to poignant questions about Christian faith, including Christianity's complicity with injustice and harm. The anthropological perspective can extend our capacity to look at what is real and try to understand it. It can strengthen resolve against the temptation to minimize or look away. Christian anthropologists can inspire patience and diligence in exploring complex concerns. They model ways to sustain deep personal Christian commitment alongside academic curiosity and ethical concern.

It's your turn: How do you see a religion (Christianity or any other religion) using power for good? How do you see a religion using power for bad? How does this shape your faith?

a. Naomi Richman and J. Derrick Lemons, "From Rupture to Repair," *The Australian Journal of Anthropology* 33, no. 3 (2023): 337–48.

b. J. Derrick Lemons, "The Room Where It Happened: How Evangelical Leaders Used a Closed Door Meeting to Change Sentiment for Donald J. Trump," *The Australian Journal of Anthropology* 33, no. 3 (2023): 349–59.

c. Naomi Haynes, *A Divine Season: Christian Nationalist Activism in Zambia* (Princeton University Press, 2026).

d. Jonathan Miles-Watson, "Transformed Ecologies and Transformational Saints: Exploring New Pilgrimage Routes in North East England," *The Australian Journal of Anthropology* 33, no. 3 (2023): 412–27.

Aminta Arrington

Aminta Arrington conducting fieldwork with the Lisu, a tribal group dispersed throughout southwest China, eastern Myanmar, and northern Thailand. Arrington lived with the Lisu in woven bamboo huts on steep mountain inclines and participated in their village life: planting corn, feeding animals, eating food cooked over a fire, and washing dishes. She went to church five times a week, sitting on hard pews and singing hymns in four-part harmony! Her book *Songs of the Lisu Hills: Practicing Anthropology in Southwest China* (Pennsylvania State University Press, 2020) documents her time among these people.

Political Organization

Anthropologists model systems of political organization with the typology of bands, tribes, chiefdoms and kingdoms, and states. Developed by anthropologist Elman Service, this typology highlights the correlations between economic strategy and political form (see table 7.1).[6] Today, however, there are no bands, tribes, chiefdoms, or kingdoms that exist apart from the influence of states. Anthropologists see societies blending political and subsistence strategies in adaptive ways in both politics and economics. Nonetheless, Service's fourfold typology continues to serve as a general model of political organization.

Bands

The **band** is the most ancient political system; it was used by many of our human ancestors and is still used by some groups today. Bands typically consist of fewer than one hundred members, most of whom are related to one another through kinship. Band membership is flexible: New members may

6. Elman Service, *Primitive Social Organization: An Evolutionary Perspective*, 2nd ed. (1962; repr., Random House, 1971).

Table 7.1 Political Organizations

Political Organization	Size	Leadership	Social Organization	Division of Labor	Political Power	Level of Organization	Subsistence System	Conflict Resolution
Band	A few hundred	Temporary and informal, decisions by consensus	Egalitarian	Members are able to do the same task, but tasks may also be divided by gender	Decentralized, informal, and based on charisma	Local	Foraging	Informal sanctions, persuasive power, violence is interpersonal and informal
Tribe	Several hundred to several million	Informal election of elders based on unique qualities rather than family name or social status	Strong kinship ties, age-set systems	Commonly based on kinship, age, and gender	Decentralized, based on kinship and charisma	Local, but can create regional associations for temporary purposes	May be associated with subsistence system	Reliance on skilled negotiators and supernatural mechanisms of guilt determination; use of warfare/violence, especially ritualized violence
Chiefdom-Kingdom	Population becomes more highly concentrated	Leadership that is an inheritable office; not based on ability	Hierarchical social statuses based on household, lineage, and clan; also determined by relational distance from the chief or king	More specialized; food surpluses are redistributed using systems of tribute and taxation	Centralized, inheritable	Relatively permanent regional associations	Pastoralism, horticulture, or agriculture	More formal; rules and punishments decided on by ruler; war is waged more frequently and on a larger scale than tribes
State	Highly concentrated; today, some populations are over a billion	Authority rests in institutions and offices	Social status primarily based on economic status and ability	Highly specialized	Highly centralized, bureaucratic	National and international associations	Primarily agriculture	Highly formal rules and sanctions decided on by institutions and offices

be included, and current members may leave with relative ease. Among the nomadic Ju/'hoansi people of the Kalahari Desert areas of southern Africa, extended families stay together for as long as the gathering and hunting in the area can support everyone. As resources diminish, seasons shift, or conflicts arise, some family members may leave to find another cluster of extended kin with whom to live. Today, many Ju/'hoansi people have assimilated into Namibian or Botswanan society, some have blended their band organization with participation in the state, and a small number continue to live in the bush, fairly isolated from state politics.[7]

Leadership in band societies is usually temporary and informal. A person takes leadership in a particular situation because of the needs of the group or the person's gifts and abilities. A good hunter might take the lead with his hunting party, but when the group is choosing a place to live, they may ask a woman who is known for her ability to choose settlement sites that are safe from bad weather and predators. Because there are no formal offices for leadership, decisions are generally made by consensus. This does not necessarily mean that everyone has an equal ability to influence a decision. The use of persuasive power (described above) strongly influences whose opinions matter at any given time. Coercive power may be used as well—such as beating a family member or physically fighting when a verbal argument escalates—but it, too, is informal and personal rather than institutionalized.

In bands, the egalitarianism seen in the division of labor extends to the realm of authority and decision-making as well. Because almost every adult can do what every other adult of their same sex can do, there are few socially recognized reasons for one person to exert power over another. Each member of the community is free to choose to go along with someone else's plans or not. Political organization never moves beyond the local level, since the ability to influence comes from face-to-face interactions. Band-level political organization works most easily with foraging subsistence systems that encourage direct and individual interaction with one another for survival.

Conflict resolution in band societies happens most frequently through informal sanctions such as talking, joking, mocking, shouting, or fighting. Bands are highly effective at avoiding and resolving conflict by relying on communication and **fissioning** (splitting up a group when conflict arises). For many people around the world, their friend group operates similarly to a band. Leadership is typically shared depending on the circumstance. Conflict is resolved informally—through conversations, joking, and group

7. Richard Lee, *The Dobe Ju/'hoansi*, 4th ed. (Wadsworth, 2013).

consensus. If one person or a small group of individuals try to exert power inappropriately, others in the group can choose to leave.

Tribes

In popular usage, the term "tribe" usually evokes images of Indigenous groups in Africa, North America, or the rain forests of South America.[8] Media may use "tribe" to refer to any language or ethnic group with a distinct identity, or even friendship or family groups within modern societies. In terms of political organization, however, "tribe" has no specific racial, geographic, or cultural connotation; its meaning is related to forms of leadership and association. Many groups called tribes in the media, or even by members themselves, do not fit the anthropological definition of a political tribe.

A **tribe** is a decentralized political system that may be associated with any economic form. Earlier in the twentieth century, tribes were often associated with pastoralism and horticulture, but today tribes rely on mixed-subsistence strategies that blend pastoralism, horticulture, agriculture, and even some foraging. Several tribes may be united as a society by culture, language, or heritage, such as the twelve tribes of Israel. Each tribe has its own leadership, usually based on personal ability; there is no central government to enforce decisions for the entire society. In the contemporary world, a tribe may function internally with decentralized political leadership, even as the entire tribe must contend with the centralized leadership of the state or states that control its territory.

The Ikalahan, an ethnolinguistic group mentioned at several points in this text, are organized as tribal communities in a traditional territorial homeland in the uplands of the northern Philippines.[9] The Ikalahan are organized into settlements, where each homestead is affiliated with a particular community. Around the Ikalahan territory are other tribal groups (such as the Ifugao, Ibaloi, Ilongot, and many others), each with their own language and identity. Each Ikalahan community has designated elders, but this is not an elected position or formal office. Today, there are government officials among the Ikalahan—as required by the Philippine state—but the communities continue to recognize their elders. One missionary-anthropologist who lived in an Ikalahan community for more than fifty years described how someone becomes an elder: "Being an elder means everyone waits. It's just that simple! You don't

8. In many mainstream Western media reports, conflicts in Africa are often called "tribal" conflicts, while civil unrest in Europe, such as in the former Yugoslavia, Chechnya, or the Basque country, are termed "ethnic" or "political" conflicts.

9. The Ikalahan are also known as the Kalungoya.

start talking unless all the elders come, so people will say, 'We have to wait for Manong Rosario,' or someone will say, 'We cannot start yet. Manang is not here yet!' So you might not even know you are an elder until you see that people wait for you to come before they start talking about anything."[10]

For the Ikalahan, like many other traditional tribal communities, leadership adheres to particular people based on unique qualities rather than an office, family name, or automatic social standing. Being an Ikalahan elder, whether man or woman, generally means that people see that you are a good parent, that your fields are well kept, that you do not drink too much, and, these days, that you are a sincere Christian. Of course, members may disagree about who satisfies these criteria, and conflict may ensue as members debate who should be considered an elder and who should not. The Ikalahan will say, however, that it is generally obvious who has earned the right to be heard and who has not.

In this way, tribes have leadership structures similar to those in bands. However, whereas bands are entirely local, tribes can create regional associations for temporary purposes. Often in response to external threats, several local communities create alliances outside the local place to defend themselves, wage war, or engage in economic exchange or religious ceremonies.

Like the local group, regional groups are typically organized by kinship. Someone in one community can identify a friend or potential ally by finding the kinship relationship. For example, my brother's wife's sister's uncle's wife's nephew can introduce me in a community where I may not know anyone personally, but by establishing the kinship connection, we can consider working together on a particular task. In addition, tribes may use **age-set** systems, social groups consisting of people of the same sex and similar age that link members of different communities as allies and friends. Among several pastoralists of East Africa, such as the Maasai and Nandi, age-sets may be formed through rituals whereby the young men become a set and enter a warrior phase. From that moment on, the men are linked to one another, even as they are dispersed in various communities. They can rely on members of their age-set and coordinate with them for the good of their separate communities.

Conflict resolution within tribes is mostly informal, handled through talking, joking, and other forms of interpersonal interaction. Because people are bound to the tribe of their family, they are less likely to move away to avoid or reduce conflict, as in a band. This necessitates some formal mechanisms for conflict resolution, such as skilled mediators, judges, and courts. During their

10. Delbert Rice, interview with Brian M. Howell, July 28, 1990. The Ilokano terms *manong* and *manang* can be translated "older brother" and "older sister," respectively. They are markers of relative age and respect.

tribal period, the Israelites relied on judges to resolve disputes, using techniques such as the bitter water ordeal described in Numbers 5. In this ordeal, a woman accused of infidelity would drink bitter water; if she was sickened, she was believed to be guilty, but if she was unaffected, she was innocent. Such conflict-resolution mechanisms seem odd to most contemporary readers of Scripture, many of whom rely on legal conflict resolution typical of state societies. But for tribes, skilled negotiators and supernatural mechanisms of

The Twelve Tribes of Israel Become a Kingdom

Judges 19–21 tells a grisly tale. The tribes of Israel shared a common culture, language, and religion, but they had no centralized political system. A man from one tribe, a Levite, had a second wife (or concubine) who ran away from him. He followed her to her father's house and reclaimed her. At this time, the Israelites were considered a dispersed tribal society. As the Levite and his wife traveled back home, they spent the night in Gibeah, a region within the territory of the tribe of Benjamin. The Levite thus chose to stay among fellow Israelites—members of the larger tribe of Israel.

The men of Gibeah (not Benjaminites) demanded sex with the Levite. In a display of perverse hospitality, the man hosting the Levite and his wife offered his own daughter and the Levite's wife to the violent crowd. The men of Gibeah refused the offer, so the Levite pushed his wife out the door in order to preserve himself. The men raped and killed her.

When the Levite returned home with his deceased wife, he cut her body into twelve pieces and sent the pieces throughout the territory of the Israelites, one to each tribe. Her body became a means of mass communication that brought together a dispersed tribal society for the temporary purpose of waging war. Most of the tribes of Israel agreed to work together in warfare, but the Benjaminites sided with the people of Gibeah. The Israelites subsequently waged war against their own and defeated the tribe of Benjamin—though they eventually restored it to the tribal collective.

Judges 19 begins with the words: "In those days, when there was no king in Israel . . ." (NRSVue). The book of Judges ends with a similar statement: "In those days there was no king in Israel; all the people did what was right in their own eyes" (Judg. 21:25 NRSVue). The story is a cautionary tale of the interpersonal violence, mayhem, and war that can happen in tribal society. A wife was lost, which threatened family and lineage stability, and an entire group (the Benjaminites) was nearly lost, which threatened tribal solidarity and strength.

This story does not condemn tribal political organization wholesale; tribal organization is effective and sustainable. Rather, it was a specific story told by and for the Israelites as they were coming to terms with massive changes in their economic and political lives. By highlighting terror, destruction, and intertribal warfare, Judges 19–21 served as a legitimating narrative for Israel's shift from a tribal political system to a kingdom.

It's your turn: What is a question or concern you have about politics in the world today? Why is it important to you?

guilt determination work well. At times tribes also turn to warfare. Warfare, however, involves a massive commitment to organize various tribes together in a common cause and to likely lose members of the population, so it is not an option used lightly.

Chiefdoms and Kingdoms

Like the term "tribe," the word "chief" is often misunderstood. The stereotype of the chief often conjures Hollywood images of Native Americans with eagle-feather headdresses or rotund African leaders surrounded by servants. Although chiefdoms have existed among some Indigenous North Americans and in sub-Saharan Africa, chiefdoms and kingdoms take a variety of forms across cultures.

In anthropological terms, **chiefdom** and **kingdom** refer to the same system: political organization involving an inheritable office, often passed through a family line, in which power adheres to the occupant of the office rather than being a product of individual gifts, abilities, or qualities. This represents a centralization of political power that allows for relatively permanent regional associations.

The chiefdoms of Polynesia have long been studied by anthropologists. Raymond Firth's fieldwork in Tikopia, an island in Melanesia (though it is classified as a Polynesian island) measuring three square miles, is an early example. In the 1920s, there were about twelve hundred people living on Tikopia, and though Europeans had explored the island, most Tikopians had very limited contact with the outside world. Island chiefs in Tikopia were seen as religious leaders who were descendants of important ancestral deities. Chiefs had broad religious, economic, political, and interpersonal authority. All the people of the island were organized into hierarchical social statuses based on household, lineage, and clan. The island had a very strong, interlinked social organization and a hierarchical, hereditary political system based on chiefs.[11]

Anthropologists debate the features that distinguish chiefdoms from other forms of centralization such as kingdoms and states.[12] With respect to structure, there is almost total overlap between chiefdoms and kingdoms.[13] In both,

11. Raymond Firth, *We the Tikopia: A Sociological Study of Kinship in Primitive Polynesia*, 2nd ed. (1936; repr., Routledge, 2004).

12. Peter Skalnik, "Chiefdoms and Kingdoms in Africa: Why They Are Neither States nor Empires," African Studies Centre Leiden, February 21, 2022, https://www.ascleiden.nl/news/chiefdoms-and-kingdoms-africa-why-they-are-neither-states-nor-empires.

13. As with "tribe" and "ethnic group," the distinction between "chief" and "king" resides in the desire of the speaker to suggest something more or less "civilized" or familiar, as opposed to a particular distinction of political organization.

a family or individual is vested with authority. The personal power and status of all members of the society are understood in terms of relational distance from this person. The sister of the king, for instance, would have more power than the cousin, great-aunt, or mother's sister's husband's niece. The office remains the locus of authority even if the individual is not particularly capable. Some system of inheritance regulates passage of office to a designee when the officeholder dies or abdicates.

Today, chiefdoms have largely given way to other forms of political organization. Kingdoms still exist, at least in name. In Britain, for instance, a monarchy continues that is based on authority vested in a lineage. The United Kingdom is a state, however, with a political system that blends the kingdom and the state. The constitutional monarchy relies on leadership from the monarch (as head of state) with the prime minister (as head of government).

YOUR TURN

Make Something Happen

You may not think of yourself as being in a position of power. It's easy to see how parents, teachers, supervisors, police officers, or politicians have power, yet each person—even you—has power that they use to influence others.

Anthropologists study power on grand and global scales, looking at nation-states, multinational corporations, and how globalization creates new flows of power. They also look at power in everyday life in local fieldwork settings. Fieldworkers reflect on their own power as well because doing fieldwork involves influencing others, if only to convince them to participate in an interview.

Using participant observation, make something happen. Fully participate but also observe and take notes on what you do and how others respond.

First, decide what you want to make happen. Persuade your friends to try a new food or to go outside with you. Convince your teammates to try a new technique or strategy. See if you can get a group of people to do something fun, challenging, spiritual, or scholarly—something they wouldn't otherwise do. Consider something that people might resist or question, which will give you more chances to practice using power to influence them. Keep it positive! Power can be used to persuade people to do antisocial things as well as prosocial things. For this exercise, consider something you think would be good for others.

Now, put your plan into action. Notice how others respond.

- What power moves do they use to resist your offer, or join in, or to persuade others? Notice what you do, as well.
- What new strategies do you adopt as the situation progresses?
- What did you learn about power?
- How is power in everyday life like and unlike power on a grander scale?

Around the world, kingdoms continue to be important political units, but like tribes and bands, they must accommodate the overarching power of the state.

Chiefdoms/kingdoms can consolidate control through coercive measures that bands and tribes do not have. Like modern states, the chiefdom/kingdom system allows for higher population concentrations as the division of labor becomes more specialized. Segments of the population work to provide food surpluses that are redistributed through systems of tribute or taxation to the population working in other capacities. Centralization of political power allows for the formation of alliances and militaries that support the coordination of large populations into a specialized and generally highly stratified economy.

People living under chiefdoms and kingdoms continue to resolve interpersonal conflicts by interpersonal means. Conflict resolution also becomes more formalized than in bands or tribes. Rules developed and delivered by chiefs or kings regulate interactions between groups of higher and lower status, serving to reinforce social stratification. When rules are breached, leaders are able to inflict punishment or encourage reconciliation, but the imposition of sanctions is largely dependent on the ruler rather than a body of law to which the ruler is also subject. The use of coercive force for control within society is common in chiefdoms/kingdoms. External conflicts also escalate as chiefdoms and kingdoms wage wars at higher frequency and in larger scale than tribes or bands.

States

The **state** is a highly centralized form of political organization in which authority rests in institutions and offices. Although individuals may be elected to these offices or appointed based on their personal qualities, the ideology of the state asserts that the office itself, rather than the individual who happens to occupy it, is the real locus of power. In democratic systems, such as the United States, the explicit ideological position (often expressed in a constitution) is that individual members of the society agree to yield their own power to those who hold these offices. The people should trust the person in office, and the office itself, to represent their interests. When individuals leave office, power passes to the person who takes the office next. The state may or may not have such democratic ideals, however. Many states neither reflect the desires of the majority of the people nor protect their interests. Centralized forms of government sometimes result in a small group holding power over the majority (**oligarchy**).

The distinction between chiefdom/kingdom and state is less about structure and more about ideology and culture. The chief/king requires cultural legitimacy rooted in the identity of the individual, to some extent. For example, the kingdoms of medieval Europe used the idea of "blood" to determine who was eligible to rule. It was for this reason that some royal families of Europe violated incest rules—even those formally decreed by the church—because to marry someone too far removed from the family would have meant the dilution of royal blood. Many chiefdoms and kingdoms throughout the world have operated on similar principles, limiting political authority to particular families.

States, on the other hand, grew out of modern ideologies of law as a transcendent reality. In Europe, these political ideas grew from the Protestant Reformation, during which Roman Catholic thinkers such as Martin Luther began to question the legitimacy of the church regulating access to the Bible, knowledge of God, and salvation. Religious changes carried political implications as people rethought the relationship between individuals and institutions. This shift in thinking brought about profound changes in the way millions of Europeans imagined their relationship to political power. Over several hundred years, through events such as the Thirty Years' War (a bloody conflict waged by Christian reformers), the signing of the Peace of Westphalia to end that war (a collection of treaties establishing territorial boundaries of citizenship for the first time in Europe), and the American and French Revolutions (wars in which citizens challenged their rulers), Europeans came to new understandings of political organization.

Today there are many examples of the dominant logic of the state becoming intertwined with chiefdoms, kingdoms, tribes, and bands. Among the old monarchies of Europe, the monarch has largely become a ceremonial position stripped of formal political authority. In other places, however, monarchs or chiefs maintain a great deal of real political authority. In the kingdom of Bhutan, the king works with a parliament but retains official authority to dismiss those leaders and act on his own.

In many countries where a state system was imposed by a colonial power, the official government is a modern state even as many people at the local level continue to operate according to persuasive leadership in a tribal system, an inheritable system of chiefs, or even the consensus and context-dependent leadership of band systems. In Ecuador, some Amazonian bands live fairly isolated from contact with the state. Nonetheless, they are still Ecuadorian citizens, even if they don't think of themselves as such. Bands such as the Cofán and the Waorani have been drawn into interactions with the state because of oil development in the Amazon rain forest. Having negotiated the right to live on ancestral lands, the Waorani people saw oil drilling as an incursion into their territory, but the Ecuadorian state asserted that the Indigenous people had only surface rights to the land. The state claimed the legal right to subsurface resources such as oil and could grant legal access for development to oil companies without Waorani consent. The Waorani quickly had to learn to mobilize with other affected groups in their region and throughout the world. They began working the political system as Ecuadorian citizens. They continue to adapt politically, retaining elements of band organization when possible and incorporating elements of state organization as necessary.[14]

There is no such thing as a society without a political system. Even the most informal and flexible systems are based on shared understandings and practices that are systematic and that serve to distribute and manage power in groups and society. Anthropologists also agree that there is no system in which people cannot abuse one another, misuse power and authority, or otherwise act in selfish and cruel ways. Across cultures and throughout time, people recognize and negotiate legitimate and illegitimate forms of power.

Christians and Politics

Just as Scripture reflects a variety of economic systems, so, too, are the pages of the Bible filled with various political forms. The nomadic pastoralist families of Abraham's day were tribes. They later developed into a kingdom that relied on both pastoralism and agriculture (see 1 Sam. 9). In the New Testament, the Roman Empire (an empire is a type of state) was the political context for Jesus's ministry and the development of the early church.

The New Testament teachings of Jesus and Paul encourage believers to take a variety of stances toward existing political structures. They do not argue for a single political system that is ideal for all times and places. Jesus taught his followers to "give back to Caesar what is Caesar's and to God what is God's," suggesting that his followers can live in the state system of the Roman Empire even as they serve God (Mark 12:17). Christians have used this teaching to support the notion of Christians holding political office, both contributing positively to a good political cause, on the one hand, and merely tolerating an existing political structure, on the other hand. Jesus, in his overturning of the tables in the temple and his own childhood refugee status (his parents escaped political oppression by fleeing to Egypt), also demonstrated the importance of challenging unjust religious and political leadership.

Believers have relied on these stories to support Christian contributions to both political stability and political protest. Paul tells the early Christians that they should live according to the laws of their society. Although he encourages believers to avoid some parts of the legal system (1 Cor. 6:1), he also argues

14. Clayton Robarchek and Carole Robarchek, *Waorani: The Contexts of Violence and War* (Wadsworth, 2002).

that believers can and should be subject to the laws and systems in which they live (Rom. 13:1–6). At the same time, Paul's teachings about the equal value of men and women, slaves and free persons, and Jews and gentiles (Gal. 3:28) have inspired believers to challenge political systems that discriminate on the basis of gender, ethnicity, or race.

No form of political organization is inherently more "advanced" or more suited to following Christ than another. The fact that terms such as "tribe" and "chiefdom" may carry negative connotations, rather than being seen as complex systems of governance well suited for local communities, reflects ethnocentrism in language and a preference for the state form of organization. Reading the Bible with an anthropological perspective can challenge this ethnocentrism because it records stories and teachings that come from tribe, kingdom, and state contexts.

Within all forms of political organization—bands, tribes, chiefdoms/kingdoms, and states—Christians can engage political power in faithful ways. The church is always a community set apart, yet it exists only in particular political and cultural contexts. Christians should not deny the place of power and politics in human life. Instead, we should think deeply about how Christians can engage, use, and understand power to encourage a vibrant life in Christ for believers and to contribute to the common good for all.

TERMS

age-set: A social group consisting of people of the same sex and similar age within a tribe.

authority: The right granted to exercise power.

band: The most ancient political system, in which power and authority are organized in informal, decentralized ways.

chiefdom/kingdom: A system of political organization involving an inheritable office, often passed through a family line, in which power adheres to the occupant of the office rather than being a product of their individual gifts, abilities, or qualities.

coercive power: The use or threat of force, legitimate or illegitimate, by individuals or groups.

counterhegemony: An ideology or movement that challenges a reigning hegemony.

fissioning: Splitting a group into numerous smaller groups. A practice used by foragers to reduce group size and reduce conflict.

formal negative sanctions: Fines or other punishments meted out for breaking official rules, meant to encourage or discourage particular behavior.

formal positive sanctions: Official rewards for socially desirable behavior.

formal sanctions: Social sanctions that are approved or delivered by institutions holding official power.

hegemonic power (or **hegemony**): The dominance of ideas or culture, such that a social or cultural status quo is maintained.

informal sanctions: Positive or negative actions or words intended to shape behavior. Informal sanctions are not approved or delivered by official organizations such as a government.

oligarchy: Within a centralized form of government, a small group holding power over the majority.

persuasive power: The use of words, relationships, and actions that influence others.

political anthropology: The study of power and authority, and systems of organizing these in social life.

politics: The distribution, understanding, and use of power in social groups.

power: Influence or control over the behavior of others.

social sanctions: The responses, positive and negative, that people receive for their behavior.

state: A highly centralized form of political organization in which authority rests in institutions and offices.

tribe: A decentralized political system usually associated with horticultural and pastoral modes of subsistence.

DISCUSSION QUESTIONS

1. What is one way that God's power is like human power? What is one difference?
2. Tell a story about someone using persuasive power. Did they succeed or not? What factors make persuasion more or less likely to work?
3. What is one way in which being a Christian should be the same in all societies? What is one distinctive Christian practice or belief that would be especially important in a band? In a tribe? In a chiefdom/kingdom? In a state?

ANTHROPOLOGY AND SCRIPTURE

Jesus's Power and Authority

He went down to Capernaum, a city in Galilee, and was teaching them on the Sabbath. They were astounded at his teaching because he spoke with authority. In the synagogue there was a man who had the spirit of an unclean demon, and he cried out with a loud voice, "Leave us alone! What have you to do with us, Jesus of Nazareth? Have you come to destroy us? I know who you are, the Holy One of God." But Jesus rebuked him, saying, "Be quiet and come out of him!" Then the demon, throwing the man down before them, came out of him without doing him any harm. They were all astounded and kept saying to one another, "What kind of word is this, that with authority and power he commands the unclean spirits and they come out?" And news about him began to reach every place in the region. (Luke 4:31–37 NRSVue)

At the beginning of this passage, Jesus amazed people by teaching with authority. Authority is the right granted to exercise power, and in Jesus's day, Jews recognized the authority of certain religious officials who were trained and seated in official roles. Jesus spoke as if people ought to recognize and accept his power, though he didn't have an official religious role.

When Jesus cast out the demon, he was continuing to claim authority and escalate its meaning by displaying power in action. Power is the ability to influence others, and Jesus demonstrated his ability to influence even demons in the supernatural realm. People were amazed because Jesus's words and actions disrupted their sense of what was expected. Jesus came to teach and to cast out demons, but he also came to change culture. Through the incarnation, Jesus lived within a local culture, but he was strategic about disrupting fundamental elements of culture like power and authority. He was showing people how to include God—the true God—in their understandings and in their daily lives.

We all have realms of life in which we have influence and power where we, too, may be called to disrupt the typical relations of power.

Informal Sanctions and Gossip

For I fear that when I come I may find you not as I wish and that you may find me not as you wish; I fear that there may perhaps be quarreling, jealousy, anger, selfishness, slander, gossip, conceit, and disorder. (2 Cor. 12:20 NRSVue)

The Bible condemns gossip as a sin. But what really is gossip? If I share a story about something funny—maybe a little embarrassing—my friend did, is that gossip? If I talk about something I personally witnessed, versus something I heard secondhand, is that gossip? Is gossip only talking about bad things? Untrue things?

Perhaps the better question to ask is why gossip is considered a sin. In the list above, many of Paul's concerns about the church in Corinth—quarreling, factions, disorder—are about social order and group cohesion. Gossip fits in this list because Paul recognizes gossip as a means of social control, a negative informal sanction used to control others' behavior.

When anthropological perspective aids biblical interpretation, it becomes clear that gossip is wrong for several reasons. The person spreading gossip may be poorly motivated, seeking to undermine the social standing, reputation, or even humanity of another member of the community. The person being gossiped about may feel hurt or angry. Gossip is wrong because it intentionally hurts another person and diminishes their place in the community.

Using informal sanctions is not sinful in and of itself. Jesus spoke words of encouragement and rebuke to persuade people to live rightly. Paul encouraged the churches to exhort, rebuke, and correct other members of their community. Informal negative sanctions—which may include talking about other people—should correct a person's behavior or attitude and restore their place in the community. In contrast, gossip is destructive talk designed to demean another person and fracture the community.

In any community, each of us should examine our own behavior to see if we are exerting social control through informal sanctions in ways that restore individuals and edify communities, or if our words tear down, disrupt, and cause harm.

8

KINSHIP AND MARRIAGE

After studying this chapter, you should be able to do the following:

1. articulate the importance of kinship and marriage in social organization
2. compare and contrast the various descent systems
3. understand anthropological approaches to the study of marriage
4. describe the variety of family systems present in the Bible

CHAPTER OUTLINE

Introduction

Family is important in every culture, but there is wide variation in how people conceive of family relationships, relate these to personal identity, and organize their social lives around them.[1] In the Philippines, most families have several children, and birth order is considered an important aspect of a person's identity. A question that is rather complicated in English—"Where do you fall in the birth order of your siblings?"—can be asked very simply in Tagalog: "*Pang-ilan ka ba?*" The frequency and ease with which this question is asked in the Philippines reflects the importance of sibling relationships in personal and social identity. In Korea, along with many other countries, the family name (or last name in English) is the first part of a person's name. Lee Chun Kee refers to a person who was named Chun Kee by his parents but whose family name is Lee. Placing the

1. Some early influential studies of kinship include works by Lewis Henry Morgan, Alfred L. Kroeber, and A. R. Radcliffe-Brown. For later work on the anthropology of kinship, see Robin Fox, *Kinship and Marriage: An Anthropological Perspective* (Cambridge University Press, 1983); David Murray Schneider, *A Critique of the Study of Kinship* (University of Michigan Press, 1984); Marshall Sahlins, *What Kinship Is—And Is Not* (University of Chicago Press, 2013).

family name before the given name emphasizes the importance of family identity. Among the Kikuyu of East Africa, along with many other groups, once a person has a child, they are no longer called by their given name. They become "mother of (eldest child's name)" or "father of (eldest child)." This custom, known as **teknomymy** (tek-*nom*-in-ee), bestows an identity based on parenthood.

Anthropologists study many dimensions of family life, including how people define family relationships, how they practice marriage, where they live, how family relationships shape (or don't shape) social organization, and how people pass on culture through families. Kinship studies analyze the structure, process, and meaning of family relationships. In this chapter, we define kinship and then consider the two major areas of kinship study: descent and marriage. We conclude with a discussion of family forms found in biblical cultures.

Kinship

Kinship refers to the ways in which people selectively interpret the common human experiences of reproduction and nurturance. Humans everywhere make more humans, and every society has systems for answering the big questions of how our relatedness matters: Who should marry whom? To whom do these children belong? Who is responsible for the care of these children? Where should wives, husbands, boy children, and girl children live? The answers allow people to organize themselves into groups and know who to trust, who to help, and who might be a threat. Kinship rules govern, among other things, inheritance of political position and property, ritual and religious responsibilities, marriage, territorial distribution, dispute resolution, and land ownership.

Kinship is foundational in band and tribal societies. In societies where most members do the same work and have roughly the same social status, people are known primarily by kinship relations. Kinship status identifies people not just in the family sphere but also in religion, politics, and economy. A person has status, reputation, honor, and even selfhood by virtue of their place in a system of relations.

In contrast, in highly stratified societies with a complex division of labor and multiple political institutions, a person's kinship status is just one of many identities (though it is often a very important one). A person may also carry religious, professional, political, and leisure statuses (for more on roles, see chap. 4). People experience distress when roles collide, such as when family responsibilities interfere with a professional role or a religious identity causes family conflict. Some people even reject their given kinship identity and live without significant ties to their families of origin.

Whether they are of European, African, Latin, Asian, or Indigenous ancestry, most North Americans have roots in places where kinship powerfully influences identity. But modern capitalism rewards individual mobility and the willingness and ability to relocate. Though some families prize physical proximity and may arrange their lives to stay close together, most families set up separate households of parents and children—the nuclear family—and move this relatively small group in response to educational and economic opportunity. They may maintain important ties to family who live far away—new immigrants, for instance, often share resources with relatives still in their place of origin—but the household itself is composed of a fairly small group of people. Similar to foragers in this respect, many people in large-scale societies today who pursue upward mobility in the global economy emphasize the nuclear family as the primary kin-group comprising a household.

In addition to having a smaller vision of family than many other groups, North Americans are more likely to emphasize individual identity over family identity. When asked for an introduction, a North American will likely begin with his personal (first) name, describe personal qualities (what he enjoys doing, where he works), and later describe his family. "Family" may include those who share his household, parents and siblings, a spouse and/or children, and perhaps a dog or cat. North Americans are unlikely to talk about grandparents, cousins, aunts, and uncles when introducing themselves, unless those individuals live with them or someone asks specifically. Many North Americans distinguish immediate family from extended family in terms of reciprocity obligations and emotional ties.

Descent

Descent is a social rule that assigns identity to a person based on their ancestry. Descent systems vary widely across cultures but may be organized into two main types: unilineal descent and cognatic descent. There are three types of unilineal descent systems: matrilineal, patrilineal, and dual. Cognatic descent reckons identity through both maternal and paternal ancestors in two primary ways: bilateral and ambilineal (see fig. 8.1). There is variation in how particular systems are understood and practiced around the world.

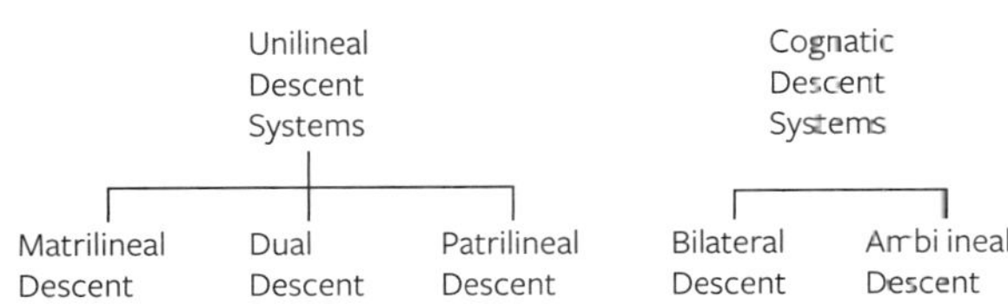

Figure 8.1. Descent systems

Unilineal Descent Systems

Unilineal descent traces relatedness exclusively or predominantly through one parent. Most unilineal societies are **patrilineal**, tracing descent through the male line (see fig. 8.2). Though this system is giving way to other practices, European Americans retain a vestige of this system through the tradition of a woman taking her husband's family name upon marriage and giving the father's family name to children. The US kinship system is no longer truly unilineal, however; this system is better classified as cognatic because we consider a person equally related to her mother's and father's families.

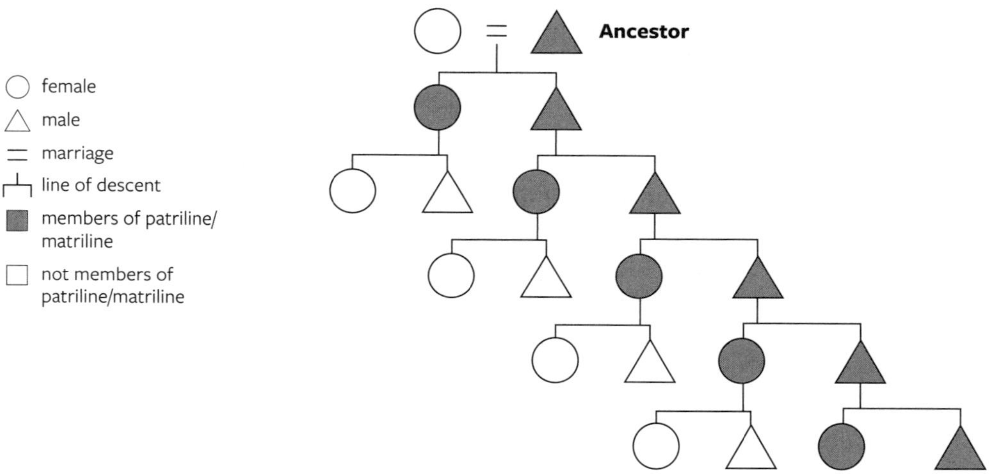

Figure 8.2. Patrilineal descent

Old Testament Hebrew culture provides a good example of a patrilineal kinship system. The Semitic cultures of the Middle East (Hebrews, Arabs, Kurds, and others) have long traced lineage through male ancestors. The metaphor for reproduction, still used in English, is "the seed and the soil." In other words, the man is thought to plant his "seed" (sperm) in the "soil" (womb) of the woman, where the seed grows into a child. Like a literal seed that contains everything necessary to create a new plant, the "seed" of the man was thought to simply need a place to grow for reproduction to occur. This cultural logic inspired Sarah to encourage her husband, Abraham, to "plant his seed" in her maidservant Hagar to produce his heir. In the logic of monogenesis, the child comes wholly from the father; the mother does not contribute anything to the physical being of the child any more than the soil would influence what kind of tree grows from a particular seed (see also Gen. 30).[2] Therefore, Ishmael, Hagar's son, received God's blessing along with Isaac, Sarah's son, because both were considered fully sons of Abraham. In patrilineal systems such as this one, children are *more* related to their fathers than to their mothers. Although a few women are mentioned in the important lineages of the Bible (e.g., Ruth and Rahab), it is because of what they did to preserve the male line, not because they are considered true members of the line.

Patrilineality is not the same as **patriarchy**, or social rule by men. However, in patrilineal societies, men typically do have more social and political power than women. Lineage systems do not necessarily predict sociopolitical authority, though they often do.

The second major unilineal system is **matrilineal descent**, in which descent is traced through the female line (see fig. 8.3). In these families, names and inheritance are passed through the mother. Though less common than patrilineality, matrilineality is found throughout the world, from West Africa to Southeast Asia to Indigenous North America.

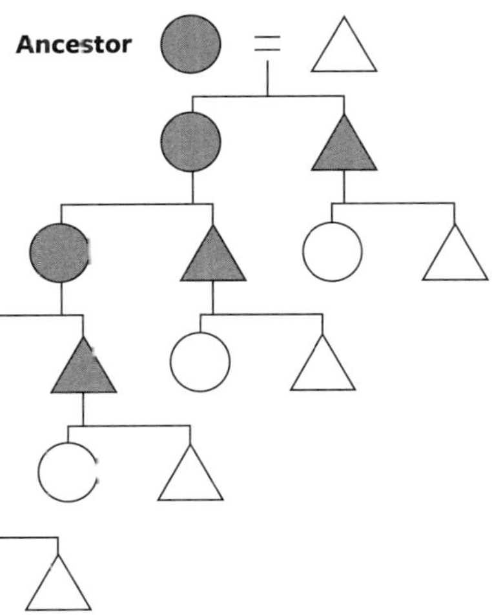

Figure 8.3. Matrilineal descent

In many matrilineal cultures, even though the family is named for the mother's relatives and inheritance is passed from mothers to daughters, the primary authority in a family rests with a male relative. The state of Mizoram,

2. This use of "monogenesis" in conception is different from the notion that humanity as a whole came from a single source or act of creation as discussed in chapter 2.

in northeast India, is the traditional home of several matrilineal groups, including the Garo. Among the Garo, the youngest daughter inherits family property. She is expected to live in the family home and care for her parents as they age. Upon marriage, her husband moves into the home and works alongside his wife caring for her parents, working the land, and raising children. The practice of a newly married couple living with or near the bride's family is known as **uxorilocal** (uhk-sohr-uh-'lo-cal) **residence**. In the case of family disputes or even child discipline, the person most likely to be called on to exercise authority is the mother's older brother, the maternal uncle. The father is primarily a nurturing presence for his children. Although individual Garo fathers have different styles, when it comes to the discipline of children, the Garo equivalent of "Just wait until your father gets home!" is "Just wait until I call your uncle to come over!"

Just as patrilineal kinship does not necessarily link to patriarchy, neither does matrilineal kinship necessarily correlate with **matriarchy**, or social rule by women. Matrilineal kinship systems typically support women in more prominent social roles in religion, politics, and economics than patrilineal ones, but these systems can also allow uncles and brothers to have more social power (as opposed to husbands and fathers in patrilineal systems). Anthropologists have never encountered a contemporary society in which women exercise the kind of control men exercise in some highly patriarchal (and often patrilineal) cultures.[3]

The third type of unilineal kinship system is **dual descent**. This uncommon system traces descent through both the mother's and the father's lines. In the case of the Yakö of Nigeria, the two lines involve different rules of inheritance. Movable property, such as cattle or personal possessions, is passed through the mother's line. Fixed property (land) is inherited through the father's line. Instead of thinking of themselves as having two "sides" of one family, members of this group think of themselves as belonging to two different families. Out of a sample of more than 175 unilineal cultures documented by anthropologist George Murdock in 1949, only eighteen (10 percent) were organized with dual descent.[4] Because there are two lines, dual descent may not seem unilineal, but anthropologists categorize dual descent this way because dual descent systems combine the rules for

3. Cynthia Eller, *The Myth of Matriarchal Prehistory: Why an Invented Past Won't Give Women a Future* (Beacon, 2000); Heide Goettner-Abendroth, ed., *Societies of Peace: Matriarchies Past, Present, and Future* (Inanna Publications, 2009); Maria Lepowsky, *Fruit of the Motherland: Gender in an Egalitarian Society* (Columbia University Press, 1993).

4. See George Peter Murdock, *Social Structure* (Macmillan, 1949).

patrilineal descent and the rules for matrilineal descent without joining the matrilineage and the patrilineage together, as cognatic descent systems do.

Cognatic Descent Systems

Cognatic descent (also called **nonunilineal**) reckons identity through both maternal and paternal ancestors. There are two major types of cognatic descent systems: bilateral and ambilineal.

Most North Americans believe in cognatic descent and rely on the rules of **bilateral descent** (see fig. 8.4). In this system, kinship exists equally through both the mother's and the father's lines. An individual in the United States, for example, is related to an ever-widening group of people on both sides of the family. Bilateral kinship terms differentiate people on the basis of gender (aunt versus uncle) and generation (great-grandmother versus grandmother) but generally do not distinguish between the mother's and the father's kindred. People distinguish between mother's and father's kin in their interpersonal relationships, of course, but this distinction is not important enough to encode in kinship terminology.

Descent rules help explain recent trends in name changes at marriage. Some North Americans continue the tradition of a wife giving up her family name and assuming her husband's surname. Some wives retain their family names, so husband and wife have different last names. Some wives hyphenate their family name with their husband's name, and the husband may or may not hyphenate. Still other couples create new last names for both husband and wife. In all these variations, however, descent rules remain firm. In fact, because bilateral kinship systems engender a sense of identity linked to both

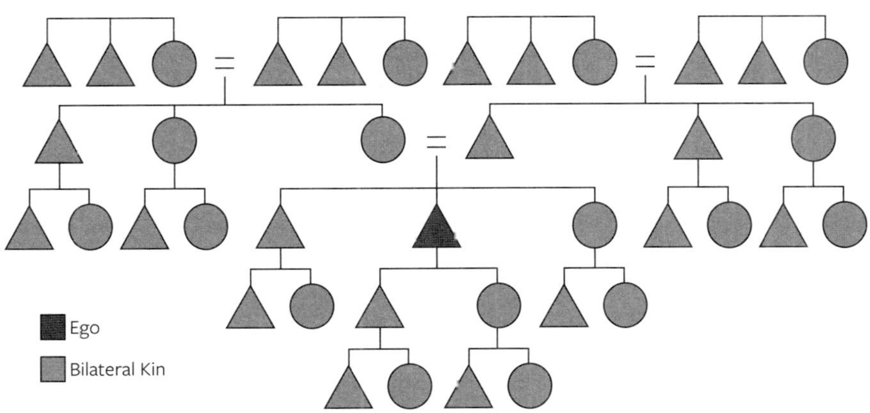

Figure 8.4. Egocentric (or self-centric) bilateral descent system

YOUR TURN

Family at a Glance

Culture is learned, dynamic, shared, power laden, and integrated. All aspects of culture are present in kinship systems. Children learn family stories when older kin share with them. Kinship systems change over time as some members pass away and as new members arrive by birth, marriage, adoption, or other means. Each member of a family has power, albeit of different kinds. One family member may have the power to tell stories, but others have the power to choose whether or not to listen carefully.

Find a family photo. It could be your own or one you find online.

- What kind of descent system is displayed?
- What kinds of marriage are displayed?
- What are the visual clues that make kinship systems visible?

Now, look for culture.

- How does this photograph portray people learning and sharing together?
- What different kinds of power do people have (and how can you tell)?

mother and father, this widens the pool of possible marital names. The couple could symbolize their union with the male name, the female name, or a new name that embraces both sides or neither side. The tradition of taking the male name is a patrilineal idea that is not necessary for kinship stability in a bilateral kinship system.

The second form of cognatic descent is ambilineal. In **ambilineal descent** systems, individuals choose a lineage on reaching adulthood, often marked by marriage. The individual may choose the lineage of their mother or father or the maternal or paternal line of their spouse. Ambilineal systems, then, look like unilineal systems because they trace ancestry through one line, but this system is considered cognatic because the lineages are open for the choosing. In light of considerations such as property, kin relationships, and personal ties, the individual may decide to live with their father's or mother's group after marriage, or may simply take the name of the group desired for affiliation. In either case, children are seen as related to both parents equally and choose a lineage when they reach adulthood.

Functions of Descent Systems

Kinship connects with many other areas of life. Three of the most important are inheritance, territory, and conflict resolution. Inheritance rules are often a function of kinship. In the Western tradition, patrilineality shaped

Rob McKee

Rob McKee (far right) served with SIL International working toward Bible translation in the Mangbetu language. He also conducted dissertation fieldwork on Meegye-Mangbetu death compensations. The Mangbetu believe that when a person dies, there is structural, custodial responsibility for the death regardless of how it occurred. Most typically, the father's family group is responsible vis-à-vis the mother's group and so has to compensate the mother's group.

practices such as the oldest son inheriting family property on the death of his parents, or the oldest son being the heir of a royal dynasty. Biblical accounts reflect the same concerns. An example is the story of Jacob and Esau, twins who were destined to follow a strict rule of primogeniture, or priority of the firstborn. In collusion with his mother, Jacob (the second-born twin) convinced Esau to renounce his birthright and tricked their father into passing the inheritance to him, the younger twin. Jacob's trick was an offense against his brother, and by violating the rule of primogeniture, it was also a transgression of the kinship system that organized their family life. Seen in another light, however, Jacob and his mother were working to preserve their patrilineal lineage. By marrying Canaanite women, Esau had violated the Hebrew preference for cousin marriage, a preference that strengthened the patriline by marrying within it. When Jacob received his father's blessing, he made a point of promising to marry within the patrilineal kin group (see Gen. 27:1–28:9).

Kinship also organizes the distribution of territory. The clans of Jacob's lineage were given specific territorial claims based on ancestry from one of Jacob's twelve sons, as described in the book of Joshua. The book of Judges describes how the leaders of various factions within the lineage, known as **segments**, engaged in warfare with Canaanites or even other Hebrew lineages for possession of territory. Leadership of those territories was also assigned and legitimated through kinship. Even today, from the highlands of Papua New Guinea to the plains of East Africa, clan affiliation determines territory.

In addition to inheritance and territory distribution, kinship helps regulate social conflict. Knowing that someone is related means that although two people may not know each other personally, there is someone connecting them they both *do* know. Where there is no kinship connection, or the kinship is weaker or more distant, there is less trust and a greater possibility of conflict or disregard.

Unilineal descent systems seem generally better suited to influence a wide variety of social behavior. In addition to inheritance, territorial distribution, and conflict avoidance or resolution, kinship may also be a significant factor in land ownership, political representation, and ritual observance (as in the case of the Levites described in Num. 3 and 4). Cognatic structures often serve fewer roles in society since their more diffuse organization influences political and economic spheres minimally. Marriage, however, is shaped by both systems.

Marriage

If we ask students in our classes to imagine who their parents would pick as spouses for them, they may name criteria important for both their parents and themselves (attractiveness, compatibility, common religion). Students sometimes note that their parents take other concerns more seriously than they do (earning potential, reproductive potential, or the character of the prospective spouse's parents). Mostly, students make it very clear that they wouldn't want their parents to pick their spouse for them. Romantic ideals of finding a soul mate, or "the one," animate Western movies and popular music. In Shakespeare's *Romeo and Juliet*, young lovers defy the wishes of their families and ultimately give their lives for true love. This story captures the Western imagination and resonates with a deeply held cultural value that love conquers all.

For people in many cultures, however, the notion of pursuing marriage primarily for personal motives represents a neglect of family; it is the height of selfishness, irresponsibility, and immaturity. For most of human history, and still today in many cultures, marriage is primarily a social, economic, and political connection between two families rather than the free choice of two individuals. While Western marriage priorities such as companionship, love, and sexual fulfillment are by no means found only in Western societies, other cultures would add economic security, continuation of a lineage by producing heirs, social status, and political alliances to the highest priorities and purposes of marriage.

Marriage is a publicly recognized social or legal union that creates a socially sanctioned context for sexual intimacy, establishes the parentage of children, and creates kinship. Marriage produces relatives. **Affinal** (a-ˈfi-nul) **kin** are relatives created through marriage. "Affinal" is related to the word "affinity," meaning attraction. Birth and adoption also create relatives, and people related by birth or adoption are called **consanguineal** (kon-sang-ˈgwin-ee-uhl) **kin**. Consanguinity means "of the blood." Marriage is important for both the partners and their families. The quality of consanguineal bonds is affected for better or for worse when a family member links with another family through affinity. Thus, parents and even the wider community are often intimately involved in selecting marriage partners for young people. Many societies have specific rules about who should marry whom and how the arrangement should be made.

Every society has **incest taboos**, prohibitions against marriage or sex between two categories of related persons. Universal incest taboos include prohibitions on parents marrying their own children, siblings marrying each other, and grandparents marrying grandchildren. Beyond that, however, rules for marriage avoidance and marriage preference vary greatly.

Because the marriage of two individuals creates bonds between two families, many families would prefer to promote marriage between people who are *already* related. Cousin preference seems to be rooted, in part, in the desire to have stronger relationships within the family or to keep inheritance within a clan. **Cross-cousin marriage**, a preference for marriage between cross-cousins, means a man should marry his mother's brother's daughter or his father's sister's daughter. The "cross" refers to the opposite-sex sibling of the person's parent. **Parallel-cousin marriage**, a preference for marriage between parallel cousins, directs a man to marry his mother's sister's daughter or his father's brother's daughter (see fig. 8.5). "Parallel" refers to the parent's same-sex sibling.

Biblical cultures offer many examples of cousin marriage in which parents work with their siblings or other relatives to find

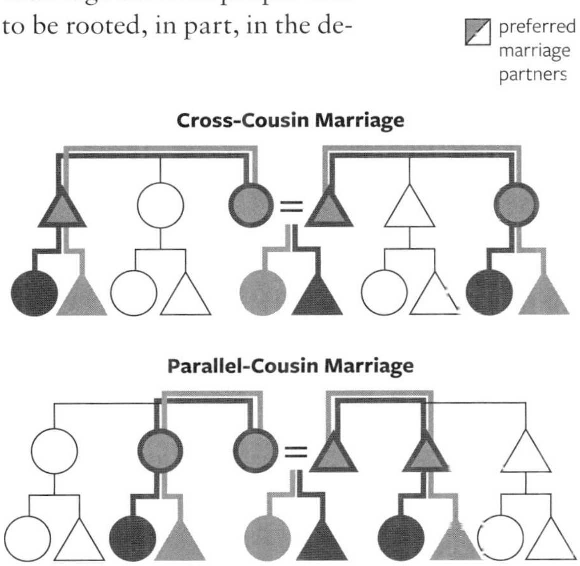

Figure 8.5. Cousin marriage

good matches for their children. Seeking marriage partners within the family assures there will already be a level of trust and familiarity among the families, hopefully making life easier for the young couple. Jacob, for instance, was the son of Isaac and Rebekah. Isaac instructed Jacob to marry the daughter of Rebekah's brother, Jacob's cross-cousin. Jacob eventually married two sisters, Rachel and Leah, both his cross-cousins, because of his uncle's trickery. In this case, marrying within the family made life more difficult for Jacob because he had to provide fourteen years of brideservice (described below) instead of seven, but it also contributed to his personal wealth. Additionally, the practice ensured patterns of descent and inheritance that were desirable to the broader kin group.

Marriage and Economic Exchange

Marriage exchange involves exchanges of material resources between families before, at, or after the wedding. The three major types of marriage exchange are brideservice, bridewealth, and dowry. **Brideservice** requires the groom to work for the bride's kin for a certain period before or after marriage. **Bridewealth** (also called **brideprice**) is an amount of money, possessions, or property given by the groom and his kin to the wife and her kin before, at, or after the wedding. The word "brideprice" carries the connotation that the groom is purchasing the wife, which is not what the practice really means. "Bridewealth" is a synonym that highlights the value of the bride. Losing the bride represents a loss of wealth to her family; that is, the service, employment, companionship, offspring, and other resources she could have given to her consanguineal kin will now go to her affinal kin. An exchange of wealth between families recognizes the value of the bride to both sets of kin.

Genesis 29 describes the brideservice transaction between Jacob and his uncle Laban. They agreed that in exchange for working for Laban, Jacob could marry Laban's daughter Rachel at the end of seven years. This arrangement would solidify trust and relationship between Jacob and Laban and would also give financial gain to Laban in exchange for the loss of a daughter and the companionship and household labor she represented. When Rachel married Jacob, she would leave Laban's patriline and join the patriline of Jacob (Gen. 29:19). Her children would belong to Jacob and his ancestors, not to her and her ancestors. Of course, in this case, Laban used another marriage preference—that the older daughter marry before the younger—to insist that Jacob works *another* seven years to marry Rachel (Gen. 29:26).

In other cases, families use bridewealth to mark marriage. Bridewealth exchanges may be symbolic, or they may involve substantial goods.

Anthropologist and former missionary Jon Arensen observed bridewealth exchanges among the nomadic Murle. The Murle are pastoralists whose traditional lands range across parts of South Sudan and Ethiopia. As with all pastoralists, the labor of the family is critical to maintain the herd, which provides almost all the family's resources. Cattle represent wealth and are crucial to survival. When it is time for a family to arrange the marriage of a son, they seek out a family with a marriageable daughter and begin to negotiate with her parents over an appropriate bridewealth, which for the Murle always means a number of cattle given in exchange for the marriage. To Westerners, this often appears as buying a wife (and equating women with cows), but the Murle do not think of it this way. They recognize that in this marriage the families will be united, and the cattle represent something tangible to mark the connection.

The Murle word for relatives, *atiinok*, comes from the word for cattle, *tiin*. To be related means "to have cattle between us."[5] This occurs when, upon marriage, the groom's family sends the agreed-upon number of cattle to the bride's family. While this may seem like a great deal for the bride's parents, they do not simply keep the new cattle. Twenty years earlier, when the father of the bride got married, he had to go to his relatives and borrow cattle from multiple families for his own bridewealth. These families remember the debt, and once the marriage of the man's daughter is complete, they come back to get the cattle they loaned to him twenty years earlier. Now, the dozen or so families who loaned the young groom his bridewealth are connected to the dozen families who collect on the twenty-year-old debt with the bride's father. Divorce becomes difficult when it involves giving back twenty cattle that, in the subsequent years, have been herded across hundreds of miles and perhaps died, been eaten, or exchanged again for another marriage. Bridewealth encourages stability of marriage and family by creating links between multiple segments of various clans.

An opposite form of exchange is the **dowry**, the practice of a bride's family providing resources, wealth, or gifts to the groom and his family upon marriage. This has been common in many parts of India, Europe, and other strongly patrilineal societies in which people understand the groom to be taking over the care of the bride from the bride's father. For the husband taking on the "cost" of caring for the wife, the dowry is meant to symbolize the gratitude of the bride's family while also providing material resources to the newly married couple. Sometimes the dowry remains the bride's property as

5. For further analysis of Murle language and social categories, see Jonathan E. Arensen, *Mice Are Men: Language and Society Among the Murle of Sudan* (International Museum of Cultures, 1992).

a kind of insurance against divorce or abandonment, particularly when the dowry consists of items such as gold jewelry or household goods associated with women's work (e.g., kitchenware). This sort of dowry is common in many Middle Eastern societies.

Stability and Flexibility in Kinship

At first glance, kinship systems may seem like rigid systems of traditions and rules. Kinship systems provide stability and belonging, but they also must adapt when life doesn't go as planned. There are many reasons why cultures develop new or alternative ways to join kinship networks. The kinsman redeemer is an Old Testament example of a culture creating a way for a patrilineal kinship network to adapt to the loss of a man who hadn't established a lineage.

Ruth, a Moabite, married Mahlon, coming into the patriline of Elimelek, husband of Naomi. When Mahlon died without providing heirs, it left the already-widowed Naomi destitute and vulnerable in a male-dominated society. Neither Ruth nor Naomi had a male relative linking them to the wider patriline. Rather than accepting Naomi's offer to leave the family and return to her parents (essentially restarting her life), Ruth elected to honor her connection to her dead husband and his family, meaning her mother-in-law, Naomi.

This decision left her extremely vulnerable in a patrilineal system. The birth of sons guaranteed the continuation of the family. Sons inherit land from the patriline. Women without male relatives had, essentially, no legitimate claim to economic resources.

When Ruth and Naomi returned to the land of Judah, they found that they did have a connection to Elimelek's family. When Naomi learned that Boaz, Elimelek's relative (in the patriline), lived in Judah, she knew he *should* serve as the "kinsman redeemer," marrying and impregnating Ruth so that she would have a child who was part of the lineage, reconnecting Ruth, Naomi, and even Ruth's dead husband, Mahlon, back to the lineage. She would be brought back in from outside the family.

Naomi believed Boaz to be honorable and likely to do the right thing. She sent Ruth to him at night so that, if he were an honorable man, he would impregnate her and "redeem" her back into the family. What made Boaz the right choice for Ruth was not principally his physical attractiveness or personal wealth but that he was a link to the lineage.

Boaz told Ruth that there was a man more closely related than he—meaning the closer relative should take Ruth, provide her with children, and bring her into his household. The risk to that man was that, were Ruth to have male children, those children would inherit part of whatever he owned. This meant his current children would receive less. He would also have the added economic responsibility of caring for Ruth, her mother-in-law Naomi, and any children Ruth might bear. That man passed on his responsibility to Boaz, who did the right thing by taking Ruth as one of his wives.

Ruth is honored for her righteousness in continuing the line of Jacob. That line led to King David and eventually to Jesus. Ruth's faithfulness is singled out for mention in the genealogy of Jesus (Matt. 1:1–17).

It's your turn: Consider your family, a family you know, or a family in general in the society where you live. What is a circumstance that the usual kinship pattern can't quite handle? How does the kinship system adapt to handle this circumstance?

Although Western conceptions of marriage as the free choice of two individuals have made marriage exchange largely a thing of the past in the United States, remnants of the practice remain. A man is expected to buy an expensive item (the ring) in exchange for a woman's agreement to marry him. The tradition of the bride's family paying for the wedding expenses resonates with the notion of dowry. With the average US wedding costing many thousands of dollars, this can represent a significant financial burden.

Plural Marriage

Plural marriage, or **polygamy**, is a form of marriage in which one person is married to two or more persons. The two major types of plural marriage are polygyny and polyandry (see fig. 8.6). **Polygyny** (puh-'lij-uh-nee) is the marriage of one man to two or more wives. **Polyandry** is the marriage of one woman to two or more husbands. Marriage exchange is one of the reasons that plural marriage often represents wealth or brings prestige. If marriage requires bridewealth, only men of considerable means can afford more than one marriage. Additional wives and children provide more labor, however, which should allow the man to regain what had been given in brideprice. Polygyny is the most common form of plural marriage. It allows a man to develop alliances with multiple families through his wives and affinal relatives. King Solomon's three hundred wives, recorded in Scripture, were entirely about the alliances such marriages created. It is possible that an important ruler like Solomon wouldn't even know all his wives, nor would they necessarily be grown women. Some neighboring rulers may have married their young (even infant) daughters to a powerful king such as Solomon simply to be able to claim him as a relative. This extreme form of polygyny emphasizes the economic and political benefits of marriage. Most polygynous marriages in the world are between a man and two or three wives, and each relationship carries a degree of intimacy and companionship.

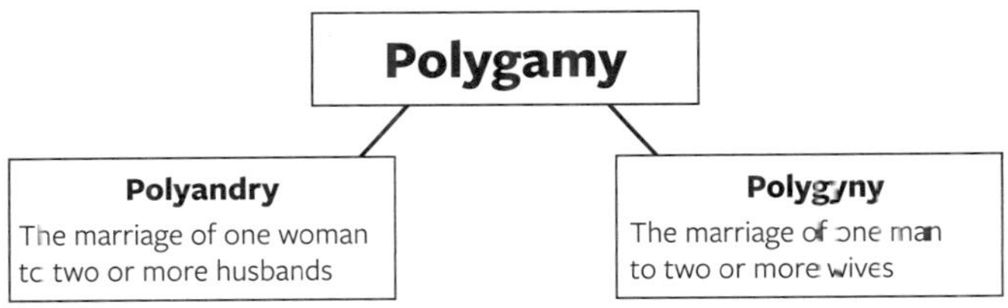

Figure 8.6. Types of polygamy

The other form of plural marriage, polyandry, involves one wife with multiple husbands and is relatively rare. The most well-known manifestation of the system occurs in the high Himalayas of Tibet and Nepal. Here several men, usually brothers, share one wife. Frequently, the oldest brother will marry, and his younger brothers will live with him and his wife. When those younger brothers are old enough, they will marry the wife. One theory as to why this form of marriage is adapted focuses on the need to keep the small amount of arable land within families. It also may be adapted to keep population density low. Men travel extensively in their subsistence work as well. Husbands essentially rotate through the home, some being home and some traveling at any given time.

Family in the Bible

When it comes to kinship, the stakes are high. Societies must have functional marriages and families to survive. Kinship patterns are a fundamental part of enculturation. People are socialized to believe that their ways of marrying, raising children, charting ancestry, and relating with kin are good. This easily becomes ethnocentrism, believing that one's own culture is superior, the norm against which all other ways of life are measured. Judgments about family are some of the most common stereotypes and insults that people turn to when encountering cultural differences. "*They* don't raise their children well." "*Their* marriages aren't as stable as ours." "*They* don't care for their elderly." For Christians, it can be tempting to use religion to bolster ethnocentrism. It is all too easy to assume that God's sense of good and normal is the same as ours.

Christians in the United States may think that a bilateral kinship structure emphasizing the nuclear family represents God's intent for all families everywhere. While it is true that the Genesis account declares monogamy as God's creational intent for marriage, it would be a stretch to suggest that God prefers **neolocal residence** (the practice of a newly married couple living separate from both partners' parents), or that the nuclear family pattern common in contemporary industrial societies is more biblical than unilineal family compounds of extended family living together.

Using Scripture to promote one specific kinship system is difficult. Patrilineality and even patriarchy is dominant among the societies represented in Scripture, and polygyny is common. Scripture never explicitly condemns polygyny, and God is even compared to a polygynous man with Jerusalem and Samaria as his two wives (Ezek. 23). Paul writes that male leaders in the church should be the "husband of one wife," but he does not explicitly extend this to all Christians (Titus 1:6 CSB; see also 1 Cor. 7:1–7). Biblical texts refer to kinship forms and practices familiar to their original audiences, using stories and metaphors of brideservice, cousin marriage, polygyny, and patrilineality. Drawing applications from these contexts for another time and place is a complex cross-cultural task.

Family forms are adaptive. People innovate marriage practices, child-rearing strategies, and household arrangements that suit their geography, political conditions, and social organization. The family forms of God's people shifted as Israel lived as a tribe, then a kingdom, then a diaspora, and then a minority group within an empire. Kinship system seems less important in Scripture than the relationships and behaviors between kin. Paul instructs those in the church to care for their relatives, "especially for their own household" (1 Tim. 5:8). At that time, most households consisted of older members (grandparents, aunts, uncles) and many younger ones (nieces, daughters-in-law), not just the nuclear family.

Scripture emphasizes kinship *behavior* over kinship *rules* or structure. The metaphor of family is used to describe the nation of Israel, and then Jesus's followers in the New Testament era. This illustrates the closeness of bonds within those groups and the mutual responsibility of the members. The relationship of Jesus and the church is compared to a marriage as a model of oneness. God is called "our Father" and compared with earthly fathers and mothers for God's people to understand him as the source of life. The use of "brothers and sisters" in the church conveys the importance of relationships between believers. Scripture conveys important ethical principles but does not dictate specific kinship systems, family roles, or how Christians should think about kinship in society at large. Christians in various times and places disagree about important elements of kinship—for instance, gender roles in marriage or government marriage laws.

A general principle is clear: Scripture teaches mutual concern and sacrificial love as the norm for Christians in marriage and family life. The bonds between Christians should be like family bonds. In the church, we have bonds of commitment that are based not on our own choices and preferences but on God's work and our place within his family. Anthropologists call this **fictive kinship**—that is, kinship relationships that are real but not based on marriage or descent. This is more than a mere illustration. Paul teaches that when we become Christians, we *become* members of a family in a real way (Gal. 6:10; see also Heb. 2:11). Those of us living in Western societies where kinship has diminished in shaping behavior and identity can learn from Christians in places where kinship relations play a powerful, organizing role in daily life.

TERMS

affinal (a-ʹfi-nul) **kin:** Relatives created through marriage.

ambilineal descent: A type of cognatic descent system in which individuals choose a lineage upon adulthood (often marked by marriage).

bilateral descent: A type of cognatic descent system that traces relatedness equally through both the mother's and the father's lines.

brideservice: A duty of the groom to work for the bride's kin for a certain period of time before or after marriage.

bridewealth (also called **brideprice**)**:** An amount of money, possessions, or property given by the groom and his kin to the wife and her kin before, at, or after the wedding.

cognatic (also called **nonunilineal**) **descent:** A system of descent that reckons identity through both maternal and paternal ancestors.

consanguineal (kon-sang-ʹgwin-ee-uhl) **kin:** Relatives related by birth.

cross-cousin marriage: A preference for marriage between cross-cousins. A cross-cousin is the child of one's mother's brother or father's sister.

descent: A social rule that assigns identity to a person on the basis of her or his ancestry.

dowry: The practice of a bride's family providing resources, wealth, or gifts to the groom and his family.

dual descent: A form of unilineal descent in which descent is traced through both the mother's and the father's lines. The person belongs to two separate families.

fictive kinship: Kinship relationships that are real but not based on marriage or descent.

incest taboo: Prohibition against marriage or sex between two categories of related persons.

kinship: The ways in which people selectively interpret the common human experiences of reproduction and nurturance.

marriage: A publicly recognized social or legal union that creates a socially sanctioned context for sexual intimacy, establishes (in whole or in part) the parentage of children, and creates kinship.

marriage exchange: The practice of exchanging material resources between families before, at, or after a wedding.

matriarchy: Social rule by women.

matrilineal descent: A form of unilineal descent in which descent is traced through the female line.

neolocal residence: The practice of a newly married couple living separately from both partners' parents.

parallel-cousin marriage: A preference for marriage between parallel-cousins. A parallel-cousin is the child of one's parent's same-sex sibling (mother's sister's child or father's brother's child).

patriarchy: Social rule by men.

patrilineal descent: A form of unilineal descent in which descent is traced through the male line.

plural marriage (also called **polygamy**)**:** A form of marriage in which one person is married to two or more persons.

polyandry: The marriage of one woman to two or more husbands.

polygyny (puh-ˈlij-uh-nee)**:** The marriage of one man to two or more wives.

segment: A faction within a lineage.

teknonymy (tek-ˈnon-u-mē)**:** The practice of referring to adults with children as the mother/father of the child in place of the parent's given name.

unilineal descent: A descent system that traces relatedness exclusively or predominantly through one parent.

uxorilocal (uhk-sohr-uh-ˈlo-cal) **residence:** The practice of a newly married couple living with or near the bride's family.

DISCUSSION QUESTIONS

1. Why is kinship a cultural universal? What social and personal needs are met through kinship?
2. How has marriage in your society changed in your lifetime or in the lifetime of your parents? How might an anthropologist study these changes?
3. Review the "Family in the Bible" section. What are some guiding principles for how Christians today can apply scriptural insights to their societies? What are some guidelines for taking cultural difference (between biblical cultures and a contemporary society) into consideration?

ANTHROPOLOGY AND SCRIPTURE

Adoption into God's Family

> Blessed be the God and Father of our Lord Jesus Christ, who has blessed us in Christ with every spiritual blessing in the heavenly places, just as he chose us in Christ before the foundation of the world to be holy and blameless before him in love. He destined us for adoption as his children through Jesus Christ, according to the good pleasure of his will, to the praise of his glorious grace that he freely bestowed on us in the Beloved. (Eph. 1:3–6 NRSVue)

Paul begins his letter to the Ephesians with a family metaphor. He says that God is our Father who chose to adopt us as children in God's family. Ephesians 1 goes on to describe how adopted children now qualify for inheritance: the inheritance of redemption. The original recipients of this letter would have appreciated the significance of adoption into a powerful man's family. God the Father is willing to fully accept newcomers, not just as charity cases or outsiders but as full family members who will become heirs to the Father's wealth (in this case, spiritual wealth). The implications for life in the church are immense: Believers should treat one another as siblings, with all the rights, obligations, respect, and concern that they show their consanguineal siblings. And they should establish their own identities in terms of their patriline that stems from God the Father.

How does the idea of adoption into God's family affect our relationship with God? With other members of the church? How should it?

The Patrilineal Descent of Jesus

> An account of the genealogy of Jesus the Messiah, the son of David, the son of Abraham.
>
> Abraham was the father of Isaac, and Isaac the father of Jacob, and Jacob the father of Judah and his brothers, and Judah the father of Perez and Zerah by Tamar, and Perez the father of Hezron, and Hezron the father of Aram, and Aram the father of Aminadab, and Aminadab the father of Nahshon, and Nahshon the father of Salmon, and Salmon the father of Boaz by Rahab, and Boaz the father of Obed by Ruth, and Obed the father of Jesse, and Jesse the father of King David. (Matt. 1:1–6 NRSVue)

When an American Christian hears the beginning of the book of Matthew, the likely response is a yawn. We'd rather skip to the exciting part later in the chapter, when Jesus is born. Jews and Jewish Christians in Matthew's original context, however, would sit up on the edge of their seats when they heard the beginning of a genealogy and say, "Tell us more!" This passage goes on for seventeen verses, detailing the genealogy of Jesus from his father Joseph back through King David to Abraham.

Understanding genealogy and its powerful message requires an understanding of patrilineal descent. For Jews at that time, identity was reckoned through patrilineal descent, so establishing Jesus's identity as the fulfillment of the promise to Abraham required a linkage of Jesus to Abraham. The genealogy meets these cultural expectations, but it complicates them as well. The genealogy includes several women, asserting their importance in the history that leads up to Jesus even though their inclusion wouldn't be strictly necessary in a patrilineal genealogy. And though Jesus is linked to Abraham through Joseph, he wasn't born of Joseph's seed. Jesus is the one promised through this lineage, but he cannot be said to belong to the lineage alone. His true paternal ancestor is God the Father, which extends the promise of inheritance to all people.

In US society, in which people use cognatic descent to establish identity, people are interested in both Jesus's mother and Jesus's father. We can appreciate the importance of the promise extending through Abraham and David, but a genealogy of many, many generations of male ancestors is not the way we begin an exciting story. Reading the genealogy of Matthew 1 with an understanding of the kinship structures of Jews and Jewish Christians in the original context illuminates the incarnation: God becoming fully human, coming from a human woman but a spiritual father, coming to live in culture, be part of a family, and fulfilling a promise to become the ancestor from which the whole world can inherit eternal life.

9

RELIGION AND RITUAL

After studying this chapter, you should be able to do the following:

1. understand how anthropologists study religion
2. define religion, ritual, and myth
3. analyze religion as a cultural system
4. explain the relevance of anthropological study of religion for Christian life

CHAPTER OUTLINE

Introduction

The word "religion" appears only a few times in the Bible. In most English translations of Scripture this word appears in Acts 25:19, 26:5, and James 1:26–27. The most well-known use of this word is in James 1:27, where we read, "Religion that is pure and undefiled before God the Father is this: to care for orphans and widows in their distress and to keep oneself unstained by the world" (NRSVue). Here the Greek word translated as "religion" refers to practices of faith, or motivations to worship, what some translators render as "piety" or even just "faith." Biblical scholars and anthropologists agree that the modern understanding of religion, a realm of life distinct from other areas of life, did not exist in the ancient world. Practices of faith were so integrated into daily life that it did not make sense to talk about "religion" as a distinct sphere of life.

Religion is an important area of interest for anthropologists. When anthropologists began to systematically study cultures around the world, they saw many different ways that people imagine the immaterial world of ancestors, ghosts, gods, and other spirits. People everywhere had explanations of a world beyond what could be seen or felt in everyday life, almost always bound up with morality, family, economy, and authority. Practices for connecting with this world (such as prayer, worship, and sacrifice) were found in every society anthropologists encountered.

Some Christians find the study of religion to be uncomfortable because they are used to approaching religion only in terms of truth rather than as a social or cultural phenomenon. But learning to see Christianity in anthropological terms can help us to understand how faithfulness is *always* bound up in culture and the social context. Noticing how Christian practices vary across cultures does not mean we cannot still talk about truth. Instead, this variation shows us that Christianity, like all religions, is always part of a specific cultural context. No one is a generic Christian; rather, each of us is a specific Christian. Learning to see how beliefs and practices influence one another teaches us even more about what it is to be human and made in God's image.

In this chapter, we first describe the value of an anthropological perspective on religion. We then present some of the social functions of religion and how religion has been studied by different anthropologists. From there we explore ritual and how it intersects with religion. Finally, we offer some concluding thoughts on how the anthropological approach to religion can be helpful for the global church.

Studying Religion

Defining religion is challenging. Many definitions refer to the so-called supernatural or spirit world, calling religion something like "a worldview in which people personify cosmic forces and devise ways to deal with them in ways that resemble the way they deal with powerful people in their society."[1] But this approach already presumes religion is something inside a person's head in the form of beliefs that help people to make sense of "unexplainable" things. First, this kind of approach neglects significant systems, beliefs, and behaviors that seem like they ought to be included in the category "religion" but have nothing to do with spirits at all. For example, the teachings of the Buddha center on the belief of *anatma* (non-being). To achieve enlightenment is to realize that nothing exists—not humans, not spirits, not a god or gods—and one's goal is to join the universe in nothingness. Buddhism would not be considered a religion in a definition focused on the relation of humans

1. Robert Lavenda and Emily Schultz, *Core Concepts in Anthropology*, 8th ed. (Oxford University Press, 2025), 76.

to supernatural beings.[2] **Atheism** provides another example. Many people see atheists as practicing their own religion of *non*belief. For instance, Richard Dawkins, an outspoken atheist who has written fiery polemics against religious belief generally and Christianity in particular, has strong "faith" in his beliefs about the absence of a supreme being.[3]

Additionally, some anthropologists studying the Indigenous religious traditions of bands and tribes have argued that to say these cultures "believe in spirits" is to impose a Western conceptual framework on an irreducibly different understanding of the world. Thus, many anthropologists posit that a good definition of religion needs to encompass Buddhism, atheism, and the wide variety of local Indigenous religions, and also monotheistic religions like Christianity, Judaism, and Islam.

In an essay titled "Religion as a Cultural System," Clifford Geertz proposed a definition that encompasses many different religious systems and a variety of perspectives in studying them. He defines **religion** as follows:

> *A system of symbols which acts to establish powerful, pervasive and long-lasting moods and motivations in men [and women] by formulating conceptions of a general order of existence and clothing these conceptions with such an aura of factuality that the moods and motivations seem uniquely realistic.*[4]

Divine beings can't be observed, and anthropologists can't do fieldwork in the supernatural realm; therefore, Geertz's definition directs the fieldworker's gaze to the social dimensions of religious practices, which connect with commitments and understandings about the nature of the universe. Geertz's definition also treats religion as a major part of culture, not just a by-product of material or political life.

The benefits of this approach are twofold. First, this delineation is broadly inclusive even of traditions such as Buddhism and atheism because it is based on any conception of how the world is thought to be organized, not about spiritual beings per se. Second, it highlights the cultural dimensions of religion, the "conception of a general order of existence," and how that is reflected in the "system of symbols" of a particular religious context.

What Geertz's definition does not describe as clearly, however, are some of the social dynamics of religion and the ways religion intersects with

2. Many people who identify as Buddhist do consider ancestors and other spirits to be real agents in the world, but these ideas are at odds with the teachings of the Buddha. See Walpola Rahula, *What the Buddha Taught* (1959; repr., Grove Press, 1974).

3. Richard Dawkins, *The God Delusion* (Transworld, 2016).

4. Clifford Geertz, *The Interpretation of Cultures* (Basic Books, 1973), 90.

institutions, hierarchies, power, and social norms. Talal Asad (1932–), a Saudi-born British-Pakistani anthropologist who did his first fieldwork among Muslim groups in North Africa, argued that for Islam and other religions, Geertz's definition obscured more than it revealed. With a focus on how individuals experience the symbolic world as well as the conceptions and personal practices that give rise to these experiences, Asad argued that Geertz's definition was a reflection of Christian (and specifically Protestant) understandings of spirituality and faith. For Muslims, Asad argued, the practices and social relationships of their religion (including interconnections with politics and economics) were more important than symbols, moods, and motivations.

Together, however, both approaches underscore how people personally experience and socially express their religious lives. Texts, doctrines, institutions, and official rituals are important, but anthropologists are also interested in how all parts of religion intersect with the stuff of everyday life.

Including the Christian faith in a general definition that encompasses all religions may make it seem that belief in Jesus Christ is no different from belief in Allah, Shiva, or the ancestors. Shouldn't we keep Christianity separate, since we believe it is true? Geertz and Asad help us see that the anthropologist can learn a great deal about how people live their faith without having to judge if a religion is true or not. For example, in Geertz's definition, using phrases such as "*seem* uniquely realistic" and "system of symbols" makes religion accessible for anthropological study. A researcher may study participants' perceptions and beliefs, the symbols used in a religion, and how various religions are like and unlike one another. Similarly, for Asad, instead of asking what people "believe," the anthropologist asks what they do in the name of their religion. How are people acting in light of specific religious identities, commitments, or communities? How is power exercised in these religious contexts? What can the anthropologist observe about the ways social life is shaped by religious claims and contexts? The question of whether one religion is true is an extremely important one, but it is not one that can be answered through ethnographic fieldwork.

Christians can subject our religion to anthropological scrutiny without compromising the strength of our belief that Christianity is true. Adopting cultural relativism as a perspective does not imply that all religions are equally true (or untrue); rather, this approach highlights the ways in which each religion makes sense within its own context (for more on cultural relativism see chap. 2). In a sense, it is an application of the second greatest commandment, treating other religions with the understanding and respect that we would want our own to be treated.

Using anthropology to study our own religion as a human system can have positive effects on our understanding of God and ourselves. First, we

The Anthropology of Christianity

Anthropologist Joel Robbins conducted fieldwork in Papua New Guinea among the Urapmin, a group that converted entirely to charismatic Christianity in the 1970s, despite never having been directly missionized by Westerners. Christianity brought drastic and rapid changes in social life, such as changes in gender relations. Robbins questioned how religion can provide both social stability and social change, and how culture, in general, provides stability to social life and also provides impetus for radical and revolutionary change.

In the course of this study, Robbins noticed a lack of attention to Christianity within the anthropology of religion. Specifically, he noticed that anthropologists often avoided talking about Christianity, even when many of the people in their field sites had converted! Then, when anthropologists did study Christianity, they often saw it as a reflection of something else, such as colonialism or economic change, and did not study it as a legitimate cultural expression outside the West. Robbins argued that people around the world took Christianity seriously, so anthropologists should too.

Drawing together the work that had already been done, and inspiring many other anthropologists to do such research, Robbins and others built up the anthropology of Christianity as a respected subfield in the discipline. Some of those working in this area identify as Christians themselves, and some do not, but what all these scholars have in common is a commitment to examine Christians and their Christianity with the same seriousness, rigor, and respect shown to practitioners of every other sort of religious tradition.[a]

It's your turn: If you were an anthropologist of religion, which religion would you want to study? List three questions that could be explored with ethnographic fieldwork.

a. Joel Robbins, *Becoming Sinners: Christianity and Moral Torment in a Papua New Guinea Society* (University of California Press, 2004); Joel Robbins, "The Anthropology of Christianity: Unity, Diversity, New Directions," *Current Anthropology* 55, no. S10 (December 1, 2014): S157–71.

can learn to see that our symbols work in similar ways to other people's symbols. Human beings everywhere, made in the image of God, use material and linguistic symbols to understand the world.

Second, the study of religion can help us perceive and critique the interaction of religious symbols with other parts of social and cultural life. Some religious practices (types of music, ways of dressing, eating, or speaking) are deeply meaningful in one community or context and meaningless or even offensive in others. Close observation of worship styles can help identify how culture and religion influence each other. For example, sociologist Kersten Priest and her husband, anthropologist Robert Priest, studied a church merger of two congregations in South Carolina, one majority White and the other majority Black.[5] Theologically, these congregations agreed on all areas of Christian doctrine. However, in

5. Kersten Bayt Priest and Robert J. Priest, "Divergent Worship Practices in the Sunday Morning Hour: An Analysis of an 'Interracial' Church Merger Attempt," in *This Side of Heaven:*

bringing their congregations together, many people in the Black congregation found themselves left out of leadership positions, which tended to go to those with seminary education, who were mostly White. Although Black music was included in many worship services, some White members would make jokes about it sounding "country" or would offer warnings to avoid "performance." For the Black Christians, these remarks came across as a criticism of their community and culture. In the end, when the congregations voted whether to make the merger permanent, the majority of the White congregation voted yes, while most of the Black congregation voted no. An anthropological perspective revealed that what ultimately drove these groups apart was not difference in theology or belief but difference in practices and symbols across these two communities and how each group felt respected (or disrespected) by the other.

This example shows how an anthropological perspective can help Christians see how symbols and practices change over time and across cultures. A form of religious dance that may be considered Spirit-filled in one place may be seen as immodest in another. In US churches that are intergenerational, older people may interpret loud, fast music using drums and guitars as "worldly" and inappropriate for worship, while younger people may view organ music or hymns as irrelevant traditions embraced by those who do not care about evangelism among contemporary non-Christians. Analysis of cultural change and an understanding of how religious symbols are related to the broader culture can bring better understandings of various perspectives within the church.

Finally, the anthropological view will help us understand how all religions reflect a common humanity. Scripture teaches that people everywhere once sought God, although because of sin they often employed means that drew them away from God (Rom. 1). At the same time, the apostle Paul demonstrated that non-Christian religions serve as guideposts for people everywhere to come to an understanding of God (Acts 17). We need not categorically reject anthropological understandings of religion because they do not speak to the question of truth. Instead, we can use these humanistic views to help us better understand our created nature and ways in which our and others' cultures both enhance and inhibit our understandings of God.

Magic, Witchcraft, and Sorcery

Magic, witchcraft, and sorcery are related to religion but, within anthropology, are distinct categories. In practice, all three categories often overlap with

Race, Ethnicity, and the Christian Faith, ed. Robert J. Priest and Alvaro L. Nieves (Oxford University Press, 2007), 275–93.

religion and with each other. In many circumstances, terms such as "witch," "witch doctor," or "magic" are used to denigrate someone else's religion as irrational superstition. Some anthropologists avoid these terms to prevent such prejudice, but the concepts to which these terms refer remain important in anthropological research.

Magic refers to ritual practices that are thought to have specific effects through the activation of unseen power. For example, a person who understands magic as operative in the world (that is, a person who has a *magic ontology*) may see various phenomena in the world—sickness, misfortune, healing, even emotions such as love or attraction—as evidence that someone in the community is using magic. A specific phrase uttered at the right time by the right person may be thought to ensure healing, or a set of gestures performed correctly may be done to guarantee success in a risky endeavor. Magic is like religion in that it addresses human insecurities and fears, and it involves the invisible realm of life. Magic is often an element of religion, even though it is typically unrecognized as such. Religious people sometimes believe, for instance, that praying with specific words, or at a certain time, or with a certain posture, will increase the odds of securing the outcome they desire. Using ritual to manipulate a certain outcome is magic, even when it is practiced by religious people. Magic is unlike religion in that it is limited to specific events and outcomes; it typically doesn't involve a full lifestyle of devotion, and it has a much smaller corporate component.

Witchcraft is mystical evil done by a person without their awareness. Unlike magic, which is the conscious manipulation of spiritual/cosmic power, witchcraft is often attributed to a person who is said to possess a witchcraft "essence" that can be triggered without effort or knowledge by the affected person. For many people in North America, the English word "witch" suggests an old woman of fairy tales who lives alone and works her black magic for nefarious purposes. But anthropologists draw their understanding of witches and witchcraft from a common and widespread understanding among many societies in the world that there are people, often through no fault of their own, who *activate* malicious forces or power to the detriment of others. These witches are often socially vulnerable people of either gender, such as old people without relatives, people who live alone, or even children.

Christian anthropologist Robert Priest, along with Congolese church leader Abel Ngolo and missionary/theologian Timothy Stabell, used ethnographic fieldwork to study the explosion of witchcraft accusations aimed at children in the city of Kinshasa, the capital of the Democratic Republic of Congo and the third largest city in Africa. They found these accusations often came from stepparents or other adult caretakers in a household undergoing financial, emotional, or social stress. Among many Congolese people, witchcraft was a familiar explanation for misfortune, and stepchildren were often vulnerable targets for witchcraft accusations. In the past, traditional religious leaders would help make determinations as to the validity of such suspicions. In the

Sect, Cult, or Something Else?

Scholars classify religious movements in various ways. "New religious movements," "Indigenous" or "nativist" movements, and "millennialist" or "apocalyptic" movements are some ways scholars of religion categorize various religious movements. Two of the most common terms students have heard are "cult" and "sect." How do anthropologists differentiate between these concepts?

The word "**cult**" often brings some deeply disturbing images to mind. Film versions of cults usually show people who are brainwashed, perhaps violent, and under the complete control of a cult leader. In real life, there have been some profoundly disturbing religious movements, such as the Jonestown colony in Guyana led by a former preacher named Jim Jones. He led over a thousand people to a compound in South America where more than nine hundred ended up dying in a mass, self-inflicted poisoning. But such examples are at the extreme edge. How do scholars distinguish a cult from other religious groups?

The word "cult" used to mean any distinct religious community. The early followers of Jesus are often called the "Jesus cult" in older scholarship just because it was a distinct religious group. Anthropologists still occasionally use the term "cult" this way—to mean a specific group defined by religious beliefs and practices.

The term "cult" has taken on such negative connotations in many English contexts, however, that it is commonly used more in psychology to refer to the extreme and negative influence of a leader over a follower or followers. Anthropologists tend to avoid the term because making such a clinical diagnosis about whether the influence of a leader is negative or extreme is very difficult to do in cross-cultural contexts without deep personal and highly contextual psychological training. In other words, there is no clear definition of what a cult is across disciplines such as sociology, anthropology, psychology, and religious studies.

The term "**sect**" is still widely used to refer to (typically small) religious communities that have separated from larger groups or traditions. For example, the Amish in North America have orthodox theology by most measures, but they distinguish themselves through their distinctive clothing, avoidance of technology, and community orientation. They are often called a "Christian sect." The many different kinds of Baptists can be thought of as sects due to their separation from broader Baptist coalitions over disputed practices or theologies that they did not want to compromise.

In the end, calling a religious group a cult versus a church or religious community, or even a sect versus a religion, is more of a judgment than a simple fact. Anthropologists are more interested in the ethnographic details than in the label.

It's your turn: What are your associations with the word "cult"? Have you known a group that seemed cult-like to you in some way? What were the features you noticed?

highly Christian city of Kinshasa, pastors were often asked to fill this role, typically with no theological or seminary training on this issue to support them. As a result, these pastors would turn to traditional Congolese understandings, unbiblical or syncretic forms of prophecy, and lay leaders who often lacked accountability. Priest, Ngolo, and Stabell used anthropological techniques and concepts to help Congolese pastors find a more compassionate and biblically based approach to witchcraft accusations.[6]

In contrast, **sorcery** is mystical evil done by a person who *intended* for it to happen. A sorcerer has access to spiritual power and can activate the power to harm others. In the Western mind, the *sorcerer* is more like the witch, a person who uses mystical/magical power for evil. Like witchcraft accusations, allegations of sorcery are often directed at those who are socially marginal and may be used as a way to prevent people from engaging in behaviors that are considered socially inappropriate. Witchcraft and sorcery are linked to religion because they help address otherwise unexplainable human suffering, and they provide an account of how the supernatural and natural worlds intersect. They are unlike religion, however, in that they involve less extensive ritual, less complex theologies, and few (if any) corporate practices or institutional supports.

Today, groups such as Wiccans and other neo-pagans identify themselves as "witches" and incorporate extensive ritual, theology, and corporate practices. These are new and different forms of witchcraft that anthropologists may study as a phenomenon separate from the labeling of an individual as a witch as an explanation for misfortune.[7]

Early Anthropological Approaches to Religion

Religion was an important area of interest for early anthropologists, many of whom hadn't traveled to the cultures they studied and instead relied on reports from colonial travelers and missionaries. Using the unilinear evolutionary approach popular in his time (see chap. 2), Edward Burnett Tylor (1832–1917) saw change in religious systems as providing a prototype for cultural change generally.[8] He believed that the earliest or most "primitive" form of religion was animism. **Animism**, from the Latin word for "soul" or "life," is the idea that souls or spirits exist not only in humans but also in plants, animals,

6. Robert J. Priest, Abel Ngolo, and Timothy Stabell, "Christian Pastors and Alleged Child Witches in Kinshasa, DRC," *On Knowing Humanity Journal* 4, no. 1 (January 30, 2020).

7. See, for example, Tanya Luhrmann, *Persuasions of the Witch's Craft: Ritual Magic in Contemporary England* (Harvard University Press, 1989).

8. Paul-François Tremlett, Graham Harvey, and Liam T. Sutherland, eds., *Edward Burnett Tylor, Religion and Culture* (Bloomsbury Academic, 2017).

elements of nature, or even all of creation. In this view, the world is seen as "animated" by spirits that reside in everyday objects. George Lucas's *Star Wars* films portray animism through the idea of the Force: an impersonal power with a light side and a dark side that some gifted people can learn to control, understand, or use in various circumstances. Animistic cultures still exist today but are more often referred to as "Indigenous religions" or by the practitioners' own name for their religion.

A well-known example of animism comes from the South Pacific, where a number of groups (Tongans, Samoans, and others) traditionally believe in ***mana***, a spiritual force that imbues all living things. This force can be disturbed (to negative consequences) if people do things they should not do. Thus, the community enforces *tapu*, prohibitions against those things that disturb the *mana*. The English word "taboo" comes from *tapu*. A **taboo** is a behavior, artifact, or symbol that must be avoided in order to evade harm. Around the world today, many people continue to believe in taboos based on this idea that strong negative emotion or behavior will cause an animistic force to be activated or disturbed.

Like magic, taboo can be part of Christian religious practice. In my (Jenell's) upbringing, for example, I was warned against allowing a Bible to touch the ground. The belief was that the Bible carried a special spiritual essence, and it would be harmful to disrespect that essence by allowing the sacred religious object to touch the ground. Likewise, in my (Brian's) United Methodist church, I was taught that only ordained clergy were allowed to distribute the elements of Communion. The history and theology of this teaching are complex—and it would not be correct to say this is animism—but the logic worked in a similar way. For many members of my church, keeping the Lord's Table pure meant observing a taboo against nonclergy distributing the elements.

In keeping with the theory of unilinear cultural evolution, Tylor believed all cultures progress through a common trajectory. In his view, animism would eventually be replaced by **polytheism**, belief in many gods and goddesses. Polytheistic religions would eventually give way to **monotheism**, belief in one god, as found in Islam, Judaism, and Christianity. In Tylor's view, however, this was not the highest stage of religious evolution. Monotheism, he argued, would be supplanted by science (which Tylor equated with atheism), in which people held purely naturalistic explanations of the world.

James Frazer developed this evolutionary thinking further with his theory of magic, religion, and science as three successive stages of human intellectual development.[9] Frazer distinguished two types of magic: homeopathic magic,

9. James George Frazer, *The Golden Bough* (1890; repr., Oxford University Press, 2009).

based on the principle that "like produces like"; and contagious magic, based on the idea that things once in contact remain connected. He saw magical rituals as failed attempts at controlling the natural world that would eventually give way to religious explanations and finally to scientific understanding.

Today, anthropologists see monotheism—along with various forms of polytheism and animism—thriving in the age of science. Many scientists throughout the world are people of faith whose order and structure in the universe as reflecting God's design. Moreover, religious beliefs and practices continue to help people make sense of the world and give moral structure to our lives. The work of early anthropologists is useful insofar as it documents religious practices and beliefs that have disappeared or changed, but the theory of unilinear cultural evolution is both empirically incorrect and ethnocentric. It assumes all cultures of the world will follow a single path of progress that leads toward the philosophy and lifestyle of the European scientists who authored the theory.

Ritual

A **ritual** is any patterned, repeated, predictable action. Rituals may be religious or secular. Religious rituals include everything from folding hands and closing eyes during prayer to the complex rituals of animal sacrifice described in Exodus 29:10–14. Familiar secular rituals include a high-school graduation ceremony, a family dinner, or singing the national anthem before a sporting event. Even small interactions can be rituals. Consider how two friends typically greet each other in the United States:

"Hey, how's it going?"

"Good. What's up?"

"Not much. What's up with you?"

These are phrased as questions, but this exchange is not primarily meant to elicit information. This is a ritualized greeting through which two people communicate a connection: "I know you. You are a friend and/or acquaintance. Let's acknowledge our relationship." The ritual form allows both people to move through the interaction quickly, communicating their desire to maintain a relationship even if the exchange goes no further. In other contexts, the greeting ritual may include questions about someone's family, how well they slept or ate, or where they are going or coming from.

For some US Christians, particularly nonliturgical Protestants, the word "ritual" may be somewhat negative and associated with an adjective like "empty" or "rote." As part of a tradition that protested the institutionalization of religion, Protestants—evangelicals in particular—have historically been opposed to elevating mere form over deeper concerns of sincerity, authenticity, and a personal relationship with God. But even a nonliturgical worship service is a ritual. Members of nonliturgical churches anticipate particular elements (songs, prayers, announcements, and more), a given length of service, and a familiar style of sermon and music. People notice when these elements are changed because it disrupts the ritualized form with which they are familiar. Rituals, whether secular or religious, are performed to emphasize some fact, desire, or belief; to transform or influence the feelings or beliefs of those

Randall Collins's Theory of Ritual Chains

Every morning, Mike, Eliza, and Jin meet at the park to exercise together. They always start with a slow jog around the tennis courts, and then they take turns leading various workouts. When they're done, they go to the local coffee shop and hang out for fifteen minutes or so before going home to shower and head to work. They call themselves the "Workout Mafia" and send each other funny exercise memes or videos with health tips throughout the week.

This kind of casual ritual forms what Randall Collins calls a "ritual interaction chain."[a] Collins's theory is a sophisticated attempt to understand how human social life is constructed through the accumulation of face-to-face encounters that generate emotional energy. Rituals create the bonds that hold society together.

An interaction ritual must have certain elements: the bodily copresence of participants, barriers that separate insiders from outsiders, a mutual focus of attention on an object or activity, and a shared mood or emotional state. When these elements align successfully, they produce "collective effervescence," a term borrowed from Émile Durkheim.[b]

Collective effervescence feels good. People experience group solidarity and belonging. They feel positive emotional energy, confidence, and enthusiasm. This motivates future action. The ritual also creates and reinforces group symbols, such as the group nickname and sharing between Mike, Eliza, and Jin. Ritual also cultivates moral standards shared and enforced by the group.

The "ritual interaction chains" theory ultimately provides a bridge between microanalysis of face-to-face encounters and macro-understanding of large-scale social structures. Small-group interactions create and sustain broader patterns of social organization that characterize human societies.

It's your turn: Conduct participant observation on rituals in your own life. Identify a ritual, even while you are in the midst of participating in it. This could be a greeting, a meal, a study session, a chapel service, or a class session. What are the elements of the interaction ritual? Which aspects of collective effervescence do you feel? Which do you observe in others?

a. Randall Collins, *Interaction Ritual Chains* (Princeton University Press, 2005).

b. Émile Durkheim, *The Elementary Forms of Religious Life*, trans. Carol Cosman (1912; repr., Free Press, 1995), 22.

participating; or to give meaning to social relationships. Some scholars see ritual as the most basic building block of social life.

Theories of Ritual

Why do people everywhere find it meaningful to participate in repetitive or predictable group behavior? The first anthropological theories of ritual were those of the unilinear evolutionists like Tylor and Frazer. They believed all rituals, including Christian worship, were related to an absence of scientific understanding. People turn to magical and religious explanations because they haven't yet learned scientific explanations. Once they do, science will become dominant, and religion will fade away.

Early in the twentieth century, Émile Durkheim (see chap. 11) offered a different view. His work, *The Elementary Forms of Religious Life*, was based on ethnographic data about Australian Aboriginal religion.[10] He saw that religion isn't primarily about providing explanations; rather, religion helps to create and maintain social solidarity. It's the "glue" of society that holds things together. Durkheim noticed that when Aboriginal groups gathered for ceremonial occasions, they experienced "collective effervescence"—a shared emotional high that reinforced their sense of belonging to the group.[11] Through ritual participation, individuals transcended their ordinary, mundane existence and connected with something larger than themselves.

In rituals, people express distinctions between the sacred and the profane. Sacred objects, words, and ideas are set apart as special, powerful, and deserving of reverence. The profane encompasses ordinary, everyday experience. What makes something sacred? Durkheim argued that it is not an inherent quality but rather collective attention and emotional investment. This insight led Durkheim to a radical conclusion: When people worship sacred objects or beings, they are worshiping society itself. The gods, totems, and sacred symbols seen in rituals are representations of the social group and its values. Ritual doesn't just reflect social bonds; it creates and strengthens them. For Durkheim, whether religious beliefs were "true" in a historical or spiritual sense became irrelevant; what mattered was how ritual practices contributed to social cohesion and moral order.

Alfred Radcliffe-Brown applied Durkheimian thinking to his own ethnographic studies, arguing that rituals function to maintain social structure by expressing and reinforcing social values and relationships. Radcliffe-Brown

10. Émile Durkheim, *The Elementary Forms of Religious Life*, trans. Carol Cosman (1912; repr., Free Press, 1995), 9, 241.
11. Durkheim, *Elementary Forms of Religious Life*, 27.

Ken Durden/Bigstock.com

Batters are often known for practicing elaborate forms of magic, including taboos, rituals, and fetishes.

saw that rituals often emerge around activities that are important for social survival but involve significant risk or uncertainty. For example, agricultural societies develop elaborate planting and harvest rituals because these rituals help communities manage the anxiety associated with dependence on unpredictable natural forces.[12] Similarly, Bronisław Malinowski emphasized the psychological functions of ritual. Based on his fieldwork in the Trobriand Islands, Malinowski argued that rituals help individuals cope with emotional stress and uncertainty. He famously observed that Trobriand fishermen performed magical rituals when they fished in dangerous open waters but not when they fished in safe lagoons.[13]

These functionalist interpretations of ritual are now often considered incomplete, but they still have value (see chap. 11 for a more detailed discussion of fun). Anthropologists studying the rituals of baseball have noted actions

12. Adam Kuper, *The Social Anthropology of Radcliffe-Brown* (Routledge, 2013), especially chaps. 7 and 8.

13. Bronislaw Malinowski, *Coral Gardens and Their Magic: The Language of Magic and Gardening* (1935; repr., Routledge, 2002), 28–59.

performed by baseball players that function in much the same way as those Malinowski identified among Trobriand fishermen.[14] Players in positions who have more control over their success (fielders, catchers) have fewer rituals. Those whose success is dependent on variables outside their control (batters and pitchers) often have numerous rituals (tapping the bat three times or eating pancakes before every game), taboos (not shaving during a good streak or not allowing others to touch their favorite bat), and lucky charms or **fetishes** (items thought to bring good fortune, such as a rabbit's foot). Like the fishermen setting out beyond the safety of the lagoon, these players use ritual to face uncertainty.

In the mid-twentieth century, Claude Lévi-Strauss focused on the symbolic logic underlying ritual practices.[15] He argued that like language (see structural linguistics in chap. 3), ritual operates through systems of symbolic oppositions. Human minds naturally organize experience in terms of binary oppositions—nature versus culture, raw versus cooked, male versus female, sacred versus profane, and more. Rituals are important because they help societies deal with fundamental contradictions in human existence. For example, humans are simultaneously part of nature (as biological beings) and separate from nature (through culture and technology). Death rituals help societies manage this contradiction by transforming the natural fact of biological death into a culturally meaningful transition. Rituals also express the myths that provide the logic of a given society. A **myth** is any story of sacred or social significance. The creation account in Genesis, for example, is a myth that helps people understand male-female relations, the binary of humans and nature, spirit and material, good and evil, and more.

More recently, Victor and Edith Turner described the phases of ritual, adapted from folklorist Arnold van Gennep's work on rites of passage.[16] Rites of passage, or transition rituals, move a person from one state to another. These rituals have three phases: the separation phase, the liminal phase, and the reincorporation phase. The **separation phase** consists of marking a person as distinct from the rest of society or from their normal social role. If you consider a secular rite of passage like a graduation ceremony, the separation

14. George Gmelch, "Baseball Magic," in *Conformity and Conflict: Readings in Cultural Anthropology*, 13th ed., ed. James Spradley and David W. McCurdy (Allyn & Bacon, 2008), 322–32.

15. Levi-Strauss develops these ideas in multiple works, but an introduction to his concepts can be found in Claude Lévi-Strauss, *The Raw and the Cooked: Mythologiques*, vol. 1, trans. John and Doreen Weightman (1964; repr., University of Chicago Press, 1983).

16. The Turners use and develop these concepts in multiple publications. For a summary, see Edith Turner, "Exploring the Work of Victor Turner: Liminality and Its Later Implications," *Suomen Antropologi: Journal of the Finnish Anthropological Society* 33, no. 4 (2008): 26–44.

phase consists of the graduating students withdrawing from friends and family to gather in a specific place, sitting in a separate section, wearing unique clothing. This moves them into the **liminal phase**, where they are graduating, but not yet graduates. The liminal phase has some especially interesting features. During liminality, participants exist "betwixt and between" normal social categories, a state that is often seen as powerful, dangerous, radically free, or all of these. When groups enter liminal states, they may experience *communitas*, feelings of connection and unity that transcend everyday life. The Turners observed that pilgrims, whether traveling to Mecca or Lourdes or Mt. Banahaw, participate in a practice of separating from their "normal life," often wearing simple or uniform clothing, performing collective rituals (such as prayers, walks, or sacrifices), and even being given new or temporary names or social identities. They eventually reenter their daily life, but the liminal phase—in which they transgress social hierarchies such as wealth, education, and race—creates powerful experiences of unity and transcendence that have lasting value.[17] Retreats, like the sort many Christian youth groups go on or work colleagues have for team building, can produce experiences of liminality and *communitas*. People leave their homes to spend time in a special, set-apart place, often allowing themselves to be casual and relaxed in ways not typical to their everyday social relationships. This often leads to feelings of connection that are unlike ones easily felt in daily life. Every ritual must end, however, and the final phase, **reincorporation,** brings the initiate back into normal life. For the graduate, this is the recessional where newly minted graduates rejoin their families for photos, hugs, unzipping their gowns and taking off their hats, to begin reentering normal life, now as graduates. For newly married couples, US American tradition calls for the husband to carry his wife across the threshold of their home, symbolizing their reentry to life as a family unit. These rituals, while symbolic, serve to reorient individuals and the community around them and to create new identities and behaviors. This is why the Turners argued that anthropologists must study more than the symbolic content of rituals; they must also look for what it's like for people to experience rituals. Ritual participation doesn't just express preexisting beliefs but actively forms people's ways of thinking, feeling, and acting.

17. Malcolm X experienced *communitas* during his own hajj in 1964. After years of teaching that Black and White people could not coexist—based on his experience of racism in the United States—Malcolm X (who changed his name to El-Hajj Malik el-Shabazz) wrote that the experience of "oneness" he felt during the hajj changed his views on race, the nature of White people, and possibilities for human unity. See John Andrew Morrow, "Malcolm X: Message to Humanity," in *Malcolm X: From Political Eschatology to Religious Revolutionary,* ed. Dustin Byrd and Seyed Javid Miri (Brill, 2016), 211–24.

Christian Rituals and Symbols

In rituals and in religions, symbols convey meanings, feelings, and associations. A **symbol** is any object, sound, action, or idea to which people assign meaning. Christian symbols include the cross, a crown, a dove, and many more. But symbols are much more pervasive than just those. For instance, in many Protestant churches, the congregation sits in rows facing the front, where the pulpit or podium is centered on a raised dais or stage. But in a Roman Catholic church, the speaker's podium may be to the side,

YOUR TURN

Share a Religious Symbol

Religion is by definition shared, and so are symbols. Sharing is an irreducible part of culture. When it goes poorly, it can cause misunderstanding or even start conflict. When it goes well, it brings people together in worship, fellowship, and joy.

Symbols have all the traits of culture. They are learned, dynamic, shared, power laden, and integrated. Symbols are meaningful, but their meaning is arbitrary. If you'd like to talk with your female parent, for example, you could use the linguistic symbol "mother" (English), "moeder" (Dutch), "mãe" (Portuguese), or "okaasan" (Japanese).

A cross is a well-known symbol of the Christian religion.[a] This symbolism is *learned* when pastors, parents, and teachers talk about the meaning of the cross. It is *dynamic* because different Christian communities prefer the cross to be a certain design or shape, or to portray Jesus on the cross or not. It is *shared* in contexts where Christianity is even casually known, because the cross is understood to represent that religion. It is *power laden* as some may wear a cross to signal their identification with the majority religious group—or as dissent in a context where it is a minority. It is *integrated* when crosses show up in art, fashion, politics, economics and commerce, education, family life, and or any other cultural context.

It's your turn to share a religious symbol.

- Find a word, an image, or an emoji that has what you would consider a religious meaning. What is the symbol? What does it mean?
- After you find a symbol, share it with someone. (Keep in mind that ethical field work involves considering how your actions will affect others. Consider whether this symbol may be threatening, hurtful, or offensive to the person with whom you're sharing it.) How did you share it (in person, virtually, with an object, with a link, as an image)? How does it feel to you to share a religious symbol?
- Ask the person or persons how they received it. What did it mean to them? Was their understanding the same as what you intended? Was their response more emotional or more intellectual?

a. The association of the cross with Jesus's death and resurrection is historical. However, the Romans could (and sometimes did) configure the structures for crucifixion in different shapes. Thus, while the cross is historical, Jesus's death could be associated with any shape the Romans might have chosen, and thus it is arbitrary.

or the priest may have no podium at all, while the altar sits in the center. In the Protestant church, the centrality of the pulpit is a symbol that communicates the theological emphasis on preaching the Word. In liturgical traditions such as Roman Catholicism, Anglicanism, and Lutheranism (the latter two are Protestant), the central altar symbolizes the centrality of the Eucharist in the faith.

Dress, music, architecture, preferred versions of the Bible, and myriad other symbols make up the symbolic system of Christianity. Symbols take on meanings in religious contexts that are linked to related meanings in secular contexts. Consider the issue of what to wear to church. Many US Americans who wear business attire to work every day may feel these are secular clothes. Wearing these clothes to church may make church seem like a continuation of the workweek rather than a special time. Thus, some white-collar workers find themselves drawn to the casual services of contemporary megachurches or informal congregations in which the pastor goes by first name and everyone wears casual clothing. In this way, their church clothes symbolize the way church is a break from the workweek.

In many Black congregations, wearing casual clothes to church is considered disrespectful, if not offensive. Instead, people dress in their finest clothes. This tradition developed among a group of people who, for many

iStockphoto.com/Franky DeMeyer

The arrangement of people, leaders, and other elements are all part of the symbolism of Christianity, and the same is true for other religions.

generations, were largely prevented from entering the ranks of professional work. For those who worked in factories or on farms, putting on the "Sunday best" marked a very different moment from daily life. Pastors earned special honor in the community through titles, such as "reverend" and "bishop," and the use of last names. Older women may be called "mother," and other markers of respect and hierarchy helped to make church a place set apart from everyday life. Symbols are important because they affirm what people understand to be true about the world. As Geertz's definition of religion expresses, a symbolic system evokes moods and motivations that allow for an expression of, and understanding of, a particular conception of a general order of existence.

Rites of Intensification

Rites of intensification are rituals in which elements of society, beliefs, values, or behaviors are made more intense—and thus feel more real—than in normal life. A high-school pep rally (common at secondary schools throughout the United States) is an example of a nonreligious rite of intensification. Symbols of the school are displayed—such as a person dressed as the school mascot dancing around for the crowd—a sports team runs out to the sounds of the fight song blasted by the marching band, and cheerleaders whip the crowd into a frenzy of school spirit with chants and dances. These rituals are meant to make the students feel their school pride, and solidarity within that community, more intensely than they normally do in daily life.

Christian worship may be understood as a rite of intensification as well. This may be an uncomfortable thought as it may seem false or manipulative to acknowledge that we use symbols or movement to create a mood or make something "seem artificially intense." But when Christians select a musical style, choose specific dress, decide between the use of written or extemporaneous prayers, or inspire (or deter) clapping hands or raising arms, we are making culture; we are choosing and shaping symbols to help participants feel close to God, understand God in particular ways, and form ourselves into certain kinds of people.

Throughout Scripture, God's people are given specific actions, objects, and words to use in understanding and worshiping God. The Lord's Prayer and the Last Supper are two examples of Jesus teaching his disciples to practice rituals of intensification. While we do not set aside our beliefs in everyday life, our ability to feel the reality of those beliefs is often influenced by the physical environment (and bodily physical condition) in which we find ourselves. Rituals of intensification help reconnect ordinary life with religious belief.

Rites of Affliction

Rites of affliction are rituals directed at alleviating suffering or resolving a problem. A common Hollywood version of a rite of affliction may involve a mystical-looking person who casts a curse or performs a scripted ritual to make someone fall in love, bring fortune, or restore peace between the living and the dead. In Hollywood films, mysticism is often symbolized with old women or characters stereotyped as primal, such as traditional Africans, folk healers, or Native Americans. In many societies, rituals for the growth and protection of crops, physical healing, or the maintenance of good social relationships are so much a part of life that people do not consider them religion. The rituals would be called "farming," "medicine," or just normal family life. Among the Ifugao of the Philippines, with the planting of rice, local religious tradition would require people to sacrifice a chicken or pig and pour the blood over the *bulol*, a carved wooden statue representing the god of the harvest. The sacrifice and the sharing of meat in the community, as well as dancing and prayer, are rituals that address the risk of crop failure. Traditionally, they are thought to protect the crop from pests, bad weather, or disease. And until recently, these rituals would not be classified as "Ifugao religion," but a normal part of farming.

God's people have always engaged in rites of affliction, using physical objects and ritualized practices to address human problems. Jesus reinterpreted familiar rituals of Jewish life (most notably baptism) to emphasize the reality of God's work in removing sin and reconciling relationships. Other biblical rites of affliction involve the transference of affliction from one place to another (such as the scapegoat of Lev. 16:21), the substitutionary death of one being for another, or sacrificial offerings made as a payment on behalf of the one afflicted. The book of James commands Christians to engage in a rite of affliction, calling the elders to pray over the sick and anoint them with oil (James 5:14).

For Christians, these kinds of rites are not meant to be magical transactions in which objects or sacrifices given to God bring about a desired outcome. Instead, they are meant to focus attention on God and God's power over illness, misfortune, and sin. But when we examine these ritual practices in terms of ritual theory, we can see the ways they work in our social context to focus attention, alleviate anxiety, draw people together, and/or form us into people who look to God for healing and blessing.

Rites of Passage

Rites of passage, or **life-cycle rituals**, transform a person or people from one life stage to another. Rites of passage may involve a person moving from

Katerina Friesen

Many traditional rituals involve music and other art forms. Here missionary anthropologist Delbert Rice is dancing the Ikalahan tayaw dance to the rhythm of traditional gongs and drums.

childhood to adulthood (often called **initiation rituals**), from one family into a new one (often through marriage), or even from life to death or an afterlife. Rites of passage take the person or people through phases in which social status is thought to change. The Turners' theory of liminality is particularly influential among anthropological understandings of rites of passage.

One rite of passage familiar to university students throughout the world is the commencement ceremony. College is often a time of life that is set apart, a time of study and preparation unlike any other phase of life. On graduation day, the graduating students are separated from the other students at the college and from their families. They dress in special clothes and enter the ceremony with special music. In anthropological terms, this is the liminal period because while they have completed the necessary academic requirements, the college official has not yet declared them graduates. When the diplomas have been handed out, students move their tassels from right to left, marking a change in status from student to graduate. At the end of the ceremony, students may remove their distinctive hats and fling them in the air, representing the end of this phase of life. The reincorporation phase begins when the graduates rejoin their families and pose for photos; they may receive gifts and often have a gathering (a party or reception) that symbolically receives the graduate back into normal life. Reintegration continues with life after graduation as former students rejoin society through work, family, and adult life.

Ritual Change

Rituals, as Lévi-Stauss pointed out, are rooted in mythical logic. As the importance of a particular myth changes or wanes, so do ritual forms. In contemporary North American wedding ceremonies, many have changed the traditional vows of a bride—"love, honor, and obey"—into something more in line with their understandings of equality in husband-wife relations (e.g., "love, honor, and cherish").[18] Increasing numbers of people in US society, including Christians, question many elements of traditional marriage ceremonies. Innovation, creativity, and even idiosyncrasy flourish in contemporary US weddings.

Some of the most dramatic examples of ritual change occur when people choose to shift their religious alliances—for example, when people convert to Christianity. Among the Ikalahan of the northern Philippines, most people converted from traditional ancestor religion to Christianity in the 1960s. Many people say they did not stop believing in the old spirits, but once they learned the story (myth) of Jesus and his power over these spirits, they felt free to change their ritual lives. Instead of sacrificing carabao (water buffalo), pigs, and chickens when people were ill, they prayed to God. Instead of calling the *mabaki* (ritual leader) to request the spirits' blessing for a new home or a newly planted field, they called the pastor to pray. They moved their ritual life into the church and away from the *cañao*, or traditional ritual circle. It was not easy to decide how they might perform worship, prayer, weddings, funerals, and so forth, but they understood that rituals should point them toward God in terms that connected with their own culture and history.

In the decades since their first generation of Christian conversions, Ikalahan believers have continued to adapt, modify, and revise their ritual life to meet the needs of new generations of Christians. These first generations of Christians often collaborated with the late Delbert Rice, a North American missionary who lived among the Ikalahan for more than forty years and was trained in cultural anthropology. Rice understood that, though the people had become Christians and believed the Christian stories (myths) as central to their lives, their rituals should not necessarily be the same as those of North Americans, lowland Filipino Christians, or some other group. Today, some rituals of the

18. Contemporary US weddings increasingly, if not overwhelmingly, use unique vows written by the bride and groom, with little reflection on traditional words or patterns. This, too, is part of a changing mythology of marriage that says marriage is, first and foremost, the expression of two unique individuals choosing each other, as opposed to the affirmation of family or the community. Some still practice the tradition of "asking for the hand" of their beloved from a parent, but this is often more a formality than a true request or something where the family could officially forbid the marriage.

Ikalahan church look like what is seen elsewhere in the Philippines or even in the United States (such as their Sunday morning service of singing, prayer, and sermon). Other practices—for example, the *tongtongan*, in which people accused of severe sins or civil crimes are disciplined by the elders and church leaders in a public process of punishment and reconciliation—reflect the unique Ikalahan culture and history. By intentionally considering cultural context as they work out ritual life, often called "contextualization" (see chaps. 1 and 12), Ikalahan Christians consider how their ritual practices reflect their own experience with God.

Christians and the Anthropology of Religion

The first time many Christians meet a committed Muslim college professor or a devoutly Hindu social worker, they may be challenged by finding that someone respected, intelligent, and admirable in their ethics could be so convinced about the truth of something that is radically different from the Christian faith. This may even cause a Christian to ask, "Who am I to tell this person that what she believes is wrong? Why do I believe my religion is correct?"

Anthropology analyzes religion as a cultural system and offers holistic interpretations of how people incorporate religion into their lives. Anthropologists look at empirical data about how people live in the world and then theorize about what it means. This scientific approach doesn't answer the question of whether any specific religious belief is true. Making a religious commitment and living a spiritual life requires faith, devotion, community, and theology.

Anthropological analysis reveals how the image of God, present in every human being, drives people everywhere to seek God. Even while we have radically divergent beliefs about the details of the "really real," common patterns of ritual, myth, and practice across cultures suggest that humans are created to seek after truth and ultimate meaning (as described in Rom. 1). Humans everywhere live in communities bound together by moral orders, tell stories about how life began and what it means, and gather in observance of shared beliefs.

Those who feel called to cross-cultural missions need to understand how symbols, myths, rituals, and other practices of religion work together to help people believe. Communicating meaningfully with others requires an understanding of one's own beliefs and practices. Being able to speak to the deep concerns in someone's life involves an understanding of how the symbols and practices of various faiths seek to answer those questions.

Studying religious diversity *should* unsettle us a bit, as it makes us recognize ways in which our own religious practices reflect historical events, cultural norms, and personal preferences. God is never completely or perfectly represented in any manifestation of human devotion. Therefore, it should not surprise us that Christians have different ways of expressing their religious commitments. Nor should we be afraid of the variety of ways humans have worked out their longing to know the truth. We can explore and understand this human dimension in the many expressions of religious life around the world. Seeing differences and similarities in religions is a testament to the image of God in all of us.

TERMS

animism: The idea that souls or spirits exist not only in humans but also in plants, animals, elements of nature, or even all of creation.

atheism: The belief that no god or supernatural being(s) exists.

cult: A term denoting a socially or psychologically destructive or problematic religious group; typically used more in psychology than anthropology today.

fetish: An item thought to carry spiritual power, such as a rabbit's foot.

initiation ritual: A rite of passage (or life-cycle ritual) that moves a person from childhood to adulthood.

liminal phase: The second phase of a rite of passage, placing the initiate in a space that is "betwixt and between" the old identity and the new identity.

magic: Ritual practices that are believed to have effects on particular situations.

***mana*:** A spiritual force that imbues all living things, a belief that is part of some animistic religions.

monotheism: The belief in one god.

myth: Any story with sacred significance.

polytheism: The belief in many gods and/or goddesses.

reincorporation: The third stage of a rite of passage in which the initiate is welcomed back to the community in their new identity.

religion: A system of symbols that acts to establish powerful, pervasive, and long-lasting moods and motivations in men and women by formulating conceptions of a general order of existence and clothing these conceptions with such an aura of factuality that the moods and motivations seem uniquely realistic (adapted from Clifford Geertz).

rite of affliction: Ritual directed at alleviating suffering or resolving a problem.

rite of intensification: Ritual in which elements of society, belief, values, or behaviors are made more dramatic, intense, or real than in normal life.

rite of passage (or **life-cycle ritual**): Ritual that transforms a person or people from one life stage to another.

ritual: Any patterned, repeated, predictable action.

sect: A religious group that has broken away from, or otherwise originated in, another, typically larger, religious community or tradition.

separation phase: The first phase of a rite of passage, involving symbolically or physically separating those going through the transition from their old identities.

sorcery: Mystical evil done by a person who intended for it to happen.

symbol: An object, sound, action, or idea to which people assign arbitrary meaning; that is, there is no necessary relationship between the symbol and its meaning.

taboo: From the South Pacific concept of *tapu*, any behavior, artifact, or symbol that must be avoided in order to evade harm.

witchcraft: Mystical evil done by a person without her or his awareness.

DISCUSSION QUESTIONS

1. What is distinctive about studying religion from an anthropological point of view? How is the anthropological view different from a theological view or a historical view?
2. How does it feel to subject your own religion to anthropological scrutiny? Does scientific scrutiny demean or disrespect religion, and if so, how? Is scientific scrutiny helpful to religion, and if so, how?
3. Tell a story about a ritual that was or is important in your life. It should be a rite of intensification, a rite of affliction, or a rite of passage. It may be secular or religious. What factors make ritual meaningful for individuals and for communities?

ANTHROPOLOGY AND SCRIPTURE

Lament as a Rite of Affliction

As a deer longs for flowing streams,
so my soul longs for you, O God.
My soul thirsts for God,
for the living God.
When shall I come and behold
the face of God?
My tears have been my food
day and night,
while people say to me continually,
"Where is your God?"

These things I remember,
as I pour out my soul:
how I went with the throng
and led them in procession to the house of God,
with glad shouts and songs of thanksgiving,
a multitude keeping festival.
Why are you cast down, O my soul,
and why are you disquieted within me?
Hope in God, for I shall again praise him,
my help and my God. (Ps. 42:1–6 NRSVue)

The psalmist is despondent and complains to God about his inner state and the response of his community while he is in pain. Like other psalms of lament, Psalm 42 registers a profound complaint with God, makes a request for help, and praises God. When we read Psalm 42 alone or with a group, we are carried through the full cycle of affliction, from agony and distress to restoration and a renewed sense of God's presence. Christians throughout time have used the reading of Psalm 42 as a rite of affliction: a ritualized form of prayer and reflection that assists individuals and communities through times of suffering. Far from being empty or rote, this type of ritual renews faith by reconnecting despondent people with other believers who went before them and with God.

Religious Symbols

For just as the body is one and has many members, and all the members of the body, though many, are one body, so it is with Christ. For in the one Spirit we were all baptized into one body—Jews or Greeks, slaves or free—and we were all made to drink of one Spirit. (1 Cor. 12:12–13 NRSVue)

In 1 Corinthians 12, Paul extensively describes the metaphor of the body of Christ. Just as the body has many parts, each of which is essential, so is each person important in the church. The church is so important, in fact, that it may be likened to Christ's body. Paul uses the human body as a symbol, making it stand for something more than its literal reality.

Religious symbols help believers perceive what is "really real" about the world. The symbol of the body reminds believers that each person has an important role in the church, especially those who may be perceived as worthless or lowly. It provides a reminder that just as we need hands and feet to do our work in the world, Christ relies on his body (the church) to accomplish good works.

10

MEDICAL ANTHROPOLOGY

After studying this chapter, you should be able to do the following:

1. describe major approaches to medical anthropology
2. appreciate how medical anthropology is applied in a variety of cultural contexts
3. understand issues of power and inequality within medical systems
4. describe theological implications of medical anthropology

CHAPTER OUTLINE

Introduction

How do you know when you're sick? Is it because of how you feel? Is it when people say you look "off"? Is it when a physician gives a diagnosis? Do you ever wonder if you're truly sick or if it's all in your head? Questions like these are asked by people all over the world, and there are no simple answers. While it may not seem cultural (after all, a tumor doesn't care what you call it or how you think about it), being sick is like the rest of human experience; it is simultaneously something happening in the material world *and* a phenomenon requiring interpretation and understanding. What it means to be sick or healthy is wrapped up in understanding the body and its limits, ideas of what exists and what doesn't, and how people think of their own ability to do things (agency) and the forces that affect them beyond their own ability to respond.

Medical anthropology is a subfield of anthropology that focuses on health, disease, and illness, the cultural dimensions of health definitions and experiences, and the cultural construction of medical systems. Health care is a massive arena of employment, research and development, and technological innovation. Medical anthropologists contribute their expertise in understanding how culture influences illness and disease, and in contextualizing health interventions in cultures around the world.

In this chapter, we look at several major approaches to medical anthropology. We start by discussing ethnomedicine, the culturally specific approaches to illness, health, and healing found around the world. Then we present epidemiological and ecological approaches, in which anthropologists explore the ways social, biological, cultural, and environmental factors intersect in disease causation and the subjective experiences of illness. Next, we explore the areas of critical medical anthropology and clinical medical anthropology. Finally, we consider how medical anthropology intersects with theological concerns about the body, healing, and suffering.

Key Concepts in Medical Anthropology

Let's say you are carrying dangerous bacteria in your body, bacteria that can cause a fever as high as 104 degrees Fahrenheit (40 degrees Celsius), joint pain, diarrhea, and possibly death. And, to make matters worse, you are highly contagious. Surely you are sick. Yet what if you have no symptoms,

YOUR TURN

Being Sick

It sounds like a simple statement: "I'm sick today." An anthropological perspective reveals how health, sickness, disease, and illness are part of culture.

We use the word "sick" in our everyday lives to mean different things. A person who says, "I'm sick today!" might have a virus, an infection, a headache, upset feelings, or perhaps even an injury. Other people may or may not believe that they are sick, depending on how their symptoms fit with other people's understanding of valid sickness. A person may say, "I'm so sick of this!"—a statement that is about feeling poorly in a different way.

Listen for the word "sick" around campus or your workplace or your home. When you hear the word "sick," shift into fieldwork mode and start taking notes. When you hear a person say they are sick, ask them to tell you more.

- How did they describe their sickness? Did others show sympathy or disregard? Did others believe them or not? Did the sickness change the person's plans (to attend class, eat with others, go to work, etc.)?
- In general, how do people use the concept of sickness in their everyday lives?
- How is the concept of sickness learned, shared, dynamic, adaptive, and power laden?

despite this pathogen thriving in your body? This happened to Mary Mallon, a young Irish immigrant who worked as a cook in many private homes in and around New York City at the turn of the twentieth century. Ms. Mallon was eventually found to have one of the first recorded cases of asymptomatic typhoid. She carried active bacteria that causes typhoid fever without displaying any of the symptoms herself. She became a notorious figure (known as "Typhoid Mary") when fifty-one people became ill and several died after eating food she had prepared. Even though the New York Department of Health would eventually quarantine her for almost thirty years, she was considered a healthy person: one who was not sick, despite the threat she posed to public health.[1]

This famous case raises many questions of class, immigration status, gender, media, fame, and discourses of health. For the medical anthropologist, it demonstrates the complicated relationship between the biological components of health and the social, cultural, and institutional frames in which it exists. To analyze these aspects of health and healing, medical anthropologists use different terms to denote these related but analytically distinguishable aspects. First, they make a distinction between disease and illness. **Disease** is an abnormal condition afflicting the body that stems from a pathogenic cause: a tumor growing in someone's brain, the mucus prompted by bacterial infection, or the pathogen lurking in the body that may produce no symptoms. Disease is the realm of **biomedicine**, the branch of medicine focusing on biology and physiology. This is what most US Americans would consider normal medicine. Medical anthropologists appreciate biomedical expertise and knowledge of disease treatment, but they always want to broaden the framework to include the ever-present interactions between culture and biology.

Specifically, all these biological phenomena—the mucus, the tumor, even the asymptomatic typhoid—are understood by the person experiencing them in particular ways. The mucus becomes a "cold." The tumor is known as "cancer." The asymptomatic typhoid becomes an experience during which a physician must tell the patient that she carries the deadly bacteria and is infecting others. Each of these may elicit distinct feelings, responses, and subjective states, though they can vary widely between cultures and even between individuals. These culturally conditioned and somewhat idiosyncratic interpretations of the biological processes are known as **illness**. A person could be ill because they feel unwell but not have a disease. Illness is where the physician begins their work, says medical anthropologist Arthur Kleinman,

1. Judith Walzer Leavitt, *Typhoid Mary: Captive to the Public's Health* (Beacon, 1997).

as they begin to decode the reports of a patient to understand the biological processes (disease) underneath.[2]

Finally, the illness is also interpreted beyond the individual experiencing symptoms, by the wider society. An individual's tumor may be interpreted as part of a pattern of cancers known to be clustered around a place where nuclear testing was once conducted. A cold is passed around a university dormitory, and people post signs to wash hands or spray disinfectant in their rooms. The contagious bacteria carried by the young Irish immigrant created a public health crisis and social panic. Medical anthropologists use the term "**sickness**" to refer to the population's cultural conceptions of a condition. Disease, illness, and sickness are closely related concepts, and people use these terms interchangeably in everyday talk. For medical anthropologists, disease focuses on biology, illness focuses on the sufferer's experience, and sickness focuses on society. Consider a person who says he needs a sick day. He may feel quite unwell, but in the absence of a disease diagnosed by a doctor, society (his employer) may refuse to recognize him as sick, his insurance may refuse to pay for treatment, and his friends may consider him to be faking or to have a psychological condition. Medical anthropologists use these distinctions to research the intersections of the biological, cultural, social, and historical dimensions of health.

Around some problems, such as heart disease or Parkinson's disease, we see strong agreement between individual, biomedical, and social interpretations. Other human experiences are deeply challenging to name and interpret. For example, conditions affecting the brain and mental processes are often referred to as "mental illness." Rarely do people, at least in the English-speaking United States, use the wording "mental disease." Yet as neurologists, psychiatrists, and psychological anthropologists learn more about brain functioning, it has become clear that there are biological components to conditions such as those called schizophrenia and bipolar disorder. There is disagreement about the biological and cultural dimensions of these disorders and disagreement about whether they are even disorders. People suffering from heart disease or Parkinson's generally agree with their doctors that there is, in fact, disease present. People sometimes disagree with biomedical diagnoses of mental illness, diagnoses that refer to what they may experience as personality quirks, gifts, or creativity.

Or, to take another case, one of the most widespread medical maladies in the United States in the twenty-first century has been type 2 diabetes. Often,

2. Arthur Kleinman, *The Illness Narratives: Suffering, Healing, and the Human Condition* (Basic Books, 1988).

though not always, this is a consequence of a modern diet and other behaviors, such as lack of physical activity. The physical (biological) consequences of diabetes are very real, but the cause is not pathogenic or environmental per se. Is diabetes, then, a disease? Or something else? Or consider these important but complex examples: Is gun violence a public health problem that should be treated at the level of society or an individual problem best addressed through criminal law? Should sex offending be treated with criminal punishment, biological alteration (e.g., castration), or spiritual intervention? While we may agree that certain behaviors or human experiences are harmful, it can be very difficult to discern their cause, which connects with prevention and intervention.

Categories used by medical anthropologists, as well as those used by people at large, are part of a **taxonomy**, or a system of categorization that is always shifting as people come to view conditions and behaviors in new ways. In the United States, certain addictions, such as alcoholism and the overuse of some drugs, have become "medicalized" as these conditions have come to be known as disease. **Medicalization** refers to the process by which a particular ailment, experience, or process becomes understood as properly being in the realm of medicine. The consequence of calling alcoholism a disease is largely social and cultural rather than biological. Several decades ago, someone suffering from alcoholism was often viewed as having a moral failing, a condition that was rooted in a character flaw or moral weakness. Today, most US Americans refer to alcoholism as a disease, which allows the alcoholic to seek medical treatment and to be viewed as deserving professional help more than punishment. However, treatment remains mostly social and behavioral—through counseling, rehabilitation, and accountability (e.g., twelve-step programs such as Alcoholics Anonymous). Alcoholism is classified as a disease, but that has not produced treatments that are primarily biological, such as medication or surgery. Similarly, classifications of stress-induced conditions—including anxiety, depression, and hyperactivity—have changed over time as people have experienced and interpreted these issues in different ways. Today, most versions of these conditions would qualify for medical insurance coverage and be considered legitimate subjects for medical research and funding grants.

The changing taxonomy of medical language, including medical anthropology, shows that all meanings, including those related to health and the body, are culturally derived. The body does not exist separately from culture; from the moment of conception, a human embryo is influenced by the mother's environment, nutrition, and stress, as well as by the ways health factors and the environment affected the father's sperm long before conception.

Ethnomedicine

Ethnomedicine explores how people in specific cultural contexts cope with illness and disease. Ethnomedical study incorporates a wide variety of anthropological approaches, including ecology, epidemiology, and medical history. The study of ethnomedicine largely involves the collection of empirical data, particularly focusing on understandings of health and healing that fall outside biomedical approaches. Also known as "medical pluralism," ethnomedical studies explore the use of local knowledge in health and healing; the local explanations of illness (which include what are known as culture-bound syndromes); the specific social, historical, and cultural factors shaping the understanding, spread, and experience of disease; and the locally specific understandings of the body, on which ideas of healing and health are invariably built.

Anthropology of the Body

In the contemporary United States, and throughout much of biomedical practice around the world, the body is compared to a machine that runs on fuel and whose parts need to be serviced, repaired, and maintained. In Japan, where the integrity of the body as a whole and unbroken object has long been of paramount concern, the body has been compared to a place in the natural world that could receive knowledge, energy, or peace from outside itself.[3] Scripture calls the body a "temple," comparing it to the place where God dwells among his people (e.g., 1 Cor. 6:19–20). In each case, these basic perceptions of what a body really is shape how members of that society approach health and healing.

Consider, for example, how the body-as-machine metaphor intersects with biomedicine as practiced throughout much of the world. Medical training is organized around specializations that often focus on discrete and specific parts of the body. From cardiology (the heart) to phlebotomy (blood) to rheumatology (treatment of the immune system, particularly focused on soft tissue as found in joints), biomedicine is mostly about treating the body as a collection of components, each with its own distinct purpose and function.[4] When thinking about eating as a part of health, the biomedical system is likely to consider food as fuel. Aspects of eating, such as the social, symbolic, or

3. Hiroyuki Noguchi, "The Idea of the Body in Japanese Culture and Its Dismantlement," *International Journal of Sport and Health Science* 2 (2004): 8–24.

4. In the US system, there certainly are generalists and medical professionals who look at the person as a whole. General medicine frequently funnels patients toward specialists, and even the generalist is educated to view the body as a collection of pieces.

sacred, are less likely to be part of how those in the biomedical system advise people to organize their intake of food.

Compare this to the Confucianist-based understandings of the body found in Chinese thinking. Emphasizing the balance of the body in *yin* and *yang*—opposites such as dry and wet, flushed and chilled—ancient writings such as

Anthropology Improves Medical Care Delivery

I (Jenell) taught Cultural Anthropology for Nurses in a major metropolitan area to a diverse group of nurses (US, Liberian, Nigerian) treating a broad range of patients (from their own cultures as well as Somalian, Ethiopian, and Hmong backgrounds). These nurses were studying anthropology in order to deepen their knowledge of the cultural dimensions of medical care delivery.[a]

One of our areas of focus was how to approach cultural expressions of pain. Medical anthropologists have found that pain is an extremely difficult experience to convey to others because it is invisible. Someone can see that your arm is bleeding, but you must express pain in a convincing way for another person to "see" the pain you are in. Some cultures socialize people toward stoicism as a response to pain, while others encourage expressiveness. My students recalled women in labor who denied pain, and full-grown adults sobbing in response to a simple injection.

In the United States, we quantify pain assessment with numerical scales. It can feel impossible to judge one's own pain (Is this a six or a seven?) or to match one's feelings to images of smiling and frowning faces.

Treating pain can be as complicated as assessing it. US medicine prizes individual autonomy in decision-making, but some cultures authorize tribal or clan leaders to make important decisions for people who are not their immediate relatives. Other times, nurses may feel certain that a patient needs pain medication, but the patient may refuse (certainly the opposite happens as well).

The LEARN model helps medical professionals deliver care in culturally appropriate ways:

- **L**isten to the patient's point of view.
- **E**xplain to the patient their illness and the doctor's plan for treatment.
- **A**cknowledge the patient's understanding of what has been explained.
- **R**ecommend a course of action.
- **N**egotiate agreement with the patient.

Developed cooperatively by a medical anthropologist and a physician some time ago, this model is still used in cross-cultural medicine throughout the world.[b]

It's your turn: Consider a field of work you may pursue, or in which you could imagine yourself. How might you engage with people from other cultures in that field? How could anthropology help you interpret cultural differences?

a. Erwin Schweitzer and Margret Jaeger, "The Good, the Bad and the Grey Areas of Care: A Review of the Anthropology of Care in Health Care," *International Journal of Care and Caring* 9, no. 1 (2025): 25–39.

b. Elois Ann Berlin and William C. Fowkes, "A Teaching Framework for Cross-Cultural Health Care—Application in Family Practice," *Western Journal of Medicine* 139, no. 6 (December 1983): 934–38. The LEARN acronym is defined various ways and sometimes includes a final S ("strengthen").

the *I Ching* and the *Nei Ching* state that health is found through balancing the various aspects of the body with each other and the wider social world. The health of the individual, then, depends on balance with the natural world, as bodily health requires each part to be in harmony with every other part. In this view, the physician treating, say, the liver would need to consider it in balance with the heart, kidneys, blood, mind, and soul. A Confucian healing process may connect, harmonize, or integrate, whereas a body-as-machine approach may focus on repair or replacement of individual parts.

Medical anthropologists explore how people come to understand the body. This knowledge is foundational to promoting health in ways that fit with social conceptions of health, illness, healing, and sickness. Nancy Scheper-Hughes and Margaret Lock, two leading voices in the field of medical anthropology, write that "the body is simultaneously a physical and symbolic artifact, both naturally and culturally produced, and securely anchored in a particular historical moment."[5] As medical anthropologists consider the culturally produced ideas of the body as an individually physical, culturally meaningful, and socially embedded reality, they can better understand particular understandings of health and illness, some of which appear unique to particular cultural contexts.

Culture-Bound Syndromes

Ethnographers sometimes encounter locally distinctive maladies that seem to have little or no corollary in other places. Known as **culture-bound syndromes** or **folk illnesses**, these are collections of symptoms that appear together and are linked to locally understood causes and cures. These are typically conditions that do not seem to have a biomedical explanation or disease component, although they may have very real—even fatal—physical consequences.

One culture-bound syndrome is ***susto***, found in Latin America. This is an unusual example in that it is found across multiple cultural and linguistic groups in Central and South America. *Susto* is also known as *jani*, *pasmo*, *espanto*, or *perdida de la sombra*, depending on where it is found. The cause is generally thought to be in the nature of the soul, understood as having multiple parts or aspects that are attached to the body. In the case of *susto* (which can be translated as "fright"), a piece/aspect/part of the soul becomes lost or separates from the body when a person is frightened suddenly, has a deeply upsetting experience, or—among some people practicing traditional

5. Nancy Scheper-Hughes and Margaret M. Lock, "The Mindful Body: A Prolegomenon to Future Work in Medical Anthropology," *Medical Anthropology Quarterly* 1, no. 1 (1987): 8.

religion—upsets a spirit guardian of a river, pond, forest, or other natural feature. In each manifestation, this syndrome is characterized by depression, the neglect of daily activities, stomach and muscle pains, loss of appetite, reduced contact with others, and general anxiety or tension. And while the cure varies from region to region, some aspects of the cure are shared across regions. A healer diagnoses the problem to determine what caused the soul to detach from the body. Then the soul must be persuaded to return home through entreating the spirits or by creating a pathway for the soul to reunite to the body. Patients may be massaged and perhaps made to sweat during the process while the healer calls out to the spirit to return to the patient. The individual may be rubbed or "swept clean" of the illness using tools such as medicinal brushes, eggs, and even guinea pigs.[6]

Culture-bound syndromes are common throughout the world, including in the Western context. Conditions such as anorexia nervosa and bulimia, agoraphobia, and even colic (a condition in which a baby cries uncontrollably for hours on end, refuses to be comforted, and often arches its back in response to touch) have been identified as syndromes unique to relatively affluent or "Westernized" cultures.

As with other cultural features, culture-bound syndromes travel and change. Rebecca Lester, a medical anthropologist who originally studied anorexia treatment in the United States, conducted research in Mexico in the first decade of the twenty-first century to compare the diagnosis and treatment of eating disorders in a Mexican clinic. Although ten years earlier eating disorders were virtually unheard of in Mexico, by 2005 several residential clinics were operating throughout the country, serving hundreds of patients each year. Patients in both the United States and Mexico had virtually identical behaviors and symptomology, yet the treatment approach in the two cultures assumed very different underlying dynamics to the illness. Thus, while a condition such as anorexia seemed to travel across cultural borders and no longer be a culture-bound syndrome per se, Lester still argued that "knowledge about eating disorders is locally generated and legitimized in dialogue with particular moral and practical commitments and within complex social dynamics."[7] In other words, as the healers approached their patients, even though all were armed with the same information from the *Diagnostic and Statistical Manual of Disorders*, they interpreted the illness through locally specific and culturally particular understandings. This awareness has

6. Arthur J. Rubel, Carl W. O'Nell, and Rolando Collado-Ardon, *Susto: A Folk Illness* (University of California Press, 1991).

7. Rebecca J. Lester, "Critical Therapeutics: Cultural Politics and Clinical Reality in Two Eating Disorder Treatment Centers," *Medical Anthropology Quarterly* 21, no. 4 (2007): 370.

led medical anthropologists to develop understandings of all conditions (in biomedical, cultural, and social terms) in light of how they intersect with and spread through the local context.

Medical Anthropology in Ecological (Epidemiological) Perspective

Epidemiological or **ecological medical anthropology** analyzes how culture and environment interact to create conditions for health and disease. When Paul Farmer first arrived in Haiti in the mid-1980s, he encountered young people suffering and dying from a condition that was little understood in the medical community. At the time, biomedical experts did not yet agree on what this new and fatal condition was. Haitians, many of whom lacked access to high-quality health care, found themselves stigmatized in the global community as carriers of, or perhaps even people biologically predisposed to, this condition. This led to travel bans, exclusion from blood donation, and speculative international reports. Although Farmer could see high rates of this condition on the island, he suspected there was something more to the spread of this disease than could be found just by looking at the individual bodies of Haitians.

He paid attention to the communities and life stories of the people he encountered who were suffering from this disease. He heard familiar stories of people dislocated from their land by hydroelectric dam projects or highways and depleted land that would no longer produce a crop. He learned of young people (particularly young women) who left to find work in the capital of Port-au-Prince, only to find themselves sexually exploited or abused. These movements of poor, vulnerable people produced a unique susceptibility to an opportunistic virus which moved among destitute people through networks of economic migration that often left them exploited politically, socially, and sexually. These economic and social realities then folded into the understandings people inside and outside Haiti had of this new disease as a curse, moral failure, or social shame.

By connecting the dots between development projects, globalization, national and international migration, gender, and cultural understandings of disease, Farmer advanced both more nuanced understanding of the disease that would come to be called HIV/AIDS and strategies for prevention and treatment. This sort of research—following how diseases move, by what mechanisms, along what routes (known as "vectors"), and at what pace—is known as **epidemiology**. In biomedicine, epidemiology focuses on the biological aspects of disease spread. Is it a virus? A bacterium? Can it be airborne?

Waterborne? In medical anthropology, epidemiological approaches take those questions into account but want to understand how and why people themselves move. How do their attitudes toward the sick affect the health of patients and the spread of the disease? How do government policies that incentivize or force people to move affect the movements of pathogens?

In the case of Farmer's epidemiological study of HIV in Haiti, he reframed this disease from being primarily an individual condition that could be controlled through individual behavior, to a sickness that afflicted a population and should be considered in terms of wider social factors. Farmer's research took into account people's understandings of the disease's causation, the economic dislocation many patients experienced because of the government's "development" plans, the vulnerability of particular people within the population to sexual and economic exploitation, and the structural impediments to treatment (such as transportation, cost of care, or availability of preventive measures). In this way, he gained a holistic view of the epidemiology of HIV in Haiti.[8]

Ecological approaches to medical anthropology emphasize environmental aspects of health and disease. Patricia K. Townsend, a Christian anthropologist and the coauthor of a widely used text on ecological medical anthropology,[9] began her research among forest-dwelling communities in Papua New Guinea and Peru as a graduate student at the University of Michigan. She later conducted research at a center at UCLA focused on people with intellectual disabilities. In both cases, she used a "systems model" approach like Farmer's, where she made the links between health, community, and environment explicit.

Critical Medical Anthropology

Critical medical anthropology considers how inequalities of power, economics, and social structures shape practices and understandings of health and healing. Critical medical anthropologists work to increase equity and quality in health care access and delivery. Analysis of how economic and political power structures shape people's health status, their access to health care, and the prevailing healing systems can be done in terms of both Western biomedicine and traditional healing practices. In all these systems, specialists—marked

8. Paul Farmer, *AIDS and Accusation: Haiti and the Geography of Blame*, updated ed. (University of California Press, 2006); Tracy Kidder, *Mountains Beyond Mountains: The Quest of Dr. Paul Farmer, A Man Who Would Cure the World* (Random House, 2004).

9. Ann McElroy and Patricia K. Townsend, *Medical Anthropology in Ecological Perspective*, 4th ed. (Westview, 2003).

by symbols of power, specialized language, and arcane knowledge—control the language of, practice of, and access to health care. Access and inequality shape how people experience health and health care. Critical analysis asks how these systems are developed and maintained.

Consider, for example, walking into a hospital where biomedicine is the assumed norm for health care. How do you know who can help you? Typically, the healers (physicians, nurses, physicians' assistants, etc.) are marked by special clothing. Thirty years ago, virtually all the staff would be wearing white, a color that symbolizes purity and cleanliness. Nurses (historically a profession dominated by women) typically had a distinctive hat and feminine dress while physicians would wear a white lab coat. These days, nurses generally wear what are known as scrubs, or hospital-specific uniforms in a few particular colors (light green, blue, perhaps pink), although the physicians often still have the lab coat. Physicians are rarely in laboratories, of course, but the coat speaks of special knowledge and the training of the medical profession. In fact, most US medical schools have an elaborate ceremony when students are presented with their lab coat and allowed to wear it for the first time. Other symbols include the use of specialized language that marks the medical world as distinct (e.g., saying "stat" instead of "quickly" or "now") and the use of honorifics, notably "doctor." (This is not unlike the use of honorifics in academia, although we professors always have to distinguish ourselves as "Not that kind of doctor. You know, not the kind that helps people.")

Examination of power relationships, economic dimensions of medicine, and institutional structures around health and healing became a significant part of anthropology in 1979 when Soheir Morsy wrote a review of medical anthropology titled "The Missing Link in Medical Anthropology: The Political Economy of Health."[10] She explained that medical anthropology had long failed to take account of political economy, or the ways that money and power inequalities influenced health and healing. Medical anthropology, and studies of cross-cultural medicine generally, often overlooked "the political-economic conditions and asymmetrical power relations which underlie conditions of stressfulness associated with culturally significant afflictions."[11] By attending to political-economic conditions and power relations, anthropologists can analyze the ways medicine itself comes to be defined in a society.

10. Soheir A. Morsy, "The Missing Link in Medical Anthropology: The Political Economy of Health," *Reviews in Anthropology* 6 (1979): 349–63.

11. Soheir A. Morsy, "Towards a Political Economy of Health: A Critical Note on the Medical Anthropology of the Middle East," *Social Science & Medicine. Part B: Medical Anthropology* 15, no. 2 (1981): 160.

Anthropology and Public Health

Anthropologist Jeffery Deal started his career as a surgeon. He later earned a PhD in anthropology and, up until his retirement, served as director of health studies for Water Mission International.[a] Water Mission International customizes solutions for water problems in communities around the world. Medicine, engineering, and anthropology come together to solve problems in local communities with attention to sustainable solutions, appropriate technology, and cultural contextualization.

Deal invented Tru-D, a disinfecting device that uses chemicals and light. During the Ebola crisis in 2014, he worked with the Ebola Task Force, a global coalition of major organizations and experts, and brought his Tru-D device to Liberia. It successfully disinfected hospital environments in a number of settings and is celebrated as a contributor to the resolution of this crisis.

Deal insists that medicine and health problems are best understood with a global lens, and his passion for tropical medicine led him to serve in locations including South Sudan, Darfur, and Tanzania.

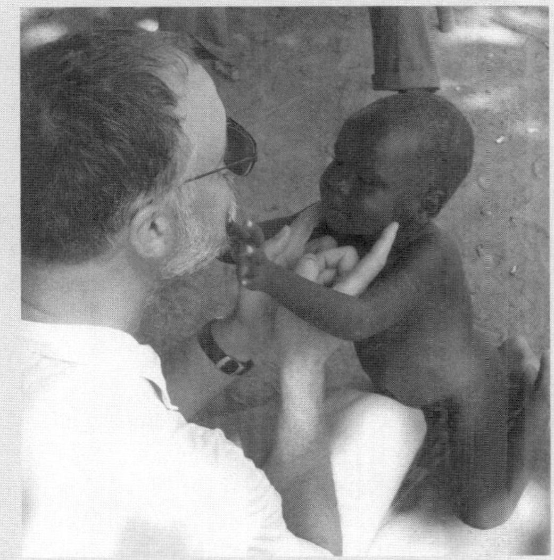

Jeff Deal

Jeff Deal examining a child.

It's your turn: Name one health challenge that you see as important on a global scale. What are two or three professions that could work together to address this challenge? How could anthropology play a part?

a. Water Mission International, accessed July 25, 2025, www.watermission.org.

Critical medical anthropology benefits vulnerable populations and communities. The Hispanic Health Council (HHC) of Hartford, Connecticut, has used critical medical anthropology in developing its programs.[12] Community-based participatory research is a type of applied anthropology in which people within a specific community determine research priorities and conduct the research themselves, with the support and participation of the anthropologist. In Hartford, community members have used anthropological research methods to explore nutrition education delivery systems via texting, how well mobile markets work for food provision, and how to incentivize quitting addictive

12. Hispanic Health Council, accessed July 15, 2025, www.hispanichealthcouncil.org.

substance use. In this setting, the very process of conducting critical medical anthropology strengthens its goals of community engagement, defining the cultural dimensions of health needs and program delivery. Critical medical anthropologist Merrill Singer is a leader in applied anthropology on an international level, and he served as director of research in the local setting of the HHC before becoming a professor of medical anthropology with the Institute for Collaboration on Health, Intervention, and Policy (InCHIP) at the University of Connecticut. In his work with the HHC, and now with InCHIP, he seeks to understand the health issues of urban populations, such as nutrition, prenatal care, addictions, domestic violence, and AIDS—all of which have complex determinants and exist in a broader social environment of inequality and racism.

Clinical Medical Anthropology

All anthropological research seeks to improve human life, but medical anthropology has clear applications toward this end. Medical anthropologists, no matter their theoretical or methodological approach, can contribute to a better understanding of how health systems work and help practitioners do their work more effectively. **Clinical medical anthropology** is the most direct application of anthropological research toward this end. Like development anthropology (see chap. 12), clinical medical anthropology makes direct contributions to people seeking health and well-being, however they define it.

When public health officials identified high levels of lead poisoning among Latino children in a community in southern Texas, they pursued the usual suspects: lead paint in the homes and lead from industrial contaminants in the soil. None of these were the cause. They questioned parents about the children's diet and couldn't discover anything unusual compared to other Latino communities where there was no lead poisoning. Public health officials invited an anthropologist, Robert Trotter, to conduct research in the community, searching for the source of the lead. Using ethnographic techniques, Trotter spent time with families. After some time, he discovered that many of the families gave a home remedy to children and infants when they came down with *empacho*. *Empacho* is a digestive problem principally symptomized by constipation. The treatment for *empacho* was a poultice, or liquid mixture, of traditional herbs. The public health officials had known this was a common practice in many communities, and the mixture had been tested to see if it contained any traces of lead. However, they did not test the pots that were commonly used to make the solution. In this community, these pots came from a town in Mexico where many of the local families had connections, and the potters there had adopted a new glaze that had high lead content. Encouraging the potters to change their glaze resolved the problem and safeguarded the health of hundreds of children. While the solution turned out to be a simple one, the problem was difficult to identify without entering into the community and observing the practices and understandings of health firsthand—that is, anthropologically.

Paul Farmer, the anthropologist who developed an epidemiological approach to HIV in Haiti, also used his anthropological understanding of health to develop more effective interventions globally. Farmer, along with his partners Jim Kim and Ophelia Dahl, founded Partners in Health (PiH), an international medical organization that helps communities throughout the world develop and access effective health care. In many places they work, such as Haiti, Rwanda, and Peru, PiH has used anthropological knowledge to advance a strategy of community health workers who are able to provide health care more effectively, and generally at far lower cost, than technologically based, capital-intensive strategies. Community health workers, PiH discovered, identify health concerns much earlier than doctors based in clinics that may be far from communities that need them or may be inaccessible because of cost or social barriers. Moreover, community health workers have been able to identify treatments, preventive measures, and local resources that physicians are rarely trained or equipped to discover. Acting almost as clinical medical anthropologists themselves, community health workers have, in some instances, proved more effective at elevating health outcomes in poor communities than the biomedical infrastructure in relatively more wealthy communities where people access the "best" care in the world.

Similar to community health workers, medical missionaries often provide direct care to local populations in remote communities with little regular access to health care. Some Christians trained in nursing or medical care go on to study medical anthropology or public health to strengthen their capacity to assess and deliver health care in culturally appropriate ways.[13]

Christians, Health, and the Body

Adam and Eve, existing in perfect union with God before sin entered the world, are depicted as "naked and unashamed," completely comfortable in the bodies God created. When Christ returns, Scripture teaches us, he will raise us to new life in bodies that will be redeemed, restored to perfect physical

13. See Vincent Gil, "A Centenary Retrospective: Christian Medical Missions and Medical Anthropology," *On Knowing Humanity* 8, no. 2 (2024): 12–19.

bodies (although Rev. 7:9–10 suggests we'll get some robes). Though we often experience pain, disappointment, shame, and fear because of our bodies, this was not God's original intent for us, and our bodies will one day be redeemed. We will not flee our bodies for some noncorporeal existence as ghosts or angels. We will be redeemed bodies, completely happy, comfortable, and healthy.

While many US Christians easily imagine the life of faith as disembodied, developing the life of the spirit internally or ethereally, Scripture offers many stories of the life of faith embodied. Both the creation narrative and Song of Songs describe human bodies as in harmony with spirit and soul, to the delight of humans and of God. Other stories describe war, rape, dismemberment, disease, and death, and the horror, grief, and longing provoked by bodily suffering. Roman Catholic Christians have a practice of meditating on Jesus on the cross, which helps the believer to resonate and empathize with Jesus's tears, thirst, bleeding, suffering, and dying.

As Christians, we need to think about the body in ways that affirm the goodness of our physical being while seeking its healing when it reflects the fallen state of disease, pain, or weakness. In all the things bodies do—eat, sleep, have sex, raise children, dance, play games, get cancer, or twist into pretzels at Cirque du Soleil—Christians need to consider how we are using our bodies to reflect God's purposes.

Many Christians work in health and health care, whether in a clinical biomedical setting, in research, through missions, or in what has come to be called **alternative medicine** in the Euro-American context (e.g., chiropractic care, naturopathy, or so-called Eastern medicine). A medical-anthropology approach opens a perspective on the wider social context that shapes how we consider what *is* medical, how people can or should experience health, and what are more effective ways to deliver medical care. To glorify God in our calling, whether that is as a healer or just a person with a body, we can use medical anthropology to enlarge this view of what health and healing are meant to be.

TERMS

alternative medicine: A term applied in biomedical contexts to forms of medical interventions considered outside mainstream scientific practices.

biomedicine: A view of medicine that understands disease as having a unique physical cause within the body.

clinical medical anthropology: Medical anthropology specifically applied toward the improvement of health outcomes and practical results.

critical medical anthropology: Medical anthropology focused on the ways inequalities of power, economics, and social structures shape practices and understandings of health and healing.

culture-bound syndrome (also called **folk illness**): An affliction suffered by certain groups of people who use specific cultural tools to deal with and explain their symptoms, the suspected causal agents, and preferred treatment.

disease: An abnormal condition afflicting the body, stemming from a pathogenic cause.

epidemiological or **ecological medical anthropology:** An approach to medical anthropology that analyzes how culture and environment interact to create conditions for health and disease.

epidemiology: The study of the incidence, distribution, and spread of disease in a population.

ethnomedicine: Culturally specific approaches to illness, health, and healing found around the world.

illness: The state of unwellness, or the subjective interpretation of symptoms and suffering.

medical anthropology: A subfield of anthropology that focuses on health, disease and illness, the cultural dimensions of health definitions and experiences, and the cultural construction of medical systems.

medicalization: The process by which a particular physical ailment, experience, or process becomes understood as properly being in the realm of medicine, as it is understood in a particular society.

sickness: Cultural conceptions of a condition held by a population.

***susto*:** A culture-bound syndrome in Central and South America believed to be caused by soul separation resulting from a sudden or traumatic fright.

taxonomy: A system of categorization. As applied to medical anthropology, the ways conditions, syndromes, or processes are grouped vis-à-vis medical knowledge.

DISCUSSION QUESTIONS

1. How do you define "health" or "well-being"? These conditions are experienced by individuals, but they also relate to social and cultural contexts. What conditions need to be in place for an individual to experience health or wellness?
2. Jesus performed many acts of healing in his ministry, although he did not physically heal everyone with whom he came into contact. How do you believe Jesus would define "health"?
3. Think of something besides addiction or childbirth that is medicalized. What are the consequences (good or bad) of this process? How/why do you think it happened?

ANTHROPOLOGY AND SCRIPTURE

Good Medicine

> A cheerful heart is a good medicine,
> but a downcast spirit dries up the bones. (Prov. 17:22 NRSVue)

A strictly biomedical perspective would not classify a cheerful heart as medicine. Cheer doesn't repair broken bones, cure cancer cells, or kill viruses.

Yet, the readers of this proverb would have recognized that humor, happiness, and joy seem to help people who are sick. Discouragement, loneliness, and negativity seem to make sickness worse. Anthropologists respect such a perspective as an element of ethnomedicine. Cultures around the world use whatever is available to care for people who are sick, including happiness.

It would be foolish to treat pneumonia with comedy, of course. But today even biomedicine recognizes that humor, happiness, touch, and companionship have measurable effects on the empirical measures of health.[14] Indeed, a cheerful heart is a good medicine.

Jesus Healed Many People

> When Jesus entered Peter's house, he saw his mother-in-law lying in bed with a fever; he touched her hand, and the fever left her, and she got up and began

14. See, for example, Fabio Scorsolini-Comin and Manoel Antônio dos Santos, "The Scientific Study of Happiness and Health Promotion: An Integrative Literature Review," *Revista Latino-Americana de Enfermagem* 18 (2010): 472–79.

> to serve him. That evening they brought to him many who were possessed with demons; and he cast out the spirits with a word and cured all who were sick. This was to fulfill what had been spoken through the prophet Isaiah, "He took our infirmities and bore our diseases." (Matt. 8:14–17 NRSVue)

Jesus healed many people in the course of his ministry. Anthropology can help us read and interpret these stories that happened long ago in a society where people had different understandings of sickness.

Jesus cured Peter's mother-in-law's fever with his touch. Then she got up and began to serve him. This doesn't make sense in biomedical terms, which require a researchable cause-and-effect relationship that can be replicated. The Bible tells the story as a miracle—the whole point is that the healing happened outside the bounds of normal science. This story also tells us about health and why we should treasure it. Peter's mother-in-law used her restored health to serve the Lord.

In the next vignette, Jesus cast out demons with a word and cured the sick. Again, this doesn't make biomedical sense. It doesn't make sense in the original context either, in terms of the culture's ethnomedicine. Miracles disrupt what people expected to happen and the ways they thought curing and healing could occur. These miracles were partly for the sake of the afflicted, but they had another purpose. Miraculous healings helped people see that Jesus fulfilled the prophecy of Isaiah—that he was, indeed, the Messiah.

11

THEORY IN CULTURAL ANTHROPOLOGY

After studying this chapter, you should be able to do the following:

1. explain the role of theory in anthropological research
2. identify key theoretical perspectives in anthropology
3. discuss how Christians can engage anthropological theory in thinking about faith and society

CHAPTER OUTLINE

Introduction

Everyone has a theory of culture. Every time someone uses the word "culture," they do so with an implicit view of what culture is and how it works. If we say we respect culture or want to protect culture, change culture, or avoid culture, we are invoking a theory of culture. Most of the time these theories are implicit. They are based on what we've been taught about what people are, why they do what they do, and how culture influences them. Anthropologists examine these assumptions and systematize their understandings into scholarly theories of culture.

This chapter presents theory in cultural anthropology. First, we define "theory" and describe the social philosophies that provide foundations for anthropological theory. Then we turn to early anthropological theories that are important in the history of the discipline. We then go on to describe several important streams of contemporary theory, including positivist anthropology, symbolic anthropology, and postmodern anthropological theories. Finally, we describe some of the problems and possibilities for Christians as they work with anthropological theory.

Theory in Anthropology

Anthropologists were among the first social scientists to conceptualize culture and describe its dynamics. For anthropologists to make sense of what they see, they need an explicit theory of why things happen and what they mean. For example, an anthropologist might observe people shopping and note the items purchased. The anthropologist then asks a question, for instance, "Why do people buy what they buy?" or "What are the meanings attached to the process of 'shopping' or the products?" The people themselves may answer, "Because it's fun" or "That's what people here do." The anthropologist considers the people's own views of their behavior and also considers scholarly theory. Are consumption patterns created by rational actors who know what they want? Are their purchases a result of socialization in which they've been taught to buy that thing? Are people in the society encouraging others to buy it? Do people seek to impress their friends and neighbors to achieve social prestige? Theory helps the anthropologist move beyond impressions or opinions to a more systematic explanation.

In popular language, calling something a "theory" means it is a guess or just one person's opinion (e.g., "My theory is that professors don't have enough to read; that's why they assign these papers"). In science, however, theory represents the highest level of scientific explanation. A **theory** is a formal description of some phenomenon in the world that explains how that thing works. Strong theories explain data in a comprehensive and persuasive way. As new data are discovered, a strong theory explains the old data as well as the new.

Consider, for instance, theories about why objects fall to the ground when dropped. The Greek philosopher Aristotle (384–322 BCE) believed all objects want to return to their natural place. This means that if a solid object, such as a pen, rolls off a desk, it drops to the ground because it is seeking the center of matter at the center of the earth; it just wants to go home. According to this theory, gases, steam, smoke, and the like seek their natural place in the heavens; therefore, they go up. And water falling on the earth runs back to the sea (the source of its elemental home).

This theory made good sense of the data known by the ancient Greeks, but as new knowledge of astronomy emerged, the old theory didn't explain the new data. For example, more sophisticated observational data appeared to demonstrate that, instead of the stars moving as if the earth were the center of the universe, the earth moves around the sun. Later Greek and Arab astronomers began to suggest the existence of a force of attraction between planets and stars. In the seventeenth century, Isaac Newton (1642–1727) took all the data he knew—from Aristotle through Avicenna, Copernicus, and Galileo—and developed his universal theory of gravitation. Later, in the twentieth century, Albert Einstein (1879–1955) radically revised Newton's theory with the theory of general relativity. What made each version of this theory work (and rise to the level of theory) was its ability to explain what people observed in the past, explain anomalies in the new data, and help predict what would be seen in the future.

A theory can never be proved once and for all. Theories are always being contested and refined, replaced by new theories that explain everything the old theory did, plus anything the old theory could not. Some scientists, such as Karl Popper, posit **falsification** as the principle of science: that is, scientific theories cannot be proven, only falsified.[1] Thomas Kuhn, however, argued that theories are not falsified but replaced.[2] Theories may be well established, such as germ theory or atomic theory, or they may be more contested, such as string theory and theories of the multiverse. What makes a theory accepted is its ability to bring empirical data together into an explanatory whole, as well as its persuasiveness within a particular paradigm or worldview of both science and society.

Within cultural anthropology, numerous theories are employed at the same time. Anthropologists choose theories based on factors such as their research interest, fieldwork context, and personal values. One important factor that shapes an anthropologist's choice of theory is whether they are seeking a nomothetic explanation or an idiographic explanation of the phenomenon in question. A **nomothetic explanation** is a generalization, a natural law that predicts and explains culture change and human behavior. Just as chemists use the scientific method of hypothesis testing, this sort of anthropological theory presents testable theories of culture change or social organization. This was the primary approach of early anthropologists, and many continue to view the discipline primarily in these terms. Their work often involves the study of material and measurable aspects of social life.

An **idiographic explanation** provides a rich description of a particular case. The understanding gained from such work is not meant to be directly compared across contexts or generalized to all contexts. Instead, it provides a detailed understanding that becomes background for future research on related issues in other settings.

Research that is directed toward idiographic explanation relies on theory differently than research designed for nomothetic explanation. Consider this

1. Karl Popper, *The Logic of Scientific Discovery* (1959; repr., Routledge, 2002).
2. Thomas Kuhn, *The Structure of Scientific Revolutions* (1970; repr., University of Chicago Press, 2012).

analogy of how a medical researcher works versus a physician in a typical doctor's office.[3] The medical researcher wants to investigate what causes a disease: Does virus A cause disease B? Hypotheses are tested in the laboratory. If the data don't support the hypothesis, it is revised or discarded in favor of a new hypothesis. The physician, however, examines a person who presents symptoms: sore throat, fever, achy joints, red blotches. Physicians ask questions and compare what they see to other patients or case studies written by other physicians who have seen similar symptoms. Their goal is to understand this patient, including the patient's history, context, and personal characteristics. They will incorporate the lab researcher's findings as appropriate. Their detailed study will become part of the medical knowledge that will help other physicians see how this disease is similar and distinct in the experience of other patients.

The medical researcher is more like an anthropologist seeking a predictive generalization (nomothetic explanation), and the physician is more like an anthropologist developing a rich ethnographic description of a culture (idiographic explanation). Geertz argued that "in ethnography, the office of theory is to provide a vocabulary in which what symbolic action has to say about itself—that is, about the role of culture in human life—can be expressed."[4] Over the years, social and cultural theory has served the purposes of both prediction and description, and anthropologists continue to incorporate both into research today.

Anthropologists cannot conduct "theory-free" research. All researchers—in disciplines ranging from biology and physics to psychology and anthropology—conduct research in terms of theory.[5] In nomothetic research, data are brought to the theory to test the validity of the theory. In idiographic research, ethnographic data are interpreted through a theoretical perspective to create a convincing explanation of phenomena such as social or cultural change, politics, religion, or any other realm of human life. Subsequent anthropologists investigating similar phenomena may apply the same theory or a new one as a way of adding to the "consultable record of what [humanity] has said."[6]

3. This analogy is taken from Clifford Geertz, *The Interpretation of Cultures: Selected Essays* (Basic Books, 1973), 26–27.

4. Geertz, *Interpretation of Cultures*, 27.

5. Grounded theory (GT) is considered by some to be an exception. GT encourages anthropologists and other qualitative researchers to gather data first and develop theory as it emerges from the data. Whether or not this is "theory-free" research is arguable. For a description of GT, see Kathy Charmaz, *Constructing Grounded Theory*, 2nd ed. (Sage, 2014). For a critique, see Gary Thomas and David James, "Reinventing Grounded Theory: Some Questions for Theory, Ground and Discovery," *British Educational Research Journal* 32, no. 6 (2006): 767–95.

6. Geertz, *Interpretation of Cultures*, 30.

Foundations of Anthropological Theory

Concepts of culture have existed since ancient times. Herodotus (ca. 484–425 BCE) wrote about the various *nomoi* (norms/customs/culture) of various Greeks (the Athenians or Spartans), people of present-day India, and Egyptians, noting their varied practices and ideas. Yet most scholars of his work would agree that he did not use the term to refer to culture in the sense cultural anthropologists do today.[7] A modern understanding of "culture" as something that can be scientifically studied as a dynamic, integrated, shared, power laden, and learned phenomenon is a more recent development.

Like other social sciences, anthropology has roots in the eighteenth century, when European philosophers wrestled with the rapid social changes caused by the Industrial Revolution. Millions moved into cities for factory work. Globalization was exploding. Through colonial expansion, Europeans were exposed to new information about the world and embedded in new economic relationships. From that time until the present, scholars have scientifically theorized about how best to understand cultural and social diversity and change. Karl Marx, Émile Durkheim, and Max Weber are three philosophers who provided intellectual foundations for cultural anthropology.

Karl Marx

German philosopher and historian Karl Marx (1818–83) constructed a complex theory to explain and predict the development of all human societies. According to him, societies moved through stages of development driven by economic relations. Capitalism, in rapid development during his time, represented one stage of development that he said would eventually give way to communism. This communitarian social arrangement would provide human beings with economic equality and social harmony.

In one of his earlier works, *The German Ideology*, Marx explained his belief that human beings gain consciousness through working together.[8] He argued that stratification of work and wages results in social-class stratification, in which classes struggle against one another for control of economic resources. Class conflict fuels social change. He argued that every society and every form of social and cultural life in history could be understood in terms of the economic systems and conflict they produce. His most significant work, *Capital: A*

7. Sally Humphries, "Law, Custom, and Culture in Herodotus," *Arethusa* 20, no. 1/2 (1987): 211–20.

8. Karl Marx, *The German Ideology*, ed. C. J. Arthur, trans. W. Lough, C. Dutt, and C. P. Magill (1932; repr., International Publishers, 1972).

Critique of Political Economy, is a detailed explanation of capitalism as a system of exploitation in which those who own the "means of production" (such as land and factories) extract surplus value from workers by compensating workers with wages far below the value of goods and services produced with their labor.[9]

For later anthropologists, a significant element of his theory was his view of human nature. Unlike Christian views of human beings as originally good but now sinful, Marx began with the idea that human beings are, at root, socially created, inherently neither good nor bad. Human nature, he argued, is a flexible capacity that changes over time. Anthropologists have often started in a similar place, leading them to embrace a cultural relativist approach (see chap. 2).

Anthropologists have also drawn from his idea that social conflict, caused by inequality, is a key organizing principle for culture. As anthropologists have studied diverse societies, they document the ways that inequalities underlie social conflict and change, including those between genders, ethnicities, races, classes, and other social statuses.

Émile Durkheim

Some fifty years later, French scholar Émile Durkheim (1858–1917) also faced the question of how to understand European industrial societies.[10] Like Marx, he believed that researchers could discover laws of social life and could use those laws to make predictions about social change. He argued that scientists could apply the same rigorous methods to the study of society as they used in physics, biology, or chemistry. Like other thinkers of his day, he believed that societies evolve from simple to complex. He wrote that European societies had advanced from the simple (what he called "elementary" or "primitive") forms to the complex. Unlike Marx, who predicted utopia after an exploitative and oppressive capitalist phase, Durkheim did not place any value judgment on capitalist industrialism.

For both Marx and Durkheim, things such as religion and the arts are products of underlying social or material causes, not reflections of spiritual or metaphysical reality. Durkheim argued that social organizational forms do not originate from some other cause, such as economic relations. He called society "a thing in itself," or *sui generis*. This meant society is not the outcome of individual choices all added together. Rather, society is the thing that creates those individual choices in the first place. Studying individual thought (psychology)

9. Karl Marx, *Capital: A Critique of Political Economy*, trans. Samuel Moore and Edward Aveling (1867; repr., International Publishers, 1967).

10. Émile Durkheim, *Suicide: A Study in Sociology*, trans. John Spaulding and George Simpson (1897; repr., Simon and Schuster, 1997).

or individual economic choices (as most economists did in his time) would not explain why society and culture looked as they did. What can be studied, he believed, are the unique forms of social life, or what he called "social facts," that differentiate one society from another. Durkheim said society is like an organism with various parts that all work together for the health of the whole. Durkheim's theory gave rise to the notion of a "social structure" that helped social scientists, including anthropologists, to see how explanations of cultural differences could not be explained by individual choices but rather at the level of society, social facts, and larger social structures.

Max Weber

Max Weber (1864–1920), a German social philosopher and contemporary of Durkheim, also wanted to explain the rapid changes in European societies. In contrast to Durkheim and Marx, Weber argued for the power of ideas in shaping social organization. That is, unlike Durkheim and Marx, who sought to reduce social analysis to single, material variables, Weber believed a multivariate approach was best.

Weber is particularly known for his analysis of modern industrial capitalism, in which he connected the ethos of investment, frugality, and discipline necessary for the growth of capitalism to the doctrine of predestination as articulated by John Calvin.[11] Weber emphasized the "Protestant Ethic"—the belief that members of God's elect should live disciplined lives focused on the afterlife rather than on enjoyment of life in the present. This is often misquoted as the "Protestant *work* ethic," or an idea that Protestants work harder than other people. But this was not what Weber said. He argued that it was the religious conviction that the elect carry out their earthly lives with an emphasis on eternal life, denying pleasure in this world, that created the conditions for what he called "economic rationalization." In other words, the idea that the elect—those predestined by God to go to heaven—would behave in a certain way caused them to reshape their economic lives. It was this ordering of economic and social life that produced industrial capitalism. Weber's analysis was geared toward explaining modern Western cultural and social life, but his use of religious, philosophical, and political ideas as foundations for cultural change became an important philosophical touchstone for later anthropological theory.

A key concern for all social theorists is the relationship between society (the large-scale organization of social life) and culture (the ideas, symbols, and interpretations people have about the world). Some theorists, such as

11. Max Weber, *The Protestant Ethic and the Spirit of Capitalism*, trans. Talcott Parsons (1905; repr., Scribner, 1985).

Choosing Theory

When I (Brian) started graduate school, I knew I wanted to study the relationship of Christianity and social change, but I did not know *how* I wanted to study it. At Washington University in St. Louis, where I did my graduate work, I had two prospective advisers, both excellent faculty members, with different theoretical perspectives. I arrived planning to work with one who employed rational-choice theory in her work. This perspective tended toward positivism and nomothetic explanations. She was a brilliant scholar and, at first, this seemed good. As I went on, however, I felt that this perspective did not allow me to consider aspects of Christianity that I found most interesting, such as how people experience their relationship with God and the ways people negotiate the meanings of their faith together.

The other faculty member, with whom I eventually worked most closely, studied Islam in Southeast Asia using an approach that employed Weberian and post-structural theory. This view emphasized how ideas, language, and culturally specific views of the world shaped human life and action. This professor did not ignore economic influences, but these were not the factors he found most helpful in explaining how the people he studied practiced Islam in their context.

Eventually, I found the Weberian and post-structural approaches to be more helpful theoretical perspectives to explain how the Southern Baptist Christians of the northern Philippines (where I eventually did my research) interpreted their Christianity.[a] My choice of a theoretical framework guided my entire research project, leading me to ask questions I would not have asked had I employed another theory and to leave aside methods that would have been central to rational choice theory (such as statistical analyses). Although I sometimes wonder what direction my life would have taken had I become a rational-choice theorist, all anthropologists eventually choose the theory that seems best given their interests, dispositions, and research questions.

It's your turn: Choose a topic you could study using ethnography. If you relied on Durkheimian theory, what question would you ask about this topic? What question would Weber ask? Marx? Write three questions about your research topic, one from each of these major theoretical perspectives.

a. Brian M. Howell, *Christianity in the Local Context: Southern Baptists in the Philippines* (Palgrave Macmillan, 2008).

Marx, gave absolutely no power to culture in shaping how people live. Marx's theory is sometimes called mechanistic insofar as it argues that all human ideas, symbols, art, religion, and even family systems are products of material relations.[12] There is an almost mechanical cause-and-effect relationship between the material world and the ideas humans have.

Other theorists said culture and ideas are the only *real* influences on human life. A contemporary of Marx, Wilhelm Dilthey (1833–1911), argued that

12. See Jeffrey Alexander and Steven Seidman, *Culture and Society: Contemporary Debates* (Cambridge University Press, 1990), 1–30.

humans only ever understand the world through the symbols and ideas in their minds. Therefore, just as Plato argued that there are perfect and immaterial "forms" behind the manifest material world and its diverse expressions, Dilthey argued that the symbolic world (culture) is actually "more real" than the material world in which we live.[13]

Today, many view these eighteenth- and nineteenth-century theories as too simple, interpreting complex processes through just a few variables. For example, those anthropologists who use Marxian theory today see culture as an independent influence on human life, rarely as one that is *wholly* a product of material relations. Yet the underlying emphases brought forth by Marx, Durkheim, and Weber have remained important in the development of many schools of thought and anthropological theory.

Early Anthropological Theories

Influenced by Marx, Durkheim, and Weber, anthropologists working in the early years of the discipline developed various theories of culture. They were trying to understand and explain cultural diversity, the scope of which was becoming clear to Europeans and Americans because of colonialism and globalization. They were also interested in culture change, particularly general rules for what they saw as cultural development. This section surveys five important early anthropological theories these early anthropologists developed: unilinear cultural evolution, diffusionism, historical particularism, functionalism, and structural functionalism.

In the tradition of Marx and Durkheim, early scholars of cultural diversity explained the development of culture in general, universal terms. **Unilinear cultural evolution** (introduced in chap. 2) posited that all cultures evolve from simple to complex along a single line of progress. This approach sought to make "objective" comparisons of different societies by placing each on a continuum of development. The British anthropologist Edward B. Tylor (1832–1917) constructed his scale largely according to religion. He believed levels of religious development could be used to classify particular stages of cultural progress (see chap. 9).[14] American anthropologist Lewis Henry Morgan (1818–81), reflecting a more Marxian emphasis on economics and material life, used technological features (such as the presence of ceramics

13. Wilhelm Dilthey, "The Construction of the Historical World in the Human Studies," in *The Philosophy of History in Our Time*, ed. Hans Meyerhoff (Doubleday, 1959).

14. Edward B. Tylor, *Anthropology: An Introduction to the Study of Man and Civilization* (Appleton, 1916).

or metallurgy) to classify cultural development on a scale from "savagery" to "barbarism" to "civilization," including such subdivisions as "upper savagery" and "lower barbarism."[15]

A competing explanation at the time, **diffusionism**, stated that cultural artifacts or activities (known as **cultural traits**) spread from more advanced to less advanced societies. In this view, people do not innovate cultural traits; rather, they borrow cultural traits from other societies. Strict diffusionists afforded virtually no role to creativity, innovation, or adaptation in culture.

Each of these theories offered a mechanism and explanation for the ethnographic data of cultural diversity and the observation that cultures had changed over time. Today, however, both cultural unilinear evolution and diffusion have been critiqued for their ethnocentrism and racism, as well as their failure to account for new historical and cultural data. These theories were ethnocentric because they used their own cultural norm as the standard by which other cultures were interpreted and judged.

Most forms of diffusionism and unilinear cultural evolution were eventually discredited as cultural anthropologists and archaeologists accumulated more data from diverse cultural contexts. It became clear that not all societies moved through the same stages of development. The old theories were not sufficient to explain the new data, so new theories emerged. Franz Boas (1858–1942) was a German émigré to the United States who originally trained as a physicist before turning to anthropology. Sometimes called the founder of American anthropology, Boas founded the anthropology program at Columbia University, the first PhD-granting anthropology program in the country. He challenged both the unilinear and diffusionist theories, arguing that they relied on speculation and circular reasoning rather than careful data collection.[16]

Boas's theory of independent cultural adaptation, which came to be called **historical particularism**, argued that each culture is a unique representation of its own history and context. Boas and his students, such as Alfred Kroeber (1876–1960), Ruth Benedict (1887–1948), and Margaret Mead (1901–78), stressed the historical, context-specific, and environmentally responsive aspects of cultural development. They amassed large amounts of ethnographic data through long-term fieldwork to support their conclusions. Their work is sometimes referred to as "salvage anthropology" because these

15. This is not to say that Morgan drew on Marx's writings. Marx's colleague and collaborator Friedrich Engels used Morgan's writings in an explanation of the development of family. The work of Morgan and other unilinear evolutionists expressed similar theoretical presuppositions and arguments about human life. See Lewis Henry Morgan, *Ancient Society* (1877; repr., Belknap, 1964).

16. Franz Boas, *Race, Language, and Culture* (Macmillan, 1940).

anthropologists were preserving as much cultural knowledge as possible at a time when Indigenous cultures, especially in North America, were thought to be either dying out or were becoming assimilated. Some have argued that Boasian anthropology is "atheoretical" (that is, without theory) since it emphasizes specificity over generality, but following Durkheim, Boas believed cultures could be studied scientifically. Though he and his students were suspicious of generalized theories of human cultural development, Boas believed that by collecting enough ethnographic data, patterns would emerge, leading to law-like (nomothetic) explanations of social life.

British anthropologists in the early twentieth century also started rejecting unilinear and diffusionist approaches as ethnographic data began to contradict these views. Bronisław Malinowski (1884–1942), a Polish ethnologist who later taught at the London School of Economics, became a prominent figure in the development of anthropology when he argued that the cultural traits of non-Western people should not be viewed as undeveloped. Instead, they should be seen as adapted to the needs of the environment. Malinowski became stranded in the British-controlled South Pacific when, during a trip there, the outbreak of World War I made him an "enemy combatant." Unable to leave, he spent several years on the islands, during which he learned the language and became intimately acquainted with the lives of the people there. His first book, *Argonauts of the Western Pacific*, became a classic owing to its extraordinary level of detail and almost storybook quality.[17]

Functionalism, the theory that emerged from this research, argues that culture develops in response to human needs and the environment. Malinowski came to believe that all the diverse customs and behaviors of cultures around the world served a function, meeting people's need for food, comfort, reproduction, safety, relaxation, movement, and growth. They were different around the world because people lived in different environments. Rather than viewing band and tribe societies as irrational, underdeveloped, or primitive, and industrialized societies as advanced or civilized, Malinowski argued that all cultures could be understood in terms of how they meet human needs.

Alfred Radcliffe-Brown (1881–1955), a colleague of Malinowski, advanced a similar theory. Radcliffe-Brown, however, drew more heavily on the work of Durkheim, emphasizing the life of the society over the individual.[18] Radcliffe-Brown's early work among the Andaman Islanders far off the coast of Thailand employed ethnographic data to demonstrate how the cultural traits

17. Bronislaw Malinowski, *Argonauts of the Western Pacific: An Account of Native Enterprise and Adventure in the Archipelagoes of Melanesian New Guinea* (Routledge & Sons, 1922).

18. Alfred Radcliffe-Brown, *The Andaman Islanders: A Study in Social Anthropology* (1922; repr., Free Press, 1964).

deemed primitive by evolutionists and diffusionists preserved the cohesion of social order. His theory, **structural functionalism**, argued that the functions of beliefs or behaviors should be understood not as meeting individual needs but as supporting a social need for order and cohesion.

Both the Boasians in the United States and the functionalists and structural functionalists of Britain pushed anthropologists to emphasize ethnographic fieldwork and the collection of empirical data to support conclusions and theory. Original fieldwork became the standard for becoming an anthropologist; no longer could anthropologists base their research on travelogues, missionary letters, or other secondhand information. The emphasis on society in British anthropology and culture in US anthropology, however, became a strong division between the two. British scholars believed the US emphasis on culture undermined the status of the discipline as a science by emphasizing an immaterial quality (culture) over the concrete (society). US researchers, however, saw their work as scientific because it relied on ethnographic data to document and interpret culture.

In the second half of the twentieth century, division continued between anthropology as a science in search of nomothetic explanations and anthropology as a process of interpretation and cultural understanding. In early anthropology, this was a division between US and British approaches. Later, it became a division between positivist anthropology on the one hand and interpretive theories on the other.

Positivist Anthropology

In the United States, Boas and his students worked to discredit evolutionary and racist views of cultural difference. But the questions those scholars asked were still important. Why do certain cultural traits exist? How and why do cultures change over time? Are processes of change unique to each culture or common to all? Those who sought to answer these questions with a more scientific approach, seeking universal, nomothetic explanations based on empirical evidence, were called positivist anthropologists. One branch of positivist anthropology includes materialist theories such as cultural ecology, cultural materialism, and sociobiology. Another branch of positivist anthropology includes structuralism. All forms of **positivism** are based on the premise that knowledge must be empirically verifiable, and ideally testable, to be considered valid.

Cultural ecology teaches that culture can be understood in terms of how people adapt to the natural environment. Leslie White (1900–1975) drew

Thomas Headland

Thomas Headland has used biometric data, environmental and ecological studies, and culture in understanding the relationship of Agta culture to the environment during his over forty years of research in the Philippines. Here he is measuring the height of an Agta woman in 1994.

on the work of Karl Marx to argue that cultures change as people develop technologies to capture energy from the environment more efficiently.[19] His contemporary Julian Steward (1902–72) disagreed that these developments are universal stages but agreed that material life is the basis for cultural change.[20] Their work contributed to the development of cultural ecological theory, an approach that emphasizes how human interaction with the material environment (human ecology) drives cultural change.

Later anthropologists developed the overall perspective of cultural ecology into more specific theories, including cultural materialism and sociobiology. **Cultural materialism** theorizes that culture is driven by the material, ecological, and economic adaptations humans make. Marvin Harris (1927–2001) argued that humans unconsciously use a cost-benefit analysis to adapt cultural beliefs toward economically rational ends.[21] These adaptations could survive beyond their usefulness, in some cases, but understanding cultural traits and culture change should be derived from an understanding of how behaviors, beliefs, and institutions benefit (or benefited) people in basic material ways.

19. Leslie White, *The Evolution of Culture: The Development of Civilization to the Fall of Rome* (McGraw-Hill, 1959).
20. Julian Steward, *Theory of Culture Change: The Methodology of Multilinear Evolution* (University of Illinois Press, 1955).
21. Marvin Harris, *Cows, Pigs, Wars, and Witches: The Riddles of Culture* (Random House, 1974).

Figure 11.1. A cultural materialist interpretation of the sacred cow

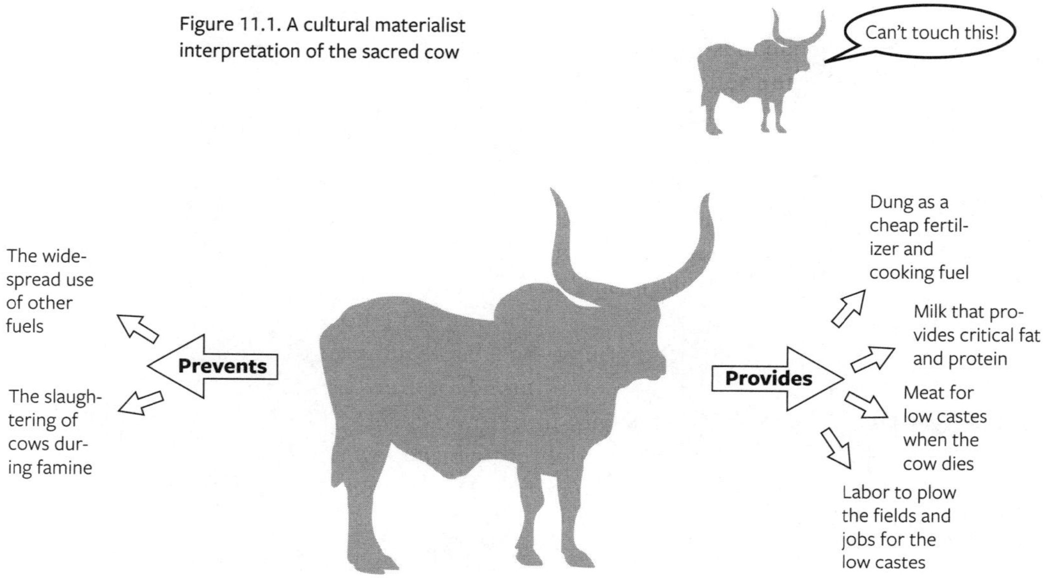

Marvin Harris argues that to replace these functions with a Western-style industrial complex powered by fossil fuel energy would be ecologically disasterous and economically unstable.

One of his famous examples is the sacred cow of India. To many outsiders, this seemed an example of "irrational" religious behavior in which people held beliefs destructive to their very lives. Harris pointed out that when the belief that cows are sacred is viewed in the ecological and economic context of India, there were very good reasons for *not* killing cows, even when people were starving (see fig. 11.1). First, they power agriculture by plowing. Second, their dung becomes fertilizer for the crops. Moreover, dung is used as a cooking fuel that burns longer and at lower temperatures than other fuels (e.g., wood), making it easier for those responsible for cooking to be involved in other productive activities at the same time. In addition, the disposal of dead cows is carried out by the low-caste members of society, who are allowed to eat the meat, providing them with valuable protein. In short, Harris argued, if people were to eat their cows to address food needs in the short run, it would jeopardize the entire society over the long run. Beliefs that promote the sacredness of cows, he contended, are a rational adaptation meant to preserve the population of cattle through difficult economic times.

Sociobiology is a theory that takes materialist explanations of culture to an extreme. **Sociobiology** teaches that culture is rooted in the human drive for evolutionary advantage and genetic survival. For example, sociobiologists have argued that women are more selective about sexual partners and enforce monogamy because they have a limited number of ova (eggs) for use in reproducing. Since men can ordinarily produce sperm throughout their lives, they gain reproductive advantage by having as many sexual partners as possible, making them prone to infidelity and proponents of polygyny. Ethnographic data have been used to support this idea, although strong sociobiological accounts of human sexual decision-making can be contradicted by other ethnographic examples. Moreover, while this theory works to explain some sexual behavior or gender stereotypes, it is often less helpful for addressing questions of religious practices, political conflict, or cultural change.[22]

Structuralism is a positivist theory that links the material to the cultural in a different way. **Structuralism** teaches that human biology, specifically brain structure, drives culture. Working from the linguistic approach of Ferdinand de Saussure (chap. 3), anthropologist Claude Lévi-Strauss (1908–2009) believed that the human brain operates using rules of opposition (see also the discussion of structuralism and ritual in chap. 9).[23] Language, with its orderly rules of grammar, is one manifestation of this tendency to structure life in oppositions such as cold and hot, raw and cooked, or nature and culture. Culture, Lévi-Strauss argued, reflects this structuring in all cultural forms from kinship terminology and political systems to mythology and religion.

Structuralism was enormously influential in the 1960s and found an eager audience in other disciplines. Historians, literary scholars, and sociologists appreciated the power of structuralist explanations to make subjective analysis more objective and scientific. Structuralists in every field argued that myths, works of art, literature, and more could now be studied with scientific rigor by uncovering and mapping the structure found within them.

There are significant differences between cultural ecology, cultural materialism, sociobiology, and structuralism, but these positivist approaches to anthropology work from the idea of naturalism. **Naturalism** is the belief that natural phenomena that can be touched, seen, or otherwise physically experienced are all that exist. Although naturalism does not view religion or the supernatural world as real in and of itself (religion is often interpreted as just an expression or aftereffect of natural phenomena), Christian scientists often work fruitfully within naturalistic scientific paradigms. Christian

22. For an example of sociobiology, see Edward O. Wilson, *Sociobiology: The New Synthesis* (Belknap, 1975). Within cultural anthropology, the field of evolutionary psychology has adapted many of the insights of sociobiology to questions of culture. This approach has drawn many adherents and critics in cultural anthropology. See Jerome Barkow, Leda Cosmides, and John Tooby, eds., *The Adapted Mind: Evolutionary Psychology and the Generation of Culture* (Oxford University Press, 1992).

23. For an example of ethnographic data interpreted with structuralist theory, see Claude Lévi-Strauss, *Tristes Tropiques*, trans. John and Doreen Weightman (Atheneum, 1974).

YOUR TURN

What Symbols Mean

Humans have a unique capacity to make, share, learn, and adapt symbols. Every word in this book is a symbol: It stands for something else, it was made and shared among people, and it could be different (in a different language). Sharing symbols strengthens human sociality, one of our most important survival skills. Symbolic anthropology focuses on this central aspect of our humanity, even viewing culture itself as a universe of symbols within which a group of people live together.

Use just one of your senses—sight—to look for symbols. If you're on a campus, you could look at decorations in a dorm, faculty doors, or posters that announce upcoming events. If you're in a classroom, look for decorations on backpacks, stickers on water bottles and laptops, or brands and designs on clothing. If you're elsewhere, pick a room and look for symbols on walls, furniture, and objects.

- Take field notes on your observations, listing symbols in two categories: clear and confusing.
- What makes you believe that you clearly understand the meaning of a symbol? What makes a symbol's meaning confusing?

sociologist Peter Berger (1929–2017) said that social scientists—even Christian ones—should employ "methodological atheism."[24] That is, even though the researcher is committed to a belief in God, the research should be done in such a way as to assume that natural laws and material phenomena are all that exist. This approach asserts that, given a consistent method, any researcher should come to the same conclusion as any other.

Many anthropologists conduct research with positivist approaches. However, beginning in the mid-1960s, other anthropologists encouraged a shift away from positivism, naturalism, and nomothetic explanations in favor of interpretive, symbolic, and idiographic explanations.

Symbolic Anthropology

Symbolic anthropology (also called **interpretive anthropology**) views culture as a system of symbols that people create, alter, and share with each other. In contrast to the Durkheimian and Marxist approaches to anthropological theory, which stressed the scientific method and objective analysis, anthropologists taking up Weber's emphasis on ideas and multicausality opened the door for new approaches. Interpretive anthropology focuses on understanding

24. Peter Berger, *The Sacred Canopy: Elements of a Sociological Theory of Religion* (Doubleday, 1967), 100.

the symbolic worlds of others and describing them in depth, minimizing the importance of constructing generalized theories of culture and culture change.

Clifford Geertz was arguably the most influential scholar in promoting interpretive or symbolic analysis as the overall agenda for anthropology. Invoking the multicausal and idea-oriented (as opposed to economics- or material-oriented) social theory of Max Weber, Geertz urged anthropologists to move away from efforts to explain and predict and turn toward description and interpretation. Geertz's work has been called "dramaturgical" because he saw human social life as akin to a drama in which people take roles and play parts on the cultural "stage." His work has also been called semiotic analysis, focusing on the signs—or meanings—people give to elements of the world around them.[25]

Mary Douglas (1921–2007), another important symbolic anthropologist, drew on structuralist interpretations of symbolic systems.[26] A devout Catholic, Douglas famously analyzed Old Testament purity laws in terms of how classifying objects, ideas, words, or people as "clean" and "unclean" served to organize society rather than to reflect anything inherent in the objects themselves. She built on Durkheim's view of society as an integrated whole, but unlike those who emphasized social institutions and practices as key to social order, Douglas focused on the ways symbolic meanings of objects and actions served this role. In a similar way, Victor Turner (1920–83), another Catholic anthropologist, analyzed cultural life in terms of what he called "social dramas," in which actions and objects were given meanings for the sake of cultural "scripts" and social order.[27]

Sherry Ortner (b. 1941), an anthropologist who has written influentially on the development of theory in the latter half of the twentieth century, points to three significant movements in cultural theory during the emergence of symbolic anthropology.[28] First is what she calls "the power shift." As anthropologists began highlighting gender, ethnicity, race, and class as constructions of inequality, they became aware of the need to account for the ways that social control—power—was integrated into cultural contexts, cultural change,

25. Clifford Geertz, *Local Knowledge: Further Essays in Interpretive Anthropology* (Basic Books, 1983).

26. Mary Douglas, *Implicit Meanings: Essays in Anthropology* (Routledge & Kegan Paul, 1975).

27. Victor Turner, *The Anthropology of Experience* (University of Illinois Press, 1986). For a deeper historical account of how Catholic Christianity influenced the work of Douglas and Turner (and his anthropologist partner and wife, Edith Turner), see Timothy Larsen, *The Slain God: Anthropologists and the Christian Faith* (Oxford University Press, 2014).

28. Sherry Ortner, *Anthropology and Social Theory: Culture, Power, and the Acting Subject* (Duke University Press, 2006), 3–5.

and even ethnographic representation itself. Second, "the historic turn" was a new emphasis on the importance of history in revealing how people's understandings and symbols change over time. Third, "the reinterpretation(s) of culture" refers to a foundational rethinking of the culture concept as anthropologists and others wrestled with the rapidly changing, globalizing, and extraordinarily diverse cultural worlds in which most people live today. These three shifts all came within the growing emphasis on symbolic anthropology as the dominant approach of anthropological research. Each of these shifts also brought in new theoretical approaches that no longer rested on the trust that human reason and scientific method alone could lead to adequate understandings of the world.

Postmodern Anthropological Theory

"Postmodern theory" is an umbrella term for theories built on the premise that positivist or so-called objective views of human phenomena are inherently limited and not unbiased in the ways proponents believe them to be. Anthropologists generally were early adopters of postmodern approaches to cultural analysis, in part because of a long-standing awareness of cultural differences. By bringing questions of power, history, and the culture concept itself into the center of social analysis, many anthropologists moved away from nomothetic explanations. Postmodernism is an expansive concept that takes on different meanings in different disciplines, but postmodern approaches in anthropology are arguably rooted in Geertz's call for anthropologists to redirect their attention from cultural explanation to cultural explication. Three important strands of postmodern theory in cultural anthropology are cultural Marxism, feminism, and perspectivalism.

Cultural Marxism (also called **Marxian theory**) draws on Karl Marx's concepts of power, inequality, and class struggle to understand cultural change. Cultural Marxists analyze all forms of social inequality, including economic disparity, inequality in social status, the oppression of women, the domination of ethnic groups, and so forth. These anthropologists are not necessarily Marxist in their politics or overall view of history.[29] Nor are Marxist theories linked to historic and oppressive governments that aligned themselves with Marx. Instead, these scholars rely on Marx's insights about social structure and culture change to interpret social inequality in the contemporary world.

29. While this distinction is sometimes made explicit in anthropology and related fields, lowercase and uppercase derivatives of the name Marx are often interchangeable in an anthropological context.

What is central to cultural Marxist theory is an attention to the ways inequalities produce tension, conflict, and cultural change.

Feminist theory often tracks with Marxian analyses, specifically highlighting gender inequalities as an analytic concept and the importance of including women's presence in cultural analysis (see chap. 5). Most anthropologists who use feminist theory are also feminist in their personal values, but feminism as a political stance is different from feminist theory as a scientific paradigm. Feminist theory says that gender categories are important to describe and analyze in ethnographic research and that women's points of view and experiences should be equally represented in ethnographic accounts. A great deal of ethnographic research assumed that men's experiences represented everyone in a culture.[30] Moreover, it was assumed that a male doing ethnographic fieldwork would have the same access, interpretation, and understanding as a female doing the same fieldwork.

Beyond recognizing gender as a key analytical category, feminist anthropologists were some of the first to emphasize the importance of recognizing power and privilege, both within the society being studied and between anthropologists, their subjects, and the readers of an ethnography. Researchers began focusing on the experiences of women in the societies they studied. They understood that inequality and differences in social power often mean that men and women do not have the same perspective or experience, even within the same society. They also contributed to the "historic turn" by highlighting the place of gender relationships in history and pointing out how the telling of history often places men's experiences and men's language as central to cultural narratives. This centering of men serves to reinforce patriarchy, or the dominance of men in social life.

In this way, feminists were among the first to argue that all scientific research, including anthropology, is always positioned. In other words, in scientific research, the identity, background, and experiences of the researcher are relevant to the conclusions and analysis being made. This gave rise to a new way of thinking about the creation of knowledge as well as the nature of data being gathered about cultures around the world.

Perspectivalism is an anthropological theory that highlights this positionality of knowledge. Also known as **standpoint theory**, this view states that knowledge is generated by a knower who is positioned in a particular place and time and therefore reflects a specific and limited perspective. Objective knowledge—conceived as knowledge that is complete and unrelated to the

30. See, for example, Annette Weiner, *Women of Value, Men of Renown: New Perspectives in Trobriand Exchange* (University of Texas Press, 1983).

identity of the knower—is not possible. Perspectivalism is a theory in other disciplines as well, such as philosophy, literature, and sociology. Within anthropology, it has led some to experiment with the form and purpose of ethnography. In the mid-1980s, James Clifford and George Marcus published a collection of essays questioning what it means to "write culture."[31] Advocating experimental forms of ethnographic writing, they suggested that traditional anthropological research obscured the voices of those being represented, misrepresenting or adding layers of interpretation between the reader and the subject. All ethnographic knowledge, Clifford and Marcus argued, is partial knowledge and must be represented as such.

Perspectivalism has influenced cultural anthropology by increasing what is called "reflexivity" in ethnographic writing. **Reflexivity** is the inclusion of the anthropologist's perspective and experience in ethnographic writing. Advocates of reflexivity argue that including first-person narrative of the experiences, feelings, and responses of the ethnographer, along with the ethnographic data, allows the reader to better understand the role of the ethnographer in the creation of knowledge. Postmodern anthropologists do not attempt to tell the objective truth about their subject; they would say this is not possible. All truth, they argue, is partial and subjective truth as researchers include some information while invariably leaving out other information. The goal of research, then, is not exhaustive truth or a complete explanation of phenomena but relatively comprehensive, ethical research presented in a way that allows the reader to understand the perspective of the researcher as well as the data.

Some fear that the abandonment of objectivity removes any capacity to assess the validity of research. Postmodern anthropological theory argues that, first, attending to standards of reflexivity, ethnographic detail, and methodology allows readers to evaluate anthropological analysis. Second, attention to comprehensive analysis, as opposed to objectivity, makes the role of theory even more important. Strong cultural anthropology is that which speaks to key anthropological questions in terms of explicit theories of culture, culture change, identity, personhood, and agency: How do concepts of time change for people who move from farm labor to factory work? What sorts of alliances and communities form among residents of squatter settlements in the slums of megacities? How do Muslims in the United States address the issues of marriage, gender, and family as a consequence of living as a religious minority in a non-Islamic country?

31. James Clifford and George Marcus, *Writing Culture: The Poetics and Politics of Ethnography* (University of Illinois Press, 1986).

Critical theory has developed as a subset of postmodern theory, specifically focusing on the ways power and inequality shape people's perceptions and thoughts, and even the basis of society itself. For example, as highlighted in chapter 10, critical medical anthropology explores the ways power relationships are embedded in medical language, practices, and institutions. Critical theory explores how these shape the ways people experience healing and

Engaging Anthropological Theory as a Christian

My (Jenell's) fieldwork in inner-city Washington, DC, was motivated by my Christian faith. Asking the question *Who is my neighbor?* led me to study how neighborhoods form over time and how people organize to improve the place they call home.

When it came to theory, however, I faced some problems. How could a Christian anthropologist rely on theories grounded in Marxism or postmodernism? I first compared Christian doctrine and Scripture with secular anthropology theories. I evaluated anthropological theories in terms of how "Christian" they were—that is, in what ways they harmonized with or diverged from Christian understandings. This approach was mistaken. First, I was comparing apples to oranges. Christianity is a living way of life, not a static philosophy or theory that can be neatly compared with modern scientific theories. Second, I had too keen an eye for difference, highlighting ways in which anthropological theories failed to align with Christian belief. This maximized antagonism, when what I wanted was a way for my faith and my anthropology to collaborate harmoniously.

In the end, I relied on Marxist theory to analyze my data. Marxian theory analyzes how social class influences all parts of life. Marxian theory certainly doesn't affirm Scripture or promote Christianity, but its detailed approach to understanding injustice helps me—as a White, middle-class, North American woman—live as a good neighbor in a world divided by class, race, ethnicity, and other social statuses. At times, Marxian theory offends my faith, such as in its tendency to denigrate the privileged social classes or its view of religion as merely a by-product of economics. At those times, I can assert my point of view in ways that can potentially shape the development of theory. Discussing and adapting theory is an essential part of developing the discipline.

I once thought that comparing Christianity with secular theories in a way that ultimately crowned Christianity the victor was a way of promoting the faith. Now I see it as a competitive approach that inadvertently diminishes the faith by reducing it to a philosophy or intellectual tool. Relying on Marxian theory to interpret data allowed me to build an anthropological argument that was acceptable in the discipline, instructed me in detailed analysis of social systems, and harmonized with my Christian values of neighborliness and care for others.

It's your turn: Which theory in this chapter stands out to you as particularly interesting? Why? Are there some anthropological questions or contexts that would be better for the theory you're drawn to, and others that would be difficult to engage with?

sickness. Critical race theory emerged from legal scholarship scrutinizing ways that law in the United States came to encode racial inequality. Critical-race theory starts from the premise that racial inequality (see chap. 4) shapes other aspects of social life and that racial inequality is not merely a social problem that can be solved with enough goodwill but, rather, a foundational injustice at the root of society.

Critical theory often has a negative ring to Christian ears since some critical theorists, like other postmodern theorists, deny the existence or accessibility of truth, and may seem to focus on inequality and group identity to the expense of individual agency and social cohesion. At the same time, many aspects of postmodern and critical thinking have proven helpful for Christians, and particularly for Christian anthropologists, who see the importance of acknowledging perspective and metaphysical assumptions, and highlighting social inequality in analysis. Though some have called critical or postmodern theory a "world view" or argued it is fundamentally incompatible with Christian thinking, critical theory is a large category of theory that can be used by Christian scholars to analyze ethnographic data and uncover social dynamics.[32]

Symbolic anthropology, critical theory, and postmodernism provide a different way to understand culture change and power dynamics, but they can seem to be limited and impervious to generalities. Functionalist, structural functionalist, and structuralist explanations of culture are comprehensive and scientific, but they often seem less able to make sense of innovation, cultural change, and human agency. Ecological, materialist, and other positivist approaches frequently produce predictive measures and falsifiable studies, but they are critiqued for ignoring agency, inequality, and power. Dialogue continues today about positivist and symbolic approaches to anthropology, both of which are vibrant.

Christians Engaging Anthropological Theory

Some Christians, such as those studying the nutritional provisions of people living in the rain forests of the Philippines or the changes in economic life spurred by new techniques of pottery production in southern Mexico, have found little intersection between their Christian commitments and the theories guiding their scientific anthropological research. Others, such as Brian

32. For an excellent review of critical race theory and how Christians may approach it, see Robert Chao Romero and Jeff M. Liou, *Christianity and Critical Race Theory: A Faithful and Constructive Conversation* (Baker Academic, 2023).

in his research on Protestants in the Philippines or short-term mission trips, or Jenell in her research on identities of race, gender, and sexuality, find anthropological theory to be a major arena for considering the intersection of Christian faith and categories of cultural theory. All professional anthropologists, regardless of research or scholarly focus, find themselves part of a larger anthropological community in which colleagues are asking vital questions about the meaning of human life, acceptable research ethics, human nature, and the assumptions anthropologists may hold about the nature of reality. Every Christian in anthropology must consider the relationship of faith and theoretical perspectives in the discipline.

Anthropologist Eloise Hiebert Meneses studies low-caste market women in India and also writes about anthropological theory. She argues that Christianity and anthropology are two distinct viewpoints, each of which calls for ultimate commitment.[33] She describes anthropology as foundationally committed to atheism, naturalism, and evolution, all three of which are incompatible with Christian truth. She argues against attempts to harmonize, integrate, or amalgamate Christianity and anthropology as if they are equals. One must be subordinate to the other, and in her view, Christianity deserves ultimate commitment. Anthropology should be taken as a secondary commitment that may be appropriated for Christian purposes. In line with her perspective, Meneses has developed explicitly Christian theories of culture that guide her ethnographic analysis.[34]

In contrast, anthropologist and missiologist Robert Priest argues for the inclusion of Christian perspectives in anthropological theory and approaches to knowledge.[35] He uses symbolic anthropology to describe the place of Christian perspectives in cultural anthropology, asserting that despite the openness of the postmodern climate to all perspectives, Christianity is too often marginalized and maligned. He presses postmodern anthropologists toward consistency, arguing that Christian perspectives should be given the same respectful attention that other religious, ethnic, political, and ideological perspectives receive.[36] Christians working across anthropology, on topics of every sort, employ a wide variety of theories in anthropology, from materialist and

33. Eloise Hiebert Meneses, "No Other Foundation: Establishing a Christian Anthropology," *Christian Scholar's Review* 29, no. 3 (2000): 531–49.

34. Eloise Hiebert Meneses, "Faithful Witness: A Postcritical Epistemology for Christians," *Direction Journal* 36, no. 2 (2007): 129–43.

35. Robert J. Priest, "Missionary Positions: Christian, Modernist, Postmodernist," *Current Anthropology* 42, no. 1 (2001): 29–68.

36. For a related argument, see Brian M. Howell, "The Repugnant Cultural Other Speaks Back: Christian Identity as Ethnographic 'Standpoint,'" *Anthropological Theory* 7, no. 4 (2007): 371–91.

ecological approaches, to feminist, cultural Marxist, and other postmodern theories. Theory in anthropology, like theory in science generally, provides a way to understand data, whether symbolic, material, or historical. For Christians, the various theoretical approaches can aid in understanding the data without contradicting or erasing faith commitments.

In recent years, several Christian anthropologists have gone beyond the use of existing theories to develop theoretical perspectives that explicitly draw on Christian categories, theologies, and epistemologies. For example, Meneses and her colleague David Bronkema at Eastern University (St. Davids, PA) brought Christian theologians, anthropologists, and missiologists together to consider how various theological concepts such as mystery, witness, and Trinity could positively contribute to the theoretical questions with which all anthropologists wrestle. With support from the Templeton Foundation, they launched the *On Knowing Humanity Journal* to publish work by Christian anthropologists who bring Christian theology and anthropological analysis together in their work.[37] Derrick Lemons, an anthropologist at the University of Georgia, embarked on a similar project with Christian and non-Christian scholars to produce a "theologically engaged anthropology." In 2018 he founded the Center for Theologically Engaged Anthropology to bring scholars from around the world together to consider the intersection of anthropological theory and Christian theological categories.[38] These and similar projects suggest Christians can bring our commitments to faith into a productive relationship with anthropological theory.[39]

37. The purpose of the *On Knowing Humanity Journal* is to promote the development of a Christian faith-based approach to anthropology. It encourages all anthropologists to incorporate insights from theology into their accounts of people and cultures and allows religiously committed anthropologists to speak freely of the ways in which their commitments inform their theory and practice.

38. Center for Theologically Engaged Anthropology, accessed July 24, 2025, https://ctea.franklinresearch.uga.edu.

39. See Philip Fountain and Sin Wen Lau, "Anthropological Theologies: Engagements and Encounters," *Australian Journal of Anthropology* 24, no. 3 (December 1, 2013): 227–34; Ian Gibson, "Pentecostal Peacefulness: Virtue Ethics and the Reception of Theology in Nepal," *Journal of the Royal Anthropological Institute* 23, no. 4 (2017): 765–82; J. Derrick Lemons, ed., *Theologically Engaged Anthropology* (Oxford University Press, 2018); Eloise Hiebert Meneses and David Bronkema, *On Knowing Humanity: Insights from Theology for Anthropology* (Routledge & Kegan Paul, 2017).

TERMS

critical theory: Any theoretical position that foregrounds power relationships, inequality, and the consequent construction of ideas, laws, behaviors, or language in that sphere of life.

cultural ecology: An anthropological theory that teaches that culture can be understood in terms of how people adapt to and interact with the natural environment.

cultural Marxism (also called **Marxian theory**)**:** A postmodern theory that draws on Karl Marx's concepts of power, inequality, and class struggle to bring attention to the ways inequalities within and between cultural groups produce tension, conflict, and cultural change.

cultural materialism: A theoretical approach that emphasizes ways in which humans adapt to the material conditions in which they live.

cultural traits: Cultural artifacts or activities.

diffusionism: An early anthropological theory stating that cultural traits spread from more advanced to less advanced societies.

falsification: The view that scientific theories cannot be proven, only falsified.

feminist theory: A contemporary theory that highlights the importance of gender as an analytic concept and the importance of including women's presence in cultural analysis.

functionalism: An early anthropological theory that purports that culture develops in response to human needs.

historical particularism: An early anthropological theory that argues that each culture is a unique representation of its history and context.

idiographic explanation: A rich description of a particular ethnographic case for the purpose of building generalizations from the specific.

interpretive anthropology: See "symbolic anthropology" below.

naturalism: A belief that the natural phenomena that can be touched, seen, or otherwise physically experienced are all that exist.

nomothetic explanation: A generalization, a natural law that predicts and explains culture change and human behavior.

perspectivalism (or **standpoint theory**)**:** An anthropological theory that highlights the positionality of knowledge; that is, knowledge is generated by a knower who is positioned in a particular place and time and who reflects a specific and limited perspective.

positivism: An approach to anthropology that involves seeking universal, nomothetic explanations based on empirically verifiable evidence.

postmodern theory: An umbrella term for theories built on the premise that positivist or so-called objective views of human phenomena are inherently limited and that they are therefore not unbiased in the ways proponents believe them to be.

reflexivity: The inclusion of the anthropologist's perspective and experience in ethnographic writing.

sociobiology: An anthropological theory that teaches that culture is rooted in the human drive for evolutionary advantage and genetic survival.

structural functionalism: An early anthropological theory that argues the functions of particular beliefs or behaviors may be understood in terms of their support of social order and cohesion.

structuralism: An anthropological theory that teaches that human biology, specifically brain structure, drives culture.

symbolic anthropology (also called **interpretive anthropology**)**:** An approach to anthropology that views culture as a system of symbols that people create, alter, and share with one another.

theory: A formal description of some phenomenon in the world that explains how that thing works.

unilinear cultural evolution: An early anthropological theory that states all cultures evolve from simple to complex along a single trajectory of progress.

DISCUSSION QUESTIONS

1. Use symbolic anthropology to interpret your classroom. What are some of the key symbols? How do they shape people's understandings, behaviors, and interactions?
2. Whose views do you find most compelling for understanding human society and culture: Marx, Durkheim, or Weber? Why?
3. How does theory work in your major? Can you perceive the theoretical orientation of your professors or of major scholars in the field? Does your major focus more on nomothetic or idiographic explanations?

ANTHROPOLOGY AND SCRIPTURE

Communion as a Symbol

> After taking the cup, he [Jesus] gave thanks and said, "Take this and divide it among you. For I tell you I will not drink again from the fruit of the vine until the kingdom of God comes."
>
> And he took bread, gave thanks and broke it, and gave it to them, saying, "This is my body given for you; do this in remembrance of me." (Luke 22:17–19)

Before he was crucified, Jesus shared a last meal with his disciples. He gave them wine and bread and told them to repeat this ritual in remembrance of him. Ever since, Christians have shared the cup and the bread with each other in the ritual of Communion.

Christians disagree about what Communion means on a spiritual level. Some believe it is a sacrament that delivers grace to the believer, and others believe it is only a symbol of Christ's sacrifice for us. Some believe the bread and wine are actually transformed into the body and blood of Jesus, and others believe the bread and wine are just bread and wine.

Symbolic anthropologists would analyze Communion as a social drama in which people use symbols to communicate important truths. The bread and wine are symbols of Jesus's life and death, used in a religious ritual that is important to Christians of all times and places. The words used in prayer and in the story of the Last Supper are linguistic symbols that give meaning to the ritual. In anthropological perspective, Communion is a social drama that uses symbols to strengthen the solidarity of the group and promote a social order. Perhaps Jesus gave us this ritual knowing that while Christians would have different theological understandings, by participating in the ritual together, we would become more unified in him. Thus, despite theological disagreements, Christians may agree that Communion serves a cultural function that is important for the strength of the church as the body of Christ.

Injustice and Theory

> For the wicked are found among my people.
> They lie in wait like hunters;
> destroyers, they catch humans.
> Like a cage full of birds,
> their houses are full of treachery;

therefore they have become great and rich;
  they have grown fat and sleek.
They know no limits in deeds of wickedness;
  they do not judge with justice
the cause of the orphan, to make it prosper,
  and they do not defend the rights of the needy.
    (Jer. 5:26–28 NRSVue)

The prophet Jeremiah describes God's anger toward the Israelites, predicting downfall and exile. This passage describes Israel's society as marked by inequality and injustice. Some people are very wealthy, and they ignore those who are poor. Some even entrap and exploit the poor. The most vulnerable members of society are not cared for, not even in public institutions devoted to justice.

If an anthropologist could do fieldwork among the Israelites at this time, they might rely on different theories to analyze the culture. Cultural materialism could help explain why social stratification had reached such an extreme point, and the anthropologist would look for environmental and ecological factors that shaped social organization. Structural functionalism could help explain how injustice stabilized society: Extremes of wealth and exploitation of the poor are wrong and unpleasant, but they can keep everyone in their place and preserve order. Feminist theory could raise questions about gender: Maybe the female orphans are treated differently than the male orphans, or maybe the human beings caught in traps for exploitation and theft are mostly male, or mostly female.

Prophetic writings inspire Christians today to address injustice and inequality in their own nations and around the world. Yet even Christians working against injustice can do more harm than good when they lack an understanding of how social problems link to other aspects of social life and culture. Anthropological theory can enrich our understanding of how injustice becomes embedded in a culture and how it can be changed, thereby helping a believer change the world with knowledge and strategy. As the writer of Proverbs taught, "Even zeal is not good without knowledge" (Prov. 19:2 CSB).

12

ANTHROPOLOGY IN ACTION

After studying this chapter, you should be able to do the following:

1. appreciate the relevance of anthropology in the world today
2. describe applications of anthropology to work and service
3. express the importance of anthropology for the global church
4. describe historic and contemporary connections between anthropology and missions

CHAPTER OUTLINE

Introduction

People who take only one anthropology course in college often remember it as one of their most interesting classes. They may recall their professor's interest in Yąnomamö violence, Melanesian museum curation, or Mexican medicinal plants. Anthropology is interesting, to be sure, but its importance is much greater than knowledge of distant people and places. Whether students are studying anthropology for a major or minor, general education, or part of a seminary program, anthropology is important and actionable in careers, Christian life and service, and everyday life.

Like other liberal arts disciplines, anthropology is not a professional program that provides certification for a single area of application. As a discipline grounded in empirical inquiry, it provides critical skills and perspectives for virtually any path a person chooses to follow.[1] Anthropology is unique, however, in

1. "Career Resources in Anthropology," American Anthropological Association, accessed July 24, 2025, https://americananthro.org/careers/careers-in-anthropology/.

being centered on diversity, culture, and human difference. For this reason, anthropology has relevance for everyone and particularly for Christians.

Many Christian colleges and seminaries offer anthropology as part of a mission studies program. The connection of cultural anthropology with cross-cultural missions is valuable. We hope every missionary preparation program includes anthropology! Most Christians, however, will spend their lives invested in everyday activities such as working, raising a family, caring for elderly parents, volunteering in a local church, and living out their Christian faith in a context similar to the one in which they were raised. What does anthropology offer them?

This chapter addresses the basic question, What difference does anthropology make? First, we describe anthropology's benefit to job seekers and college graduates. Then, we explore anthropology's usefulness in everyday life and in ministry. Next, we consider the global church and discuss how anthropology contributes to the ability of Christians to engage what has always been a cross-cultural faith. Finally, we engage the intersections of anthropology, ministry, and missions, highlighting new paradigms of mission in the church today.

Anthropology in Education

Whether a student majors in anthropology or takes just one course, anthropology can open a path into the moral, intellectual, and social development that fulfills the highest ideals of higher education. For most of human history, people learned what they needed to know directly from parents and community members. Apprenticeships, whether formal or informal, were how young people learned to be farmers, blacksmiths, potters, healers, and community leaders. Only in the past few decades has formal education, literacy, and technical academic training become normal for the majority. This has produced societies that anthropologist Joseph Henrich famously called WEIRD: Western, Educated, Industrial, Rich, Democratic.[2] These features, he argued, create new and distinct psychological and social patterns in individuals and communities. Not all societies in the world are WEIRD, but WEIRDness has infiltrated many domains.

Most people using this book will be rooted in a WEIRD society. Formal education is deeply woven into how we live. In such a context, having the ability to think scientifically, literarily, metaphorically, figuratively, mathematically, historically, and socially is a vital skill. Anthropology assists in

2. Joseph Henrich, *The WEIRDest People in the World: How the West Became Psychologically Peculiar and Particularly Prosperous* (Farrar, Straus & Giroux, 2020).

developing this skill in all these areas. Reading ethnographic accounts helps us to think systematically and scientifically about social life, noticing and learning connections between our lives and those of others. Anthropology sparks a creative and empathetic imagination as we strive to put ourselves into others' shoes, understanding how they view the world and the concepts they use. Anthropology develops our social skills in asking questions, engaging ambiguity, and enduring confusion as patterns emerge over time. As part of an educational program, anthropology can serve to develop important habits of mind.

Frank Bruni, professor of journalism and public policy at Duke University, wrote that the "soul" of university education seemed to be dying.[3] While it is true that for many decades university degrees have been rightly viewed as a means of social mobility, they were also, he argued, considered a social good. Universities, and the graduates they produced, were good for civil society, ideally making society "culturally and morally richer." But as college became more expensive and work less secure, education has become more transactional and consumer-oriented.

It is appropriate for parents and students to ask about the worth of the education they pay for, but perhaps worth needs to remain an expansive idea. A worthwhile education, Bruni argues, does more than lead to a high-paying job. It may (and should potentially) do that, but as artificial intelligence rapidly reshapes the employment landscape, education must make humans *more human*. Education, he argues, should help us develop skills in "intellectual dexterity and powers of judgment."[4] Christians would add moral development, empathy, and a sense of biblical justice to that list.

"The smartest approach to college," Bruni writes, "may be precisely the one that its trajectory of late has conspired against: range widely across subject offerings and focus not on a skill that could become obsolete but on intellectual dexterity and powers of judgment with better odds of enduring relevance." Quoting historian Jonathan Zimmerman, who teaches first-year seminars at the University of Pennsylvania, Bruni notes, "A liberal arts degree *is* a preprofessional degree—you just don't know what the profession is."[5] With its emphasis on listening, imagining other social worlds, and engaging holistically, anthropology serves as a vital piece—or even the very core—of just such an education.

3. Frank Bruni, "I'm Watching the Sacrifice of College's Soul," *New York Times*, July 14, 2025, https://www.nytimes.com/2025/07/14/opinion/college-soul-ai-education.html.

4. Bruni, "I'm Watching the Sacrifice of College's Soul."

5. Jonathan Zimmerman, quoted in Bruni, "I'm Watching the Sacrifice of College's Soul."

Anthropology in the Workplace

It may not seem that knowledge of pastoralism (chap. 6) or the ability to distinguish patrilineality from matrilineality (chap. 8) would relate to a job working in electrical engineering or nursing, yet these jobs, and most others, involve working with people. Anthropology is fundamentally about people: how they see the world and why they do what they do. Anthropology majors graduate with a bachelor's degree ready for careers, though many eventually go on to graduate school in a wide range of professional programs.

Regardless, at both the undergraduate and the graduate level, most students of anthropology work outside the academy, applying their research methods and understandings of culture to professional concerns. The Anthropology Career Readiness Network supports professionals working with anthropology undergraduate degrees and also those who have graduate degrees. Its *World of Work* blog shares career stories and professional advice.[6]

Anthropology students work in government policymaking, parks management, museums, public education, public health, and many other arenas. Job postings rarely state "anthropology major required," so job seekers must be ready to describe what anthropology is and how its key skills will benefit a position. The American Anthropological Association describes three skills that set anthropology students apart: understanding human diversity, building research skills for collecting and making sense of information, and communicating effectively. A person in an entry-level career position in the healthcare industry, for example, benefits from an anthropological view of human diversity. Anthropology majors and minors often work in the nonprofit and ministry sectors, serving people with a sound philosophy of human well-being and what it means to help. They are also equipped to self-reflect on the strengths and challenges in their own cultural context, which helps sustain work for the long term.

In the first decade of his career, Tim Garland used his anthropology major to shift from teaching at-risk students to executive corporate leadership.[7] After graduating from Wheaton College with a major in anthropology, Tim taught with the Teach for America program at a charter school devoted to students who were in the foster-care system. Students were dealing with instability and emotional-social challenges in addition to the "normal" challenges of being in high school. Moreover, the school was based on an innovative and untested model of education that was staffed by many young, inexperienced teachers (like Tim!). Tim used his anthropological training to understand

6. Anthropology Career Readiness Network, accessed July 24, 2025, https://anthrocareerready.net/.

7. "Tim Garland" is a pseudonym for a student Brian had in the mid-2000s.

what his students were going through as well as how the faculty and staff experienced this world. He recalled, "Asking questions, and questioning my own assumptions, was really critical in that setting."[8]

Later, Tim made a major career shift to a global financial corporation where he became an executive in charge of acquisitions. "Our company would buy small financial services companies in Japan, for example, and I would be the one to help them understand our corporate culture, helping them to adjust."[9] Tim's anthropology background supported his ability to perceive cultural norms, explain them across cultural differences, and develop strategies of adaptation.

Another anthropology major, some years after her graduation, wrote back to me (Brian) with this advice to pass on:

> An anthropology major will make you stand out in a job interview, but only if you can articulate its value. I can't tell you how many people say, "That sounds great. I thought anthropology was digging up bones." Develop a one-minute "elevator speech" (brief sales pitch) for yourself and practice it on as many people as you can. My elevator speech goes something like this:
>
> *I have a bachelor's in cultural anthropology. It is a great major and I use it every day! Cultural anthropology is all about how people understand the world and learning to see from someone else's perspective. I work with diverse groups of people, and I have a strong customer focus. I know how to observe and ask questions and develop creative solutions that are unique to my organization.*

The worker with an anthropological perspective is distinguished by a willingness and ability to look at circumstances in context and from many angles. Ethnographic journalist Anne Fadiman conducted fieldwork among the Hmong, a group of Southeast Asian immigrants. In *The Spirit Catches You and You Fall Down*, she recounts a situation in which medical professionals in Merced, California, misinterpreted the responses of a Hmong family regarding their daughter's treatment for epilepsy.[10]

Hmong people saw epilepsy as caused by spirits. They worried that Western medicine could cause more harm than good, so they would use it sparingly. At the time of her fieldwork, Hmong people in America were seen as irrational or simpleminded because they didn't always trust physicians or obey medical orders. Fadiman showed that the parents' choices were rooted in their love for their daughter. The parents' reluctance to trust Western medicine and

8. As reported in an alumni survey submitted September 19, 2017.

9. Personal communication with Brian Howell, April 9, 2021.

10. Anne Fadiman, *The Spirit Catches You and You Fall Down: A Hmong Child, Her American Doctors, and the Collision of Two Cultures* (Farrar, Straus & Giroux, 1997).

Christine Jeske (right) is the former director of a microfinance project in South Africa. She and her husband, Adam, have served as development workers and teachers in Nicaragua, China, and South Africa. Christine completed an MBA in international economic development and then began PhD study of cultural anthropology, researching how unemployed people in South Africa define and seek "the good life."

unwillingness to obey all the physicians' advice made sense when seen in terms of Hmong history, society, and culture.

Fadiman also described the views of physicians and medical staff who, like the parents, desperately wanted what was best for the patient. Their training, institutional context, and deeply held cultural assumptions made it difficult for most of them to understand a family that seemed to be undermining their efforts to treat the patient.

In the story, a few social workers and physicians with anthropological instincts intervened when they began to perceive the grave consequences of cultural misunderstandings. Unfortunately, too few of those involved had such insight. At many points, anthropological training could have been used to ask a key question or anticipate a misunderstanding. This might have prevented the crippling infection the little girl acquired during a hospital stay, which caused massive brain damage. Had someone in the Hmong family studied anthropology, that person might have been better able to consider the perspective of the medical personnel or explain the traditions and assumptions of the Hmong community rather than becoming fearful or hostile in the face of what appeared to be illogical or incompetent medical advice.

As a result of Fadiman's research and writing, the medical center featured in her book has become a model of culturally appropriate medicine for the country. Hmong people have now lived in the United States for decades, and the blending of Hmong and US cultures has led to better understanding over time; however, this story from a first-generation perspective is still powerful because it provides lessons for engaging new refugee and immigrant groups.

Cultural relativism—the anthropological tenet that people's ideas and behaviors make sense when viewed from their culture's perspective—and cultural sensitivity benefit virtually every occupation, calling, or context.

Anthropology in Everyday Life

Graduates who have studied anthropology often report that, in addition to influencing career and service, anthropology shaped them in ways that were beneficial to their everyday lives. One anthropology major (a student of Jenell's) later became a father, and his daughter was diagnosed with apraxia of speech, a neurological condition. He used his basic linguistics knowledge to communicate better with her. He used a fieldwork approach in his family relationships, trying to see the world from his daughter's perspective rather than simply judging or misunderstanding her based on his own perspective. He says that though he chose anthropology because of its potential for public service and career, he is even more grateful for how anthropology shaped him as a father.

Fieldwork skills and knowledge of theory are useful in everyday life. A married couple may analyze their own culture, questioning how they have been shaped by cultural expectations for household life and intimacy. Parents who are mystified by their child's behavior might use anthropological sensibilities in observing their child's school or playgroups. Neighbors who cannot understand why the people across the street eat, socialize, or speak as they do might first pursue a fuller perspective of their cultural or social background. This does not mean that every problem has an easy solution, but taking a posture of cultural relativism often yields insights that can't otherwise be seen. Seemingly irrational behavior may have a meaning or purpose that can be understood from the insider's point of view. This opens up possibilities for communication and understanding.

Anthropology in Ministry

Anyone planning to participate in ministry, whether as a professional or as a lay leader, will have challenges and opportunities in engaging cultural and social differences. The Christian church has many denominations and associations, each with distinctive theology and practices. Virtually every group and individual church has a variety of opinions about worship styles, decision-making, and outreach priorities. Political and economic changes in the broader society may result in disagreements and divisions within the church. The global church is on the move through migration, as immigrants and refugees join existing churches and establish their own. Some ethnic groups have rapidly growing churches, while others are declining.

It is not enough for Christians to be well intentioned when approaching diversity, difference, and division. Without skills and abilities, good intentions often wither or even do damage. In the case of Black evangelicals and White evangelicals in the United States, sociologists and anthropologists have described how, in spite of general theological agreement between the two communities, cultural misunderstandings and historic and current power imbalances lead to continued mistrust and separation.[11] Efforts to create racially or culturally diverse congregations, such as mergers between Black and White churches or congregations focused on "racial reconciliation," may succeed or fail in part depending on the ability of leaders and congregants to recognize and respond to power and cultural conflict.[12]

Pastors, worship leaders, Sunday school teachers, and lay leaders with anthropological perspectives will be well positioned to lead Christians past misunderstanding and toward real reconciliation and fellowship. Billy Graham, who started his ministry just as the Civil Rights Movement was beginning to take shape in the American South, was a leader among White evangelicals in supporting the movement. He integrated his rallies and leadership when many White evangelicals were still resisting the end of segregation. Even so, Graham publicly said he wished he had spoken earlier and more forcefully in support of Martin Luther King Jr. and the movement for racial equality. As an anthropology major from Wheaton College, Graham could see how racial segregation could never be reconciled with the gospel message of equality before God.[13]

11. Drew G. I. Hart, *Trouble I've Seen: Changing the Way the Church Views Racism* (Herald, 2016); Christian Smith and Michael Emerson, *Divided by Faith: Evangelical Religion and the Problem of Race in America* (Oxford University Press, 2000).

12. Kersten Bayt Priest and Robert J. Priest, "Divergent Worship Practices in the Sunday Morning Hour: Analysis of an 'Interracial' Church Merger Attempt," in *This Side of Heaven: Race, Ethnicity, and the Christian Faith*, ed. Robert J. Priest and Alvaro L. Nieves (Oxford University Press, 2007), 275–92; also Brian M. Howell, "Power and Reconciliation in an Urban Church: The Case of New City Fellowship," in Priest and Nieves, ed., *This Side of Heaven*, 293–309.

13. See Brian M. Howell, "Anthropology and the Making of Billy Graham: Evangelicalism and Anthropology in the 20th-Century United States," *American Anthropologist* 117, no. 1 (2015): 59–70.

Many ministries involve connecting across differences of subculture, ethnicity, social class, or life experience. Engaging culture, inequality, and difference with an attitude of curiosity is relevant beyond just acknowledging racial

Christians in Academic Anthropology

Christians who pursue doctoral study in anthropology follow a variety of paths toward meaningful service and careers. They earn degrees from a variety of universities and often belong to professional associations such as the American Anthropological Association or the International Union of Anthropological and Ethnological Sciences. Some work as professors, but the great majority of graduate-educated anthropologists practice anthropology in corporate, government, or nonprofit settings.

Some Christian anthropologists do basic research and teach in secular universities and colleges. Others teach in Christian colleges, universities, seminaries, and missions training schools. Many of these anthropologists choose religion as their primary area for research. For instance, I (Brian) studied how Philippine Christians interpret and practice their Southern Baptist faith in light of the local context in which they live. Others, including me (Jenell), study other dimensions of culture, such as neighborhood activism in an urban setting.

Many Christian anthropologists apply anthropology to advancing human well-being and solving social problems. Some devote their careers to international development or the alleviation of poverty. Others work in missions as missionaries or teachers. Anthropology is especially useful in mission work related to Bible translation, language preservation, development, and church planting. Some missionary anthropologists develop dual-track careers. One track involves their mission work, and the other includes ethnographic research and publishing in the secular academy. Thomas Headland, for example, did both research and missions among the Agta people of the Philippines. His work is important to the Agta themselves and to his organization (SIL International). His ethnographic writings are important to secular anthropologists who study hunter-gatherers, tropical forests, or upland minority groups elsewhere in the world.

The Network of Christian Anthropologists is a group that connects Christian anthropologists in collegial relationships and spiritual support. The Network provides a valuable forum for discussing anthropological issues from Christian perspectives.

The On Knowing Humanity Research Center at Eastern University brings together anthropologists, theologians, and others to explore humanity from an explicitly Christian perspective. Eastern University also offers a master's degree in theological and cultural anthropology.

The Christian Sociological Association is a group that connects Christian sociologists, some of whom teach anthropology courses. Anthropology fits well with interdisciplinary approaches to learning about human life and supporting human well-being.

It's your turn: Pick one area from this chapter—work, church, or everyday life. Describe one way your service could be more effective because you've taken an anthropology class.

divisions or cultural difference. Many pastors work in a context similar to their own background, but if they have attended college and seminary, they may find that their higher educational status creates a social class distinction between them and their parishioners. Using anthropological techniques and perspectives to investigate the context provides a way back into a community from which the pastor has been separated by the new social identity they have taken on. Youth ministers in the United States face a context where each generation is encouraged to differentiate itself from the previous one, so there are significant differences in the cultural contexts of youth and those even just ten years older.

Anthropology and the Global Church

Lamin Sanneh was born into a Muslim family of *Nyanchos*, an ancient royal line in the West African country of The Gambia. As a teenager, Sanneh was intrigued after reading about Jesus in the Qur'an, and he began a search to understand the man Muslims consider a prophet. Eventually he gave his life to Christ and, after studying in London, became professor of world Christianity at Yale University.

Sanneh understood, both personally and academically, the multicultural nature of the gospel. He wrote and spoke about the power of the gospel to influence local cultures. Unlike Islam, which mandates a holy language and officially endorses cultural practices rooted in the Arabian societies in which it was born, Christianity quickly broke away from its Jewish beginnings to become a religion at home in every language, culture, and context in which it was accepted. The first work of the Spirit at Pentecost was to translate the gospel into the languages of the world. The apostles then translated the gospel into multiple cultural contexts, a process that continues today. Sanneh wrote,

> Christianity's translated status exempted Christians from binding adherence to a founding culture. . . . As the religion resounded with the idioms and styles of new converts, it became multilingual and multicultural. Believers responded with the unprecedented facility of the mother tongue, and by that step broke the back of cultural chauvinism as, for example, between Jew and gentile. Christianity's indigenous potential was activated, and the frontier beckoned.[14]

Activation of this "indigenous potential" has spread the church throughout the world. Christianity has grown to become the majority religion in many

14. Lamin Sanneh, *Disciples of All Nations: Pillars of World Christianity* (Oxford University Press, 2008), 27.

places. Today, most Christians live outside Europe or North America and speak a language other than English. How does—or should—this growth affect the church as a whole?

Sociologist Robert Wuthnow notes that scholars of world Christianity often say the center of gravity has shifted from the countries of the Northern and Western Hemispheres to those in the Southern and Eastern Hemispheres (sometimes called the "Global South"). This shift, however, is more about numbers than influence. Churches of northern countries remain far wealthier,

YOUR TURN

Anthropology and . . .

Anthropology can enrich our everyday lives, our service and ministry, and our careers. People who have studied anthropology go on to work and serve in ways that may seem surprising. Cellist Yo-Yo Ma credits anthropology with shaping how he shares and makes music across the globe. King Charles III studied anthropology, supporting his understanding of colonial history and modern monarchies. Evangelist Billy Graham valued his anthropology education for opening his eyes to the importance of justice in society.

Some professionals add an anthropology master's or doctoral degree to their first line of work. Others stay connected to anthropology so they can apply their work cross-culturally. Some professions even have associations devoted to connecting with anthropology, including the following:

The Council on Nursing and Anthropology
National Association for the Practice of Anthropology
Council on Anthropology and Education
Society for Medical Anthropology
Society for Linguistic Anthropology
Society of Forensic Anthropologists
Dental Anthropology Association
Council for Museum Anthropology
Society for Psychological Anthropology
American Society of Missiology
Evangelical Missiological Society
Society for Applied Anthropology

Put anthropology to work in your future profession. Choose the prompt most suited to your interests.

- Using a search engine or generative AI, search for "anthropology and [your major or your profession]." If needed, try a variety of words for "anthropology" such as "cultural anthropology," "ethnography," or "ethnographic fieldwork." How do professionals in this area make use of anthropology concepts, theories, or methods?
- Using social media (e.g., LinkedIn) or a general online search, identify a professional in your area of interest who has a master's or doctoral degree in anthropology. How does anthropology influence their work? You may search through their professional profile, look at articles they've written, or reach out to them to ask directly how anthropology shapes their work life.

with greater educational, publishing, and media resources, and they have a much stronger voice in theological discussions than do the churches of the Global South. The fact that most Christians live in Africa and Asia does not necessarily mean that Christians in the United States or Canada have a meaningful or mutual connection with them.[15]

Wuthnow argues that focusing on a shift of power or gravity is not the best way to think about the church anyway. The church is not a club in which the majority rules. The church is a body in which each part is vital. As Wuthnow says, "A story that focuses on the withering of one appendage and the strengthening of another makes no sense. A better story acknowledges each limb or organ's dependence on others. In this story, global Christianity emerges less as a narrative about shifting centers of gravity and more about opportunities for mutual edification and interaction."[16]

Whether those interactions result in edification is up to us. Students of anthropology can use their knowledge and perspective to bless the church as a whole. Understanding the nature of language, the cultural construction of concepts such as gender and race, the material and ecological reasons for cultural practices, and the processes of cultural change will enhance the ability of Christians across the global church to truly be brothers and sisters in Christ, with mutually edifying interactions that support the family of God.

Anthropology and Missions

Anthropology in mission work focuses largely on cross-cultural communication and the translation of the gospel. **Contextualization**, along with companion terms such as "indigenization" and "accommodation," refers to expressing the gospel within the language, idioms, customs, and traditions of a culture so that Christianity can be practiced and understood as intrinsically part of the local context. When this concept was first promoted in the 1970s, many theologians and missionary leaders objected. They argued that missionaries who took culture seriously—adapting the way they communicated the gospel—risked polluting or distorting the gospel. What they did not see was how every expression of the gospel is already contextualized. The question, for missionary anthropologists, was not whether the gospel would be part of culture but whose culture it would be part of. Melanesian Christians, for instance, could not become "just Christians." If they rejected their own

15. Robert Wuthnow, *Boundless Faith: The Global Outreach of American Churches* (University of California Press, 2009), 39–47, 59–61.

16. Wuthnow, *Boundless Faith*, 61.

cultural context as "un-Christian," they simply ended up with a foreign, often American cultural Christianity in its place. The anthropological emphasis on contextualization suggests that missionaries and church leaders should encourage local believers to listen to the Holy Spirit and express Christian faithfulness in ways that emerge from within their own cultures and histories.

Connections between missions and anthropology go back to the very foundations of the discipline (see chap. 1), when some of the first professional anthropologists served as missionaries.[17] For over a hundred years, Christian missionaries have developed connections between anthropology and mission work. Linguists such as Ken Pike and Eugene Nida were widely respected in anthropological linguistics for their Bible translation and other scholarship. Later missionary anthropologists such as Paul Hiebert, R. Daniel Shaw, Charles Kraft, Miriam Adeney, and Marvin Mayers (among others) influenced missionary training programs.

Contextualization was first proposed to encourage missionaries to dissociate the message of the gospel from the (generally Western) cultural context in which the missionary had learned it. Today, contextualization has become just as important for non-Western Christians struggling to reconcile their own cultural contexts with Christian faith. Missionary anthropologist Darrell Whiteman tells of a Thai student who, after learning about anthropology and contextualization, said, "Now that I have been studying contextualization and have discovered how the Gospel relates to culture, I am realizing that I can be both Christian and Thai."[18] Many Christians throughout the world once thought that to be Christian was to wear Western clothes, sing European hymns, and eat with a fork and spoon. Anthropologically informed understandings of culture and society have encouraged new generations of Christians around the world to think about how a relationship with God should be lived out in their own context and how that relationship might transform their culture. The contextualization concept has more recently been critiqued as being insufficiently attentive to issues of power, colonialism, and history, but there is no doubt that the concept has proved extremely important in missionary anthropology and for the health of the church around the world.[19]

17. See James Clifford, *Person and Myth: Maurice Leenhardt in the Melanesian World* (Duke University Press, 1992).

18. Darrell Whiteman, "Contextualization: The Theory, the Gap, the Challenge," *International Bulletin of Missionary Research* 21, no. 1 (1997): 3. See also Darrell Whiteman, *Crossing Cultures with the Gospel: Anthropological Wisdom for Effective Christian Witness* (Baker Academic, 2024).

19. For a critique of the contextualization concept, see Brian M. Howell, introduction to *Power and Identity in the Global Church: Six Contemporary Cases*, ed. Brian M. Howell and Edwin Zehner (William Carey Library, 2009), 1–42.

Brian Howell

During his research on short-term missions, Brian spent the year with a team preparing for a trip, then traveled and worked with them to understand how the participants interpreted and subsequently represented their experience. He published his findings with an academic Christian publisher as a way to speak to both the anthropological community and the church about what short-term mission is and ways that Christians might better think about and serve others.

Anthropological contributions to missionary method and theory pushed many North American missionaries and missionary training programs away from paternalistic and culturally imperialistic means of communication. Paul Hiebert, who spent six years as a missionary in India before earning his PhD in anthropology, wrote, "It is possible for missionaries, like others, to go to another culture as tourists, noticing its strangeness but never entering and identifying with its world." Only when we enter anthropologically, he argued, can we "love humans in other cultures as people—to see them as human beings like ourselves."[20]

Many North American Christians first experience missionary work during a short-term mission trip. Some participants remember these trips as life-changing because they come to see God, others, and themselves in a new light. Christians from around the world who engage in short-term service work often encounter communities with great passion for the gospel in spite of political opposition, material deprivation, or social inequality.

20. Paul Hiebert, *Cultural Anthropology*, 2nd ed. (Baker, 1997), xxii. Hiebert uses the word "incarnational" to describe his favored approach to missions. We substitute the word "anthropological," which we believe conveys the same intent without the theological problems associated with the term "incarnational" when used to describe a missionary methodology.

Jamie Gates

Anthropologist Jamie Gates co-leads the groundbreaking research project "Measuring the Extent and Nature of Gang Involvement in Sex Trafficking in the San Diego/Tijuana Border Region." He founded and directs the Human Trafficking Research and Data Advisory Roundtable for San Diego County. In this photo, Gates is standing in solidarity with grocery workers picketing for fair working conditions.

At the same time, short-term mission trips can be confusing and frustrating. Having had just a glimpse of another culture, participants may come back wondering how to make sense of what they saw. Worse yet, after just a short time in another place, people may think they have a very *clear* understanding of that place. The trip may provide a false sense of understanding and connection when a great deal more time and engagement are needed. A short trip is often just long enough to have stereotypes reinforced, prejudices confirmed, or judgments strengthened. Christian anthropologists apply a century's worth of missiological research and experience to supporting contemporary churches in developing short-term mission trips that guide participants toward strong culture learning and relationship building.[21]

Regardless of the length of the trip, an anthropologically astute short-term missionary can learn to get beneath surface observations, asking questions and seeking to understand the context from within. This will help them to reflect on how their own culture has profoundly shaped their faith.

21. Brian M. Howell, "Re-thinking (the Social Imaginary of) Short Term Missions," in *Re-Imagining Short Term Missions*, ed. F. Inslee and A. Burns (Wipf & Stock, 2002), 147–60. See also Robert J. Priest, ed., *Effective Engagement in Short-Term Missions: Doing It Right!* (William Carey Library, 2008); and Brian M. Howell, "Mission to Nowhere: Putting Short-Term Missions into Context," *International Bulletin of Missionary Research* 33, no. 4 (2009): 206–11.

The Future of Christians in Anthropology

Though God exists outside of culture, people do not. Christians worship and pray and serve and live in specific times and places. Globalization brings us into contact with cultural influences of all sorts, both Christian and non-Christian. Cross-cultural contact is no longer the exclusive purview of missionaries and travelers. As Christians study anthropology, we can bring our insights to help the body of Christ better engage the global church, world cultures, and the globalized economy.

Christians can also contribute to anthropology itself. While an earlier generation often found professional anthropology and the academy generally hostile to Christianity, there is good reason to believe that the environment is changing. As perspectives of various sorts—racial, gender, ethnic, sexual—are acknowledged and even celebrated in the academy, Christians have joined in the conversation. Along with other explicitly religious perspectives such as Buddhism and Islam, Christianity has a seat at the table when Christians come as well-trained, creative, and skilled scholars who identify their religious perspective as relevant to their work.

We invite Christian college students, seminarians, prospective missionaries, and other interested people to keep studying anthropology. May you discover new ways to love God and people more fully, with all your strength, heart, and mind.

TERMS

contextualization: Fitting the gospel with the language, idioms, customs, and traditions of a culture so that Christianity becomes organically woven in with the context.

DISCUSSION QUESTIONS

1. Generate an example of how anthropology can be helpful in each of the following arenas: work, everyday life, ministry, global church.
2. How does your area of interest connect with globalization, people from different cultures, cross-cultural communication, or diverse languages? This could be in the workplace itself, products or services, clients, supply chains, marketing, or more. How could anthropology support your career area?

ANTHROPOLOGY AND SCRIPTURE

The Gospel in Culture

> When the day of Pentecost had come, they were all together in one place. And suddenly from heaven there came a sound like the rush of a violent wind, and it filled the entire house where they were sitting. Divided tongues, as of fire, appeared among them, and a tongue rested on each of them. All of them were filled with the Holy Spirit and began to speak in other languages, as the Spirit gave them ability.
>
> Now there were devout Jews from every nation under heaven living in Jerusalem. And at this sound the crowd gathered and was bewildered, because each one heard them speaking in the native language of each. (Acts 2:1–6 NRSVue)

The work of the Holy Spirit at Pentecost was to speak the good news in a variety of languages. People from Mesopotamia, Judea, Cappadocia, Asia, Egypt, Libya, Rome, and other places all heard about God's deeds of power in the language they knew best. The Holy Spirit comes to us in our own cultures, and this story shows the Holy Spirit working a miracle in order to communicate clearly with each person.

Lamin Sanneh says that after the Holy Spirit translated the gospel into languages by this miracle, the apostles set out to translate the gospel into cultures through mission. We continue that work today when we share the gospel with people of other cultures, appropriately translating the good news into linguistic and cultural terms that make sense in particular contexts. We also continue the work when we learn from other cultures, gaining insight into how our own culture shapes our understanding of the gospel.

Anthropology in Jesus's Ministry

> A man with leprosy came to him [Jesus] and begged him on his knees, "If you are willing, you can make me clean."
>
> Jesus was indignant. He reached out his hand and touched the man. "I am willing," he said. "Be clean!" (Mark 1:40–41)

Jesus wasn't an anthropologist, but his ministry shows why elements of the ethnographic method are so important. Jesus lived among the people he was trying to reach, sharing their daily lives. He taught them in locations familiar to them and addressed the issues that were important to them. In this case, Jesus was emotionally moved by the person he encountered, and he reached out to touch him.

Anthropologists approach people similarly, living among them and coming to understand and value their concerns. Practicing the ethnographic method can lead to a greater ability to listen, perceive, understand, and communicate effectively. It can also lead to compassion, as the anthropologist comes to really understand another person's context by living in it. The skills that characterize an effective anthropologist also mark the effective Christian; both include living among, talking to, communicating with, and caring for people in their own contexts.

ACKNOWLEDGMENTS

This book reflects the encouragement and gracious help of many colleagues, students, and editors. We are thankful to Baker Academic and Bob Hosack, in particular, for believing in the text and encouraging us in our work in all three editions. We were thrilled when the book quickly became collaborative, drawing on the expertise of Christian anthropology colleagues, many of whom are part of the Network of Christian Anthropologists. Colleagues with the Christian Sociological Association have been helpful as well, especially Matt Vos. For expert review of chapter drafts and other contributions, we thank Miriam Adeney, Kevin Birth, Dana Chisholm, Katrina Greene, Mike Jindra, Diane King, Sherwood Lingenfelter, Eloise Hiebert Meneses, Sue Russell, John Schaefer, Dan Shaw, Sarah Tobin, Christa Tooley, Todd Vanden Berg, and Steve Ybarolla.

For the first edition, Njeri Bene read two chapters and provided detailed editorial and substantive comments that were very helpful and much appreciated. For the second edition, special recognition must go to Rob McKee, who taught the book for many years and provided us detailed notes. Gene Rohrbaugh assisted greatly with the linguistics chapter. For photographs, we thank Aminta Arrington, Jeffery Deal, Murl Dirksen, Katerina Friesen, Jamie Gates, Katrina Greene, Vince Gil, Naomi Haynes, Tom Headland, Christine Jeske, Michael Jindra, Tony Kail, Rob McKee, Mari Mendez, Eloise Hiebert Meneses, and Glenn Stone. For cartoon illustrations, we appreciate James Marohn's artistry and generosity.

We are both grateful to our families as well.

INDEX